MAN, MYTH, AND MAGIC

MAN, MYTH, AND MAGIC

Beliefs, Rituals, and Symbols of Ancient Greece & Rome

Cavendish Square

New York

Published in 2014 by Cavendish Square Publishing, LLC
303 Park Avenue South, Suite 1247, New York, NY 10010

Library of Congress Cataloging-in-Publication Data

Brandon, S.G.F.
Beliefs, rituals, and symbols of ancient Greece & Rome / by S.G.F.Brandon.
p. cm. — (Man, myth, and magic)
Includes index.
ISBN 978-1-62712-566-6 (hardcover) ISBN 978-1-62712-567-3 (paperback) ISBN 978-1-62712-568-0 (ebook)
1. Mythology, Classical — Juvenile literature. 2. Greece — Religion — Juvenile. 3. Rome — Religion — Juvenile literature. I. Title.
BL723.B73 2014
292—d23

Editorial Director: Dean Miller
Editor: Fran Hatton
Art Director: Jeffrey Talbot
Designers: Jennifer Ryder-Talbot, Amy Greenan, and Joseph Macri
Photo Researcher: Laurie Platt Winfrey, Carousel Research, Inc
Production Manager: Jennifer Ryder-Talbot
Production Editor: Andrew Coddington

Photo credits: Cover photos by Achilles Hector Louvre G153/Campana Collection, 1861*; Giovanni Dall'Orto/DSC00355 - Orfeo (epoca romana) - Foto G. Dall'Orto/Own work/*; DEA / A. DAGLI ORTI/De Agnostini Picture Library/Getty Images. Albani Collection/Artemis Ephesus Musei Capitolini MC1182/Marie-Lan Nguyen/*, 1; Giovanni Dall'Orto/0456 - Roma, Museo d. civiltà romana - Sarcofago Mattei Foto Giovanni Dall'Orto, 12-Apr-2008/Own work/*, 2–3; Juan José Moral/2000px-Oidipous sphinx MGEt 16541 reconstitution/Own work/*, 7; Campana Collection, 1861/Hector Louvre G153/Jastrow/*, 9b; Gren12345/Achilles hee/Own work/*, 9t; Campana Collection, 1861/Achilles weapons Louvre E869/Jastrow/*, 10; Former collections of Cardinal Mazarin/Adonis Mazarin Louvre MR239 n3/Jastrow/*, 11t; Charles-Joseph Natoire - Vénus et Adonis/Sotheby's/*, 11b; Brandmeister/Mosaic-high res fragment/*, 12; OAR/National Undersea Research Program (NURP)/Alexander the Great diving NOAA/*, 13; Jean-Pol GRANDMONT/0 Amazzone ferita - Musei Capitolini (1)/*, 15; Acquired by Henry Walters, 1924/Beldam Painter - Three Amazons - Walters 48249 (2)/Walters Art Museum/*, 16; Sandro Botticelli/Botticelli Venus Uffizi/Google Art Project/*, 18; Jastrow/Aphrodite Sappho Chiaramonti Inv1459/*, 20; Purchase, 1880/Head Kassel Apollo Louvre Ma692/Jastrow*, 21; Napoleon Vier/Delphi temple/nl.wikipedia/*, 22; Marie-Lan Nguyen/Silver tetradrachm Athens new style reverse/*, 26t; Steve Swayne/temple of athena Nike/*, 26b; Farnese Collection/Minerva MAN Napoli Inv6319/Marie-Lan Nguyen/*, 27; John William Waterhouse/Circe Invidiosa - John William Waterhouse/*, 29; Archaeological Museum of Heraklion/P1010654bronze shield/*, 31; Olaf Tausch/Minoische Schaukel 01/Own work/*, 32; Deror avi/Armon Knossos P1060039/Own work/*, 33; Wolfgang Sauber/AMI - Stierrhyton/Own work/*, 34; Olaf Tausch/Kleine Schlangengöttin 01/Own work/*, 36; Francisco de Goya/Francisco de Goya, Saturno devorando a su hijo (1819-1823)/*, 38; Anthony van Dyck/Anthony van Dyck - Daedalus and Icarus - Google Art Project/*, 40; Thesupermat/Le Petit Palais - Protome de Déméter - IVème siècle avant JC - 002/Own work/*, 41; Rogers Fund, 1914/Great Eleusinian relief fragments Met 14.130.9 n01/Marie-Lan Nguyen/*, 43; Colin/Isis-Sothis-Demeter/Own work/*, 44; Titian/Titian - Diana and Actaeon - Google Art Project/*, 45; Albani Collection/Artemis Ephesus Musei Capitolini MC1182/Marie-Lan Nguyen/*, 47; Candelori Collection/Ariadne Staatliche Antikensammlungen 1562/Bibi Saint-Pol/*, 50; WolfgangRieger/Villa dei Misteri V - 1/*, 52; Google Art Project/Dionysus - Google Art Project/*, 53l; Jastrow/Phaler Dionysos CdM/*, 53r; Bibi Saint-Pol/hydria Antikensammlung Berlin 1984.46 n2/Own work/*, 55; Paravey Collection/Piglet carrier Louvre MNB1714/Marie-Lan Nguyen/*, 56; Castellani Collection/Epikouros BM 1843/Marie-Lan Nguyen/*, 58; Parmigianino/Parmigianino 014/*, 59; Jastrow/Skyphos Shuvalov Painter Louvre CA1588/Own work/*, 60t; Marie-Lan Nguyen/Domus di Amore e Psiche Ostia Antica 2006-09-08 n2/Own work/*, 60b; Clemensfranz/Villa Romana del Casale Schlafzimmer Mitte cropped/Own work/*, 61; Paravey Collection/Aineias Ankhises Louvre F118/Bibi Saint-Pol/Own work/*, 62; Jean-Pol GRANDMONT/0 Lupa Capitolina (2)/*, 63; Peter Paul Rubens/Peter Paul Rubens - Romulus and Remus - Google Art Project/*, 64; Leemage/UIG/Getty Images, 65; Leemage/UIG/Getty Images, 66t; DeAgostini/Getty Images, 66b; Dennis Jarvis/Greece-1172 Temple of Athena/*, 67; Jebulon/Zeus Camiros Rhodes black background/Own work/*, 68; DieBuche/Funeral mask of Agamemnon-colorcorr/Own work/*, 69; Marie-Lan Nguyen/Calyx-krater olympian assembly MAN/*, 70; Jastrow/Stater Zeus Lampsacus CdM/*, 71; Jastrow/Hecate Chiaramonti Inv1922/*, 73; rob koopman/WLANL - koopmanrob - Hekate/*, 74; Ealdgyth/Pergamonaltarhekate/Own work, 75; Diego Rodríguez de Silva y Velázquez/Velázquez - La Fragua de Vulcano (Museo del Prado, 1630)/Erzalibillas/*, 76; Marie-Lan Nguyen/Achilles weapons MNA Naples/*, 77; Coyau/Parc de Versailles, demi-lune du bassin d'Apollon, Junon, Jean-Jacques Clérion 03/CC-BY-SA-3.0/Own work/*, 79; Giovanni Dall'Orto/DSC00406 - Tempio E di Selinunte - Zeus ed Hera - Ca. 450 a.C. - Foto G. Dall'Orto/*, 80; Jastrow/Herakles Nessos Loggia dei Lanzi 2005 09 13/Own work/*, 81; Marie-Lan Nguyen/Hercules Musei Capitolini MC1265 n3/*, 82; Luis García (Zaqarbal)/Mosaico Trabajos Hércules (M.A.N. Madrid) 03/*, 83; Marco Marchetti/Marco Marchetti from Faenza - Hercules suffocates Antaeus - Google Art Project/*, 84; Mountain/Hercules fight with lion/Own work/*, 85; Stefano Bolognini/Affresco romano - eracle ed onfale - area vesuviana/Own work/*, 86; Wolfgang Sauber/MAP - Amphora Baratti 5 Hermes/Own work/*, 87l; Laitue/Hermes portant Dionysos par Praxitèle/Own work/*, 87r; cgb.fr/As frappé en bronze représentant Janus/*, 89; Charles de La Fosse/Château de Versailles, salon de Diane, Jason et les Argonautes débarquant en Colchide, Charles de La Fosse/Coyau/CC-BY-SA-3.0/*, 90; Musée du Louvre/Jupiter Smyrna Louvre Ma13/*, 93; Michel Corneille the Younger (1642–1708)/Iris and Jupiter/*, 94; Marcel Clemens/Shutterstock.com, 95t; Luis García/Lares romano de bronce (M.A.N. Inv.2943) 01/*, 95b; Giovanni Dall'Orto/0456 - Roma, Museo d. civiltà romana - Sarcofago Mattei Foto Giovanni Dall'Orto, 12-Apr-2008/*, 97; Borghese Collection/Imperial group Mars Venus Louvre Ma1009 n3/Jastrow/*, 98; Lambert Collection/Mercurius MBA Lyon L84/Marie-Lan Nguyen/*, 101; Wolfgang Sauber/Cardiff castle - Turm 4 Merkur/Own work/*, 102; Szilas/Mercury, patron of the merchants/Own work/*, 103; Wolfgang Sauber/Paphos Haus des Theseus - Mosaik Achilles 3 Moiren/Own work/*, 106; Cosimo Tura/Cosmè Tura - The Muse Terpsichore - Google Art Project/*, 107; Albani Collection/Thalia sarcophagus Louvre Ma475/Jastrow/*, 108; Luca GIORDANO Giuseppe RECCO/Luca GIORDANO - Giuseppe Recco - The riches of the sea with Neptune, tritons and two nereids - Google Art Project/*, 109t; Tony Hisgett/Neptune Roman mosaic Bardo Museum Tunis/*, 109b; Juan José Moral/2000px-Oidipous sphinx MGEt 16541 reconstitution/Own work/*, 111; Roelant Savery/Bequeathed by S.J. Ainsley/Savery, Roelant - Orpheus - 1628 (3180 A 2050)/*, 112; Giovanni Dall'Orto/DSC00355 - Orfeo (epoca romana) - Foto G. Dall'Orto/Own work/*, 113; Giovanni Dall'Orto/2158 - Taormina - Badia Vecchia - Sarcofago romano del sec. II d.C. - Foto Giovanni Dall'Orto, 20-May-2008/*, 115; Helvetiker/Pan mit Panflöte griechisch Slg Ebnöther/*, 116; Antonio Muñoz Degrain/Antonio Muñoz Degrain Nymphs bathing/*, 117; Rembrandt/Rembrandt - The Rape of Proserpine - Google Art Project/*, 118; Marie-Lan Nguyen/Persephone Hades BM Vase E82/*, 119; Mosaique romaine/*, 121; Coyau/pluto Parc de Versailles, Bosquet de la colonnade, Enlèvement de Proserpine par Pluton, François Girardon 02/CC-BY-SA-3.0/*, 122; Bibi Saint-Pol/Poseidon Polybotes Cdm Paris 573/Own work/*, 125; Szilas/Prometheus Bound/Own work/*, 126; Marie-Lan Nguyen/Prometheus Adam Louvre MR1745/Own work/*, 128; sailko/prometeo crea un uomo, 1505-07 circa/*, 129; music of the spheres/*, 130; Giovanni Dall'Orto/4666 - Venezia - Palazzo ducale - Capitello 17 - Arti liberali - Pitagoras arsmetricus - Foto Giovanni Dall'Orto, 31-Jul-2008/Own work/*, 131; Elie plus/Roman forum/Own work/*, 132–133; WolfgangRieger/Herculaneum - Casa di Nettuno ed Anfitrite - Mosaic/*, 134; bgds/Museum of Side 012b/*, 137; McLeod/Roman priest w axe/Own work/*, 138; LPLT/Villa Torlonia4/Own work/*, 140; Wolfgang Sauber/Fresko Astrologie Winter 2/Own work/*, 141; Caught between a rock and a hard place/*, 142; Marie-Lan Nguyen/Selene Terme/*, 143; Richardc39/Mark Henderson at the Merseyside Skeptics Society/*, 144; Bequeathed by Richard Payne Knight/Chrysippos BM 1846/Marie-Lan Nguyen/*, 145; Jastrow/Theseus Minotaur Ramey Tuileries/Own work/*, 146; George Frederic Watts/George Frederic Watts - The Minotaur - Google Art Project/*, 147; DEA / G. GAGLI ORTI/Contributor/De Agostini/Getty Images, 149; Werner Forman/Universal Images Group/Getty Images, 150; Jomafemag/Atlas pasa a Heracles la esfera celeste/*, 152; Brussels Manufactory - The Story of Troy. Cassandra intercedes before Priam to obtain a Pardon for Paris - Google Art Project/*, 153; Travelling Runes/Mykonos vase/*, 154; Michel Wolgemut, Wilhelm Pleydenwurff/Nuremberg chronicles f 36r 1/*, 155; sailko/Tesoro di priamo, bracciale lamellare con decorazione a spirale, dal tesoro F, orus. cat. 123/Own work/*, 156; Troy/*, 157; Szilas/Golden sauceboat with two handles-2/Own work/*, 158; Bibi Saint-Pol/Aion mosaic Glyptothek Munich W504/Own work/*, 159; NASA/Uranus - GPN-2000-000440/*, 160; Titian/Venus and Adonis by Titian/*, 161; Jebulon/Venus of Rhodes/Own work/*, 162; Rembrandt/Rembrandt - The Abduction of Ganymede - Google Art Project - cropped/*, 166; Virginia Frances Sterrett/Vfs europa-and-the-bull 002/*, 167.   * Wikimedia Commons.

Cavendish Square would like to acknowledge the outstanding work, research, writing, and professionalism of Man, Myth, and Magic's original Editor-in-Chief Richard Cavendish, Executive Editor Brian Innes, Editorial Advisory Board Members and Consultants C.A. Burland, Glyn Daniel, E.R Dodds, Mircea Eliade, William Sargent, John Symonds, RJ. Zwi Werblowsky, and R.C. Zaechner, as well as the numerous authors, consultants, and contributors that shaped the original Man, Myth, and Magic that served as the basis and model for these new books.

Printed in the United States of America

Contents

Beliefs, Rituals, and Symbols in Ancient Greece and Rome

A Reader's Guide to *Man, Myth, and Magic: Beliefs, Rituals, and Symbols of Ancient Greece and Rome*

Wherever cultures have grown up, common universal themes run through their religions and mythologies. The myths and legends of the ancient world make a wonderful, colourful tapestry expressing the variety of local experiences and attitudes. The gods and goddesses of the ancient Greeks and Romans reflect humans' desire to explain the nature of the universe and the human psyche, the mysteries of birth and death, the progression of the seasons, and so much more.

The human experience has mainly been turbulent and full of struggle. We have felt insignificant when ranged against the immensity of the universe. The other side of impotence is unlimited strength—the actions of heroes, such as the labours of Hercules, and the valour of Achilles on the battlefield until his insignificant-seeming singular weakness proved his undoing. The vast majority of the human race may be weak and vulnerable but in many cultures heroic figures emerge to echo our braver dreams.

Man, Myth, and Magic: Beliefs, Rituals, and Symbols of Ancient Greece and Rome is a work derived from a set of volumes with two decades of bestselling and award-winning history. It is a fully comprehensive guide to the myths and cults surrounding the Titans, gods, demigods, heroes, and beasts that formed the basis of the faith and day-to-day living in ancient Greece and Rome. This book in the

The Romans were keenly aware of the strength that the land imparted to its inhabitants. When they conquered and wholly absorbed another people, they ritually summoned the chief local god (or gods) from the conquered land to Rome where the alien god was properly domiciled.

Man, Myth, and Magic series provides an excellent historical perspective on the deities of ancient Greece and Rome, larger-than-life figures that had an impact on almost all subsequent Western culture, and are still studied to this day.

Objectives of *Man, Myth, and Magic*

The guiding principle of the *Man, Myth, and Magic* series takes the stance of unbiased exploration. It shows the myriad of ways in which different cultures have questioned and explained the mysterious nature of the world about them, and will lead teachers and students toward a broader understanding of their own beliefs and customs and those of others.

The Text

Within *Man, Myth, and Magic: Beliefs, Rituals, and Symbols of Ancient Greece and Rome*, expert international contributors have created articles arranged alphabetically, and the depth of coverage varies from major articles of up to 10,000 words to concise, glossary-type definitive entries in the form of short paragraphs. From Achilles to Zeus, every major figure from the mythology of both civilizations is covered, with different articles on the two versions of significant figures. This allows readers to better understand

Oedipus and the Sphinx

the differences between Zeus, who led the Greek pantheon of immortals, and his Roman counterpart Jupiter. In addition to the numerous articles on the gods and demigods, there are also several entries on key historical figures, such as Alexander the Great, Homer, Ovid, and Pythagoras, as well as the philosophical schools of thought that emerged from the era, including Cynicism, Skepticism, and Stoicism.

The work is highly illustrated, and subjects of major interest are provided with individual bibliographies of further readings on the subject at the end of each article.

What made it possible to create this work was the fact that the last century has seen a powerful revival of interest in these subjects at both the scholarly and the popular levels. This rebirth of scholarly interest has created the modern study of comparative religion and modern anthropology with its investigation of indigenous, or first, peoples and their beliefs and rituals (which are far more complex than originally believed). At the same time there has been a flourishing revival of popular interest in ancient civilizations, mythology, magic, and alternative paths to truth. This interest has shown no sign of diminishing this century; on the contrary, it has grown stronger and has explored new pathways. At the same time, scholarly investigation of our subjects has continued and has cast much new light on some of our topics. The present edition of *Man, Myth, and Magic* takes account of both these developments. Articles have been updated to cover fresh discoveries and new theories since they first appeared.

With all this, *Man, Myth, and Magic* is not intended to convert you to or from any belief or set of beliefs and attitudes. The purpose of the articles is not to persuade or justify, but to describe what people have believed and trace the consequences of those beliefs in action. The editorial position is one of sympathetic neutrality. It is for the reader to decide where truth and value may lie. We hope that there is as much interest, pleasure, and satisfaction in reading these pages as all those involved took in creating them.

Illustrations

Since much of what we know about myth, folklore, and religion has been passed down over the centuries by word of mouth, and recorded only comparatively recently, visual images are often the most powerful and vivid links we have with the past. The wealth of illustration in *Man, Myth, and Magic: Beliefs, Rituals, and Symbols of Ancient Greece and Rome* is invaluable, not only because of the diversity of sources but also because of the superb quality of colour reproduction. Gods and goddesses, heroes and demons, birth, initiation, and death are all recorded here in infinite variety, including tomb and wall paintings, and artifacts in metal, pottery, and wood. The famous architecture of Greece and Rome is well represented also, with examples of religious buildings from all over the region.

Back Matter

Near the end of the book is a glossary that defines words that are most likely new to students, edifying their comprehension of the material. The A–Z index provides immediate access to any specific item sought by the reader. This reference tool distinguishes the nature of the entry in terms of a main entry, supplementary subject entries, and illustrations.

Skill Development for Students

The books of the *Man, Myth, and Magic* series can be consulted as the basic text for a subject or as a source of enrichment for students. It can serve as a reference for a simple reading or writing assignment, or as inspiration for a major research or term paper. The additional suggested reading at the end of many entries is an invaluable resource for students seeking to further their studies on a specific topic. *Man, Myth, and Magic* offers resources for students that are extremely valuable: twenty volumes that are both multi-disciplinary and inter-disciplinary, a wealth of fine illustrations, and a research source well suited to a variety of age levels that will provoke interest and encourage speculation in both teachers and students.

Scope

As well as being a major asset to social studies teaching, the book provides students from a wide range of disciplines with a stimulating, accessible, and beautifully illustrated reference work.

The *Man, Myth, and Magic* series lends itself very easily to a multi-disciplinary approach to study. In *Man, Myth, and Magic: Beliefs, Rituals, and Symbols of Ancient Greece and Rome*, literature students will be interested in myths and legends, fairy tales and folk plays, riddles, and nursery rhymes. Math students will be fascinated to read about Pythagoras and his early contributions to the field, while students of art, sculpture, carving, pottery, and other crafts will find the marvelous illustrations and special articles on the subjects particularly helpful. Readers interested in military history will gravitate to the discussion of Alexander the Great and marvel at his accomplishments at such a young age. Students of physics, chemistry, and biology will find interesting background reading in such topics as alchemy, astronomy, and plant and animal lore. As well as its relevance to study areas already mentioned, the book will provide strong background reference in history, anthropology, philosophy, and comparative religion.

Conceptual Themes

As students become involved in the work, they will gradually become sensitive to the major concepts emerging from research. Students can begin to understand the role these two civilizations played in the development of major themes, patterns, and motifs underlying many of the world's belief systems. For example, the concept of how humans first mastered fire is covered by all major civilizations and belief systems, including the Greeks considering it a gift from the Titan who created them, Prometheus.

The trickster figure appears in folklore tales all over the world, including the Greek god Hermes, another concept worth exploring. What similarities and differences exist in the concept the Greek and Romans have used to explain creation versus other cultures? The progress of the seasons, the rising and setting of the sun, the hero's journey—all are fundamental concepts universal to all civilizations. Understanding the methods that these civilizations used to incorporate the stories and myths centred around each, can make for a keener understanding of history. All these areas are challenging ways for more advanced students to use both this individual volume and the other title selections in this set.

Dying Achilles at Achilleion, Corfu. Sculptor: Ernst Herter (1884)

Achilles

The plot of the *Iliad*, one of the most blood-drenched stories ever told, turns on the pride and the ungovernable temper of Achilles (*Achilleus* in Greek), the most formidable of the Greek champions who laid siege to Troy. 'The Wrath of Achilles is my theme', Homer begins, 'that fatal wrath which . . . sent the gallant souls of many noblemen to Hades, leaving their bodies as carrion for the dogs and passing birds.'

The *Iliad* is usually dated to the 8th century BC. It is quite possible that Achilles was originally a real man, however legendary the exploits with which Homer and later authors credited him. Homer calls him 'the great runner' for his skill as an athlete and 'the city-sacker' for his prowess as a fighter. In Hesiod, who wrote some years after Homer, he is 'lion-hearted Achilles, the destroyer of men'. Later still, as a result of the fame which the *Iliad* brought him, he was honoured in many parts of the Greek world as a hero, a being halfway between a god and a man.

At the village of Achilleum near Troy there was a temple sacred to Achilles and a statue of the hero wear-

ing, oddly enough, a woman's earring. At Elis on the Greek mainland he had a monument and on a certain day, toward sunset, the women of Elis honoured him by lamenting his death. He had a temple and a statue on Leuce,

Achilles keeping Hector's corpse

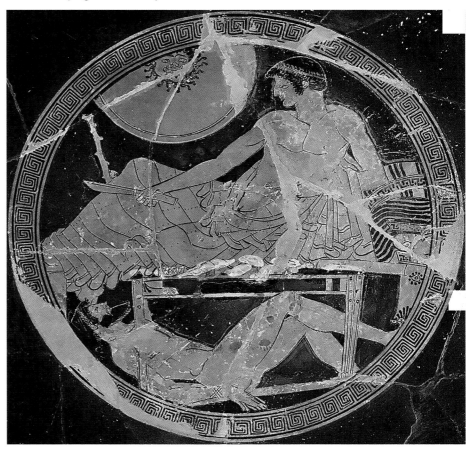

the White Island in the Black Sea opposite the mouths of the Danube, where offerings were made to him and games were held in his honour. It was said that passing sailors heard his voice across the water, reciting Homer to the accompaniment of the clash of battle and the thunder of horses' hooves.

The Wrath of Achilles

The story of the *Iliad* begins, in the tenth year of the siege of Troy, when the Greek supreme commander, Agamemnon, seized a beautiful slave-girl who had been allotted to Achilles as a prize of battle. Insulted, Achilles refused to fight any more and his absence gravely weakened the Greek resistance to fierce Trojan attacks. Agamemnon tried to make the quarrel up, offering to return the girl to Achilles with many splendid gifts. But Achilles was still nursing his fury and refused to be reconciled.

Lacking Achilles, the situation of

the Greeks now became so dangerous that Patroclus, the dearly loved friend of Achilles, went out to fight the Trojans. Patroclus was killed by the best of the Trojan warriors, Hector. When this news was brought to him, Achilles became berserk with grief and rage, and readied himself for battle—in spite of the warning from his mother, the sea-nymph Thetis, that he was doomed to die after Hector's death.

The next day, bearing new arms given to him by the gods, Achilles 'chased his victims with the fury of a fiend and the earth was dark with blood'. His horses trampled over dead men and fallen shields as he raged on in search of glory, until he found Hector and killed him in single combat, gloating over the Trojan's death agony.

Achilles maltreated Hector's corpse, dragging it in the dust behind his chariot, and he intended to throw it to the dogs to gnaw. But Hector's father persuaded him to return the body to the Trojans so that it could be decently buried.

The *Iliad* ends with the funeral rites for Hector but it is clear that Achilles has not long to live and that he will be killed by Hector's brother Paris and the archer-god Apollo. The *Odyssey* describes his death in battle, with the flower of the Greek and Trojan warriors falling round him in the struggle over his corpse. The sea-nymphs come from the ocean to weep salt tears for him and the nine Muses sing his dirge. His bones are mingled with those of his friend Patroclus and buried outside Troy.

Something Superhuman

Achilles has all the virtues of the Homeric hero. He is brave, passionate, ferocious in battle, beautiful to look at, intensely proud, and fated to an early death. His failing is his uncontrollable anger. His treatment of Hector's corpse is so savage that Homer calls it 'shameful outrage' and condemns as 'an evil thing' his slaughter of a dozen Trojan prisoners at the funeral of Patroclus. When Hector's father comes to beg for

his son's body, Achilles tries to console him and mercifully gives him the corpse. But even then he is sufficiently aware of his weakness to be afraid that he may suddenly fly into a rage and kill the old man.

Achilles' Heel

Many of the best-known stories about Achilles appear in later writings, including some which have parallels in folk tales all over the world, like the story that his mother tried to make him immortal by dipping him into a fire, but her husband thought she was trying to kill the child and stopped her. A famous variant of this is that she dipped him in the Styx, the river of the underworld, which made all of him deathproof except the heel by which she held him. It was in this heel that he received his mortal wound, from an arrow fired by Paris or Apollo.

His mother, Thetis, was so beautiful that both Zeus and the sea-god Poseidon desired her. But she was fated to bear a son who would be mightier

Thetis gives her son Achilles his weapons newly forged by Hephaestus

than his father, and when the two gods heard this, their ardour cooled, and they gave her in marriage to a mortal named Peleus. It was at the wedding of Thetis and Peleus that the apple marked 'for the fairest' was thrown among the gods, the apple of discord that caused the Trojan War in which Achilles met his death.

Achilles was only a boy when the Greek armies gathered for the siege of Troy. His mother hid him on the island of Scyros, where he was dressed as a girl and brought up with the king's daughters. But the crafty Odysseus came to Scyros bringing presents of cloth for dressmaking and also a spear and a shield. Achilles revealed himself by ignoring the cloth and seizing the weapons. What name Achilles bore when hidden among the women is an old problem. One suggestion is that he was called Pyrrha, 'redhead', for the colour of his hair.

At Troy, after the death of Hector, Achilles is said to have defeated various other notable fighters, including Penthesilea, Queen of the Amazons— a tribe of warrior women—who had come to fight on the Trojan side. When he killed her with a spear-thrust, he was so smitten by her beauty that he made love to her dead body.

Most of these later stories, to a modern eye at least, tend to lessen the stature of the hero, as compared with the picture of him in Homer. But there is a suitably grim tale in the Hecuba of Euripides. After the fall of Troy, the ghost of Achilles rose in the sheen of golden armour and stood high on the crest of his tomb, demanding his share of the spoil, in the shape of Polyxena, daughter of the king of Troy. The Greeks slaughtered the girl on Achilles' grave-mound, so that she could accompany her new master to the after-world, and the blood welled from her neck over her golden robes.

FURTHER READING: Homer's Iliad and Odyssey, *trans. R. Fitzgerald (Doubleday, 1975); M. Grant.* Myths of the Greeks and Romans *(New American Library, 1964); R. Graves,* The Greek Myths *(Braziller, 1959); and see also M. I. Finley,* The World of Odysseus*, rev. ed. (Viking Press, 1978).*

Adonis

That the name Adonis is still a byword for masculine beauty is a legacy from Greek mythology. In the myth, Aphrodite, the alluring goddess of love, falls irresistibly in love with the handsome young Adonis, but there is tragedy in store. He is out hunting one day when he is gored and killed by a boar, sent by Ares, Aphrodite's jealous lover. According to various versions of the myth, the rose springs from the young god's dying blood, or the anemone springs up from the tears Aphrodite sheds for him—or all roses were white originally, but Aphrodite pricks herself on a thorn as she runs to help her lover and her blood falls on the roses and stains them red.

Behind this poetic tale lies the ancient theme of the mother goddess and her virile lover, the dying god who

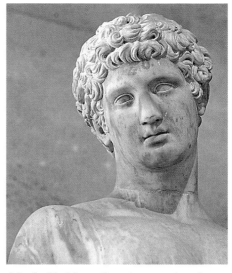

Adonis. Marble, antique torso restored and completed by François Duquesnoy, Flemish (1597–1643)

represents the vegetation which dies with every autumn and comes back to life with every spring. The Greek version tells only of the death of the god, but Adonis, whose name means 'lord', was originally a similar figure to Tammuz in Mesopotamia, the lover of the goddess Inanna or Ishtar, who rescued him from the realm of death and restored him to life.

In another Greek story, which preserves more of the dying and rising theme, Adonis is the son of a king in Cyprus or Assyria by incest with his daughter, Myrrha. The gods turn

Venus and Adonis, Charles-Joseph Natoire (1700–1777)

Myrrha into a tree—the myrrh—and in due time a beautiful boy is born of the tree. Aphrodite entrusts him to Persephone, the queen of the underworld, to look after, but she is so taken with his extraordinary beauty that she refuses to let him go. Eventually Zeus decides that the youthful god is to spend part of the year below ground with Persephone, part with Aphrodite and part on Olympus. This tale is obviously linked with the death and rebirth of crops and vegetation, and recalls the myth of the rape of Persephone herself.

Alexander the Great

Alexander the Great led his triumphant armies from Greece to the Nile and on into India, created a vast empire which no one afterward could hold together, and died before he was thirty-three. Deified in his own lifetime—he was recognized as a god by the Greek cities of the League of Corinth—his astonishing career caught the imagination of succeeding generations. Four hundred years after his death at Babylon in 323 BC, the Emperor Trajan, one of the ablest of Roman generals and rulers, went to ruined Babylon and offered sacrifice to Alexander's spirit in the room where he had died.

Legendary stories clustered round Alexander's memory like limpets on a rock and were retold for hundreds of years with alterations, additions, and shifts of emphasis. They spread across Europe and Asia, as far west as Ireland and as far east as Java.

The core of the later romance of Alexander was a book written in Greek at Alexandria after 200 BC by an unknown writer now called pseudo-Callisthenes (because the book was originally wrongly attributed to a real Callisthenes). The original is lost but four revisions of it have survived. It combined accurate historical material with legend. Later authors expanded it and translated it into other languages, with liberal additions in which they mingled material from reliable historians with imaginative fictions of their own invention and fables which were originally independent of Alexander. They often quoted letters supposedly, but not really, written by Alexander or to him.

Just as many of us now cannot feel any bond of sympathy with a character in fiction who is too far from our own likeness—a monstrous Martian or Venusian, for instance—so each different audience for the tales of Alexander made him one of themselves by giving him their own setting, nationality and outlook. As a result, he appears as an object lesson in the workings of fate, or as a saintly Christian, though he

Alexander the Great, detail of Alexander Mosaic (c. 100 BC)

lived long before Christ; as a benefactor of the Jews, an emissary of Allah, a noble medieval knight, or even as an incarnation of the Devil because he was a predecessor of the 'Antichrist' Antiochus IV Epiphanes.

At the World's End

The extent of Alexander's travels—he only stopped, reluctantly, when he had invaded India because his soldiers refused to go any further east—inspired stories about him reaching the end of the earth, where paradise, the fountain of life and other marvels were to be found.

Some of these stories were told to draw a moral. A Jewish tale in the Babylonian Talmud (before 500 AD) says that Alexander reached the earthly paradise but was turned back at the gate because 'only the just can enter here'. But he is given a mysterious ball as a present, which turned out to be an eyeball. The eye, like Alexander himself, is restlessly insatiable and tries to encompass the whole earth and yet when only a handful of dust drops on it, blinds it and blots it out; the dust, of course, being death to which all men come, even the most successful.

This story was expanded later and appears in the twelfth century in the German *Lay of Alexander* and the Latin King *Alexander's Journey to Paradise*. Alexander and his companions voyaged up the Ganges (or the Euphrates) till they came to the wall of a great city. There was no opening in the wall and they sailed on beside it for three days before they found a small window. When an old man came to the window, Alexander's lieutenants imperiously demanded tribute from the city. The old man sent them away, telling them that the city was the earthly paradise, the home of the blessed, but gave them a stone of mystic meaning as a present for Alexander.

Alexander took the stone back to Babylon, where various wise men

Sixteenth century painting of Alexander the Great, lowered in a glass diving bell

puzzled their wits to find its meaning. At last an aged Jew demonstrated with scales that the stone was heavier than any quantity of gold but if a little dust was sprinkled on it, it was lighter than a feather. The stone stood for Alexander himself. The greatest of monarchs in life, a feather would outweigh his value once dusty death had claimed him.

There is the same motif in the story of how, on the way to the Wells of Life, Alexander came to a lake in which was an island, and on the island a castle and over the castle's gateway was written, 'No man may go in to the greatest and least treasure of the world until he has passed the night of fear.' Alexander and his men spent the night beating off the terrifying and dangerous attacks of tigers and dragons, monstrous crabs, lions the size of bulls, mice the size of foxes, foul bats, and an army of wild men with six hands each.

In the morning the castle's drawbridge was lowered. They went in and saw a niche in the wall, above which was written, 'The greatest treasure and the least.' In the niche was a rich cush-

ion and on it a stone shaped like an egg. When they looked into the stone they saw everything that a man could desire in this world, and when they weighed it against gold and silver it was heavier than all their treasure. But when a pinch of dust was put in the other pan of the scales, it outweighed the stone.

Within a hundred years of his death Alexander was already said to have gone to the world's end looking for the water of life which conferred immortality—like other heroes. What was originally a separate story about 'the green one', who drank the water of life and became immortal, was tacked onto Alexander in the tale of his cook. Nearing the world's end, Alexander's expedition came to an area of many wells. The cook washed a dried fish in one of them and the fish came to life and swam away. The cook drank some of the water, became immortal and promptly turned green, the colour of vegetation which is reborn every spring. But the cook could not find the right well again. Furious, Alexander tried various methods of killing him—which all failed because he was immortal—and finally threw him into the sea, where he lives to this day as a sea-spirit.

Fiction from Fact

Many of the stories were built up around a grain of historical truth, like a pearl in an oyster. The daughter of a Scythian king, offered in marriage to the real Alexander but declined with thanks, turned into a Queen of the Amazons who visited the legendary Alexander with amorous intent. Another example is the famous story of Alexander's birth which represented him as the son of a god.

The real Alexander was the son of King-Philip of Macedon, in northern Greece, and his queen, Olympias. When he drove the Persians out of Egypt, he was accepted as Pharaoh and when he visited the oracle of the god Ammon in the desert, as Pharaoh he was formally hailed by the priest as 'son of Ammon'. On this basis, apparently, pseudo-Callisthenes and other Egyptian authors said that Alexander was not really the son of Philip of Macedon. They said that the wise Nectanebus, King of Egypt, skilled in magic and astrology, fled before the invading Persians to Macedon and told Olympias that Ammon would "bestow" a child on her, which Nectanebus, pretending to be the god and disguised as a dragon or a snake, duly did.

The legend may not be as cynical as it looks at first sight. Nectanebus may have been meant to be both himself and the vehicle of the god,

for in Egyptian belief a pharaoh was a god. Plutarch, who lived at the turn of the 1st and 2nd centuries AD, suggested that the snake came into the story because Olympias was a devotee of Dionysus and danced with snakes twined round her in the frenzy of his worship.

The Sky and the Sea-Bed

Alexander's rule of the West (Greece) as well as the East greatly impressed posterity and may account for the notion that one of his eyes was black (the West, sunset) and the other yellow (the East, sunrise). It may lie behind his Arabic title Dhul-Karnain, 'the

The Amazons were a mythical race of warrior women, whose battles with a number of Greek heroes were recorded in various local legends.

two-horned', meaning that he had subdued both horns of the sun, or the horns may be those of Ammon, whose animal was the ram. It was not unfitting to suppose that he had also gone to the limits of height and depth; and so in legend he goes down to the bottom of the sea in a green glass box banded with iron, and flies through the air in a chariot drawn by birds or griffins, which he steered by dangling a bit of liver enticingly on a spear just out of reach of their beaks.

His other feats included shutting up the savage tribes of Gog and Magog behind a wall of iron and brass, from which they will pour out to wreak havoc in the last day, a story which appears in the Koran. He made love to Candace, Queen of Ethiopia (or of India). He tamed a vicious man-eating horse which became his favourite war-charger and was called Bucephalus, 'the bull-headed', because it had horns.

He met and defeated innumerable monsters and peculiar humans, gigantic ants, female cannibals, giants with six heads, dwarves with one leg, horses with the faces of men, men with the faces of dogs, and, in the English *King Alysaunder*, the people who stand on one foot all day gazing steadfastly at the sun.

In the fourteenth century Chaucer said that the tales of Alexander were so common 'that every wight that hath discretion hath heard somewhat or all of his fortune', and Philip the Bold of Burgundy took Alexander for his hero and model in much the same way that Alexander himself had conceived a great admiration for the Homeric hero Achilles.

Waning Reputation

With the revival of classical scholarship in the Renaissance, the legend of Alexander began to go out of fashion and to be replaced by sober history. He has not lasted as well as King Arthur, about whose real life far less is known, and few of the stories about him are still common currency. He wept because there were no more worlds to conquer. When, at the height of his power, he asked the philosopher Diogenes what he could do for him, Diogenes replied, 'Move. You're standing in my light'. He cut the Gordian knot which no one had been able to untie; when he was told that whoever undid the knot would rule the East, he slashed it with his sword. But you may still be reminded of him if you hear 'The British Grenadiers' sung—'Some talk of Alexander, and some of Hercules, Of Hector and Lysander, and such great names as these . . .'

FURTHER READING:
N. G. Hammond. Alexander the Great: King, Commander & Statesman. *(Noyes, 1981).*

Amazons

The Amazons were a mythical race of warrior women, whose battles with a number of Greek heroes were recorded in various local legends. Their original home was in the gorges and forests of the Thermodon valley in Pontus in Asia Minor, and their capital city was Themiscyra on the coast of the Euxine (modern Terme, on the Black Sea coast of Turkey). According to one tradition, men were excluded altogether from their country, but for purposes of propagating the race the Amazons made an annual visit to the Gargareans in the Caucasus. Girls born of these unions were then brought up by the Amazons, each one having her right breast either burned or cut off to make it easier to hurl a javelin or stretch a bow. Boys were either put to death or sent back to their fathers. Another version has it that a number of men were kept for mating purposes, but had the status of slaves, and were allowed to perform only those tasks executed in other countries by women. Legend also has it that the legs and arms of these men were mutilated to prevent their challenging the Amazons' power.

Whether men were or were not included in the Amazon state, only women bore arms, not only defending their own country, but making expeditions of conquest into neighbouring territories. They fought both on foot and on horseback, carrying crescent shields and wielding spears, bows, and battle-axes. Their life consisted mainly in hunting and warlike exercises and the training of the girl Amazons. They were ruled by a queen, and they worshipped Ares, the god of war, from whom they were believed to be descended, and Artemis, goddess of the hunt.

Stories about the Amazons belong to the earliest Greek sagas. Homer

Marble statue of the wounded Amazon

mentions them in a way which shows that they were familiar to his audience. When in historical times the Greeks got to know the Thermodon region and found no Amazons there, they supposed either that Hercules had destroyed them all, or that they had been driven away. Thus in later legends, the Amazons were moved further and further away from their original homeland, but they were always located on the fringe of the world as it was then known to the Greeks. They were said

to be of Scythian origin from Colchis (south of the Caucasus), and there was also supposed to be a race of Amazons in Africa. They were in any case always foreign to the Greek homeland, and in Greek eyes—like all foreigners—they counted as barbarians.

Hercules, Theseus, and the Amazons

Two of their queens, Hippolyta and Penthesilea, figure in widely told Greek myths. The ninth labour imposed on

Hercules by his master Eurystheus was to take from Hippolyta her girdle, symbol of her royal power, which had been given to her by the god Ares. According to one version of the myth, Hercules withstood a cavalry charge of Amazons single-handed and routed their whole army, killing Hippolyta at the same time.

Later legends linked the name of Theseus, mythical King of Athens, with Hercules' expedition against the Amazons. Theseus carried off Antiope whose sister Oreithyia, sworn to vengeance, led an invading army into Attica. The Amazons were defeated by the Athenians after four months fighting. Some say that Antiope was killed in the fighting, but others that she survived to make a scene at Theseus' wedding (she being the mother of Theseus' son Hippolytus, though not his lawful wife), where she threatened to murder all the guests. Theseus killed her, to prevent her carrying out her threat.

In another legend, Hippolyta brought yet another Amazon force against Theseus after this wedding, and in the ensuing battle was killed accidentally by her sister Penthesilea. Pursued by the Furies of her dead sister, Penthesilea sought refuge in Troy, where she obtained purification from her blood-guilt at the hands of the aged King Priam. In gratitude she enrolled in the Trojan army, where, as the war-god Ares' daughter, she fought bravely until Achilles killed her. Achilles then wept for the lost beauty, youth and courage of the dead queen and made love to her corpse. Thersites, reputed to be the ugliest Greek at Troy, jeered at Achilles' grief and accused him of unnatural lust, whereupon Achilles killed him. This enraged some of the Greeks and Diomedes, a cousin of Thersites, threw Penthesilea's corpse into the River Scamander.

Amazons in the New World

Sir Walter Raleigh, the famous Elizabethan adventurer, explored South America in the sixteenth century and was told of Amazons:

Three Amazons. **This black-figure lekythos shows the women facing right, and they appear to march one after the other. Each wears a helmet, holds a long spear, and has a horizontal quiver. The middle figure holds both hands near her waist; the other two have one hand raised.**

Amazons in the Old World

We are told, namely, that there was once in the western parts of Libya, on the bounds of the inhabited world, a race which was ruled by women and followed a manner of life unlike that which prevails among us. For it was the custom among them that the women should practice the arts of war and be required to serve in the army for a fixed period, during which time they maintained their virginity; then, when the years of their service in the field had expired, they went in to the men for the procreation of children, but they kept in their hands the administration of the magistracies and of all the affairs of state. The men, however, like our married women, spent their days about the house, carrying out the orders which were given them by their wives; and they took no part in military campaigns or in the exercise of free citizenship in the affairs of the community by virtue of which they might become presumptuous and rise up against the women. When their children were born the babies were turned over to the men, who brought them up on milk and such cooked foods as were appropriate to the age of the infants.

Diodorus Siculus,
Bibliotheca Historica

But they which are not far from Guiana do meet with men but once in a year. At that time all the Kings of the borders assemble, and the Queens of the Amazons, and after the Queens have chosen, the rest cast lots for their Valentines. This one month they feast, dance and drink of their wines in abundance, and the Moon being done, they all depart to their own Provinces. If they give birth to a son, they return him to the father, if a daughter they nourish it and retain it. It was further told me, that if in the wars they took any prisoners that they used to accompany with those also at what time soever, but in the end for certain they put them to death; for they are said to be very cruel and bloodthirsty, especially to such as offer to invade their territories.

Sir Walter Raleigh,
The Discovery of the Empire of Guiana

The Greeks continued to circulate stories about the Amazons down to a late period. One very popular story was that the Amazon queen Thalestris visited Alexander the Great (356–323 BC) during one of his Asian campaigns, wishing to have a daughter by such a famous general. She stayed with him for thirteen days before returning to her own country. Writing more than 400 years later, Plutarch lists no less than fourteen authorities who mention this tale, though nine of them, he says, dismissed it as 'complete fiction', and it was laughed at after Alexander's death by his successor in Thrace, Lysimachus.

Slave-Girls or Matriarchs

The Amazons were a favourite subject for Greek sculptors and painters. In art of the earliest periods, they are dressed exactly like Greek warriors, but usually with one breast bare. After the Persian Wars (499–448 BC), for example, on Greek vases of the great classical period, they are represented in oriental garb, wearing caps and trousers, and pictures of them relate more and more to known legends about them. They are never depicted as having lost one breast, in spite of the Greek belief that their name meant 'breastless'.

Various explanations of the origins of the legends about the Amazons have been put forward. Some writers trace them to the armed slave-girls who were dedicated to the service of certain Asian deities, and the association of the Amazons with Artemis supports this theory. But the story is more likely to be an imaginative Greek embroidery of reports about matriarchal tribes in southwest Asia, or of tribes in which the women led a freer and tougher life than they did in Greece. Certainly the persistence of the legend right up to the 2nd and 3rd centuries AD, and its perennial popularity as a theme in the arts show that it had a deep appeal to some area in ancient Greek fantasy.

Antigone

Mythological daughter of Oedipus, the disgraced King of Thebes. Antigone has three siblings: sister Ismene and brothers Polyneices and Eteocles. Antigone is known as a tragic figure because she sacrifices her life to bestow honour on her dead brother Polyneices. After Oedipus discovers the truth about his family and blinds himself, Antigone accompanies her father in exile, finally leading him to a happy death at Colonus. When she returns to Thebes, she finds her two brothers warring for control of the kingdom. The brothers kill each other in combat, but Eteocles' army ultimately wins the war. An edict is passed that Polyneices and his allies will not be allowed a proper burial, offending an ancient custom that gives peace to the dead. Antigone violates the edict by burying her brother, is captured and sentenced to die for her crime, but hangs herself in captivity. Her story is told by Sophocles as the final installment of the Oedipus Trilogy of plays: Oedipus Rex, Oeudipus at Colonus and Antigone. Her tragedy explores the difference between human law and divine right, and has also been used by contemporary scholars to explore aspects of feminism in ancient and modern culture.

FURTHER READING: Sophocles, Robert Fagles, and Bernard Knox. The Three Theban Plays. *Harmondsworth, (Middlesex, England: Penguin, 1984); Hamilton, Edith, and Steele Savage.* Mythology. *(New York: Penguin, 1969); Söderbäck, Fanny.* Feminist Readings of Antigone. *(Albany: State University of New York, 2010); Steiner, George.* Antigones. *(New York: Oxford UP, 1984).*

Aphrodite

Aphrodite was the ancient Greek goddess of love, beauty, generation, and fertility. She was, naturally, a popular goddess and her cult was widespread throughout almost all of the Greek world. The Romans identified her with their goddess Venus. She had famous sanctuaries at Corinth and on the island of Cythera, at Paphos and Amathus in Cyprus, and at Eryx in the west of Sicily. She figures prominently in Greek mythology, beginning with the *Iliad* and *Odyssey* of Homer (8th century BC) and the poetry of Hesiod (c. 700 BC).

Despite her great popularity and important place in Greek religion and culture, Aphrodite was not in origin a native Greek goddess. Her cult came to Greece from Cyprus, where she was known as Kypfis (Lady of Cyprus). Aphrodite was probably a local Cypriot version of the great mother goddess, whose worship under various names was almost universal throughout the Near and Middle East in ancient times, and was of great antiquity. The many primitive idols found in Cyprus, depicting a naked female figure with the sexual attributes grossly emphasized, are probably archaic representations of this mother goddess, to whom the ancient inhabitants of Cyprus gave the name of Aphrodite.

The Foam-Born

There has been much learned but inconclusive discussion about the original meaning of the goddess's name. The Greeks, from the time of Hesiod, tried to explain it as deriving from the word *aphros*, 'foam', in the sense that Aphrodite was 'foam-born'. Hesiod in his *Theogony* accounts for this 'foam-birth' in a strange way. Describing the

origin of the universe, he tells how Earth gave birth to various beings through cohabiting with Uranus, the personification of Heaven. Uranus proved a tyrannous sire and imprisoned his offspring within the body of Earth, so that she groaned with the burden. Release came finally when Cronus, one of the sons of Earth, with the connivance of his mother, castrated his father. Cronus threw the severed genitals into the sea, and a white foam gathered around them, from which a maiden emerged. According to Hesiod, 'first she drew near to holy Cythera, and from there, afterward, she came to seagirt Cyprus, and came forth an awful and lovely goddess, and grass grew up about her beneath her shapely feet.'

This idyllic scene has been immor-

talized by the Renaissance artist Botticelli in his painting, *The Birth of Venus*.

This strange tale, so shocking in conception and yet so poetic in its presentation of Aphrodite, may provide a clue to the origin of some of the Greek myths about the origin of the universe. On Hittite clay tablets there has been found an even stranger and more primitive myth of a primordial act of castration: the sky-god Alalus is emasculated by a divine hero Kumarbis, who swallows the genitals and becoming impregnated by them, gives birth to the storm god. Since it is known that the Achaeans (one of the earliest of the peoples we call Greeks), had dealings with the Hittites of Asia Minor, it is possible that Hesiod drew on some tradition that derived ulti-

The Birth of Venus, Sandro Botticelli (1445–1510)

mately from this region.

The Hittite myth does not deal with the origin of a goddess like Aphrodite. But the similarity of the theme of generation resulting from the severed genitals of a god is remarkable, especially since Aphrodite personified the principle of generation. According to Hesiod's *Theogony*, Aphrodite was also called Philommedes (member-loving) because she 'sprang from the genitals'. The Christian scholar Clement of Alexandria, writing in the early third century against pagan religion, asserts with reference to the name Philommedes that in the rites of Aphrodite, her birth from the sea-foam was symbolized by the presentation of a cake of salt and a phallus.

Desire as a Universal Force

In his account of the origin of things, Hesiod still further emphasizes the fundamental sexual significance of Aphrodite by associating her with Eros: 'And with her went Eros, and comely Himeros (Desire) followed her at her birth.' The Eros of Hesiod is not the young god of love or the mischievous Cupid of later mythology. He is a powerful creative force, described by Hesiod as one who 'unnerves the limbs and overcomes the mind and wise counsels of all gods and all men'.

It is evident that Hesiod regarded the traditional gods as deifications of basic universal forces. Seeing the creation of the universe in sexual terms, as the product of the intercourse of various pairs of cosmic beings, he felt the need for some factor that would unite and make fruitful the unions of the various pairs. In Eros he saw such a factor but he probably also drew on a primitive folk-tradition, where this view already existed. The Athenian dramatist Aeschylus, in the 5th century BC, gives eloquent expression to the idea in some lines that have survived from his lost play of the *Danaids*:

'Love moves the pure Heaven to wed the Earth; and Love (*eros*) takes hold on Earth to join in marriage. And the rain, dropping from the husband Heaven, impregnates Earth, and she brings forth for men pasture for flocks and corn, the life of man.'

It would seem that the ancient Greeks had already made a god of sexual potency an agent in the creation of the universe, under the name of Eros, long before Aphrodite entered

> *She had, in fact, many sides to her nature: she was a sea goddess, a goddess of animals, of gardens, and even of death.*

their religion. Mindful of this, Hesiod evidently seeks to account for the later appearance of Aphrodite as the goddess of sexual love by using the strange and probably foreign myth of the castration of a primordial deity. By so doing he also manages to explain her non-Greek name of Aphrodite and to associate her with Eros, the older deification of the mysterious force that prompted the union of the sexes for the purpose of procreation.

Love and War

Hesiod's account of Aphrodite is especially important because, though somewhat later in date than Homer, he is aware of Aphrodite as a newcomer among the Greek deities; in the *Iliad* and *Odyssey* she has already been included in the company of the Olympian gods. Homer makes her the daughter of the supreme god Zeus and Dione, an obscure goddess. However, two small facts may preserve some tradition of Aphrodite's eastern origin. In Homer she is the wife of Hephaestus, the lame fire-god and divine craftsman, who was certainly of oriental origin. And her love affair with the

war god Ares recalls the fact that some eastern goddesses, including Ishtar of Mesopotamia and Anat-Astarte of Canaan and Phoenicia, combined the roles of goddess of fertility and goddess of war.

In the Homeric poems, Aphrodite is often portrayed in a rather undignified manner, although she is 'golden Aphrodite', the daughter of Zeus. In the *Iliad* the goddess Hera is depicted as consulting her when she wanted to beguile her husband Zeus. The goddess asks Aphrodite to give her 'love and desire, wherewith thou art wont to subdue all immortals and mortal men.' Aphrodite helps by lending Hera the embroidered girdle that adorned her breast, 'wherein are fashioned all manner of allurements'. Such a service was probably deemed proper to the goddess of love, even though it assisted in the deception of the supreme god Zeus.

But more surprising, and contrary to our ideas of the status of a goddess, are two other episodes in which Aphrodite is involved. The first occurs in the *Iliad* in a lively account of the fighting before the walls of Troy. The Greek hero Diomedes severely wounds Aeneas, a Trojan leader who was the son of Aphrodite by Anchises, a mortal man. Aphrodite, seeing her human son in danger of death, intervenes to save him. When Diomedes recognizes the goddess he is not deterred but lunges at her with his spear. Aphrodite is wounded in the wrist, and the immortal ichor, which the Greek deities have instead of mortal blood, pours out. Aphrodite gives a piercing scream, drops the wounded Aeneas and flees, while Diomedes derides her.

The idea that a goddess could be wounded by the weapon of a mortal man is certainly strange, and we can only wonder why the Homeric poet depicted the goddess of love as suffer-

ing so humiliating and painful an experience. He seems, while recognizing her divinity, to mock the idea that she should participate in war. It may be that in this way he rebuts some older tradition of a warlike aspect which the Greek Aphrodite had inherited from her eastern origins.

Even more degrading is the episode in the *Odyssey*, where a minstrel sings of the illicit love of Ares and Aphrodite. He tells how Helius, the sun god, reported their liaison to Hephaestus, the lame and deformed husband of Aphrodite. Furious at the news, the craftsman god plans the punishment of the guilty pair. He forges a net too fine to be seen but too strong to be broken, and spreads it about the bed in his house. Saying that he is leaving to visit his favourite sanctuary, he sets the trap for the lovers. Ares seizes the opportunity of the husband's departure to visit Aphrodite. Warned by Helius, Hephaestus turns back and discovers the lovers together in his bed, where they are enmeshed by the invisible but imprisoning bonds.

Hephaestus calls the other gods to witness the shameful spectacle, and he demands that Zeus pay back the bridal gifts before he releases his shameless daughter and her paramour. The sea god Poseidon finally persuades the angry Hephaestus to let the couple go, by guaranteeing the payment of damages by Ares. The extraordinary episode ends by describing the 'laughter-loving' Aphrodite's retreat to Paphos in Cyprus; 'where is her demesne and fragrant altar. There the Graces anointed her with immortal oil . . . and clothed her in a lovely raiment, a wonder to behold.'

Little, unfortunately, is known of the nature and form of the rites which were performed in the various temples of Aphrodite. At Corinth and in Cyprus she was served by sacred prostitutes; and at Abydos there was a temple of Aphrodite Porne (Aphrodite the Harlot). This connection with ritual prostitution attests Aphrodite's eastern origin; for the custom prevailed at the cult centres of many eastern goddesses.

Aphrodite, however, was also the divine patron of marriage. In Athens, under the title of Pandemos (of all the people), her cult was dignified and unobjectionable. She had, in fact, many sides to her nature: she was a sea goddess, a goddess of animals, of gardens, and even of death—there was a small statue at Delphi called 'Aphrodite by the Tomb'. This last association is not surprising, for the great mother goddess was also a subterranean deity concerned with the dead.

In mythology Aphrodite was also associated with the three Graces or *Charites* (personifications of charm, grace and beauty) and with the Hours (*Horae*), goddesses of the seasons. Various animals were connected with her (including doves, sparrows, swans, dolphins, and mussels) and forms of vegetation (roses, myrtle, cypress, and pomegranates).

Anemones for Adonis

Aphrodite's connection with Adonis (well known through Shakespeare's poem *Venus and Adonis*) reveals most clearly her original association with the Great Goddess of the ancient Near East. The story of Adonis appears in its most complete form in the *Metamorphoses of Ovid* (17 AD). Adonis is the incestuous offspring of Cinyras, King of Cyprus, and his daughter Myrrha who, in consequence of her sin, is transformed into a myrrh tree (the myrrh, exuded from the bark, is explained as the tears of Myrrha). This metamorphosis of his mother occurs before Adonis is born and his subsequent birth from the myrrh tree is significant of his origin as a vegetation god.

Grown to a beautiful youth, Adonis attracts the attention of Aphrodite, who falls passionately in love with him. Despite her warnings of the risks of hunting, Adonis is killed by a wild boar. Aphrodite is distraught with grief at his death and, to commemorate the tragedy, she causes the anemone to spring from his blood.

The death and resurrection of Adonis was celebrated annually in a ritual lamentation by women over an effigy of the dead god in many places, including Athens. In the Greek city of Alexandria in Egypt the sacred marriage of Aphrodite and Adonis was celebrated, followed next day by lamentation as an effigy of the dead god was taken out and cast into the sea. 'Gardens of Adonis' were also made, in which the forced growth of seedlings symbolized the resurrection of Adonis. The cult and myth of Adonis doubtless came to Greece from Cyprus with that of Aphrodite.

The Goddess in Art

The portrayal of Aphrodite in art deserves special notice. Greek classical art of the 5th century BC presents the goddess as a dignified figure, robed in contemporary costume, as in the famous Parthenon frieze. A delicate exception is the representation of Aphrodite rising from the sea on the Ludovisi throne, where the body of the goddess is depicted as only lightly veiled.

The first notable figure of a nude Aphrodite was made in the 4th century BC by Praxiteles. The work was commissioned by the people of Cos, who rejected it for the traditional draped figure. It was accepted by the citizens of Cnidos, and became one of the most famous statues of the ancient-world. The goddess was shown laying aside her robe, preparing for the bath; the original statue is known only through later Roman copies. The Cnidian Aphrodite inspired many later Hellenistic and Roman statues of which the Venus de Milo, now in the Louvre at Paris, is the most celebrated.

S. G. F. BRANDON

FURTHER READING: H. J. Rose. A Handbook of Greek Mythology. *(Dutton, 1959); J. Harrison.* Prolegomena to the Study of Greek Religion. *(Merlin, 1981); E. O. James.* The Cult of the Mother Goddess. *(Barnes & Noble, 1961); S. G. F. Brandon.* Creation Legends of the Ancient Near East. *(Verry, Lawrence, 1963); H. Licht.* Sexual Life in Ancient Greece. *(Greenwood, 1976); Kenneth Clark.* The Nude. *(Princeton University Press, 1972).*

Apollo

Apollo, brightest and best of the ancient Greek gods, was the god of music, archery, prophecy, healing, care of animals and young growing creatures, and from the 5th century BC, at least, he was identified with the sun.

He was the only Greek god to have specific functions in each of the domains allotted separately to the gods of the sky (Zeus), the sea (Poseidon), and the earth (Hades). His titles bear witness to these functions. He was, for example, Apollo Asgelatas—'god of radiance'; Embasios—'favouring embarkation'; and Arotrios —'god of ploughing'. His titles, of which over 300 have survived in ancient authors and inscriptions on stone, show that Apollo was a god much loved by people in all walks of life.

He was the inspiration of a great deal of ancient Greek painting, poetry, and music. More than any other figure in Greek mythology or history, he embodied the spirit of Greek civilization. In art he was depicted as the ideal type of young, virile beauty.

In historical times Apollo was worshipped by all the Greeks. He plays a prominent part in the Homeric epics, and in the *Iliad* is the ally of the Trojans. In Homer, he is usually called Phoebus Apollo—'bright Apollo'.

Other epithets associated with him refer to his deadly aim as an archer, or to his silver bow.

But this most typical Greek of gods, if he did not come originally from Asia Minor, certainly incorporated many of the features of a prehistoric non-Greek deity. It is possible that the name Apollo is of Greek origin, although modern scholars are divided as to whether the root-meaning of the word is 'strength', 'sheep-fold', or 'assembly of voters'. But at an early date the original Greek god seems to have been identified with a Hittite god named Apulunas or Appaliunaas, and the Greeks themselves associated Apollo not only with a legendary northern people, the Hyperboreans, but also with Lycia, a country in what is now southwest Turkey. Apollo's mother's name, Leto, has often been connected by scholars with a Lycian word meaning 'woman'.

Head of the Kassel Apollo type. Pentelic marble, Roman copy of the 2nd century AD after a Greek original of c. 460 BC. Found in Greece

The Greeks, however, were aware of an ambiguity in the title Lykeios (Lycian) often given to Apollo. Greek poets punned (and in ancient Greek puns had a serious, not a humourous significance) on the associations this title could have with Apollo's fame as a slayer of wolves—*lykos* being the Greek for 'wolf'.

Apollo's eastern connections partly account for an atmosphere of mystery which was another of his aspects. In time, he accumulated many exotic titles, some of them of undoubtedly non-Greek origin, and as the god of oracles he was known throughout the Greek world as Loxias—'the ambiguous one'.

Apollo and his twin sister Armetis were the children of Zeus, king of the gods, and Leto, the Titaness. According to one version of the birth myth, Delos was the only land which would receive Leto as she felt her time to give birth drawing near. Other places feared the power of the god she would give birth to. In historic times, Apollo's birth at Delos was celebrated by an important festival held in that tiny island each spring. According to the historian Herodotus, the Hyperboreans came every year with offerings which they brought all the way from their northern homeland. There was also an oracle of Apollo at Delos.

Apollo at Delphi

Apollo's most important oracular shrine, however, was at Delphi on the Greek mainland, a place which preserves to this day much, of the extraordinary, religious atmosphere which it had in ancient times. The Homeric Hymn to Apollo describes how the god came to this place 'beneath snowy Parnassus' and performed—while still a child, according to some accounts—one of his greatest exploits:

'Nearby there was a fair stream, where the Prince, son of Zeus, killed with an arrow from his bow a drago-ness, a fat, great, wild monster, who had done much harm to men on Earth and to their longshanked flocks, for she was a blood-reeking bane.'

Later tradition embroidered this story, and the female dragon became a male snake: a python, from which derived Apollo's title of Pythian, often accorded him in his connection with the Oracle at Delphi. It is often said—and the belief was already prevalent in antiquity—that the dragon or snake represented an earlier earth cult which was ousted by Apollo. But there is nothing in this original account, in the Homeric Hymn, to suggest that the dragoness was in any way oracular, or the guardian of an oracle, and the theory seems to spring from a later interpretation of what, in the first place, was a simple dragon story of a type common in Greece and elsewhere.

The Oracle was run in historical times by priests who interpreted the more or less incoherent mutterings of the Pythia, a middle-aged woman dressed by convention as a maiden, who sat on a tripod, inhaling the fumes of barley, hemp, and chopped bay-leaves burned over an oil-flame; she was believed to be in direct communication with the god. For over 1,000 years the Oracle was regularly consulted by both Greeks and Romans (and by Asians as well), who were anxious to know the divine purpose in relation to future events. The Oracle's replies were almost always obscure or ambiguous, and often wrong, but Socrates was a firm believer, perhaps because Apollo had declared him to be the wisest of all men.

The Oracle was closed for three months in winter, and during this time Apollo was supposed to be absent, visiting his special people, the Hyperboreans, who danced, sang, and feasted in his honour.

It was through the Oracle at Delphi that Apollo exercised his chief political influence in the Greek world, which can be summed up as moderate, conciliatory, and conservative. His advice

The ruins of Apollo's temple and the small *omphalos* or navel-stone which the Greeks regarded as marking the true centre of the earth can still be seen. Apollo was sometimes shown in Greek art as sitting on the stone.

was considered especially valuable by anyone intending to found a colony overseas. It was here, too, that Apollo chiefly operated as a moral force in Greek life. The three famous maxims, or 'programmes' as the ancients called them, were carved on a column in the fore-temple at Delphi: 'Know thyself, 'Nothing in excess' and 'Go surety, and ruin is at hand'. They—or the first two, at least—epitomized that awareness and moderation which are usually taken to have been the Greek ideal.

Apollo lasted at Delphi well into the Christian era. He delivered his last oracle in the year 362 AD, to the physician of the Emperor Julian, the Byzantine ruler who tried to restore paganism after Christianity had become the official religion of the Byzantine Empire. 'Tell the king,' said the oracle, 'that the curiously built temple has fallen to the ground, that bright Apollo no longer has a roof over his head, or prophetic laurel, or babbling spring. Yes, even the murmuring water has dried up.'

Wolf and Mouse God

The primitive deity who developed, partly by assimilating some of the characteristics of an eastern god, into the glorious figure of classical Greece was very probably a wolf god, worshipped by herdsmen for his power over wolves, which meant that he could keep wolves away from their flocks. In later times, Apollo's connection with flocks and herds was not emphasized as much. Apollo, in common with many other Greek deities, had a special tree which was sacred to him. This was the laurel (called Daphne in Greek). A very ancient legend tells how the nymph, Daphne, was overwhelmed by the god's amorous attentions and fled away from him. Luckily, she was turned into a laurel tree.

Apollo was known as the god of leafage, the ripener, the nourisher, the grower of things, the protector of corn, the warder-off of blight, and the averter of locusts. One of his oldest titles was Smintheus, which connected him either with the Asian town of Sminthe, or with mice, or with both. Here, as so often, a number of concepts merged into one cult name. Mice were associated with snakes, such as the one which, according to some versions of the story, Apollo destroyed at Delphi; they were also destroyers of the crops Apollo was believed to protect.

Many of Apollo's higher functions arose out of these primitive agricultur-

> *Apollo took up the role of divine founder of colonies.*

al ones. It is easy to see the connection between his care of flocks and his skill with the bow which drove away predators. Shepherds to this day are known for their singing, playing and dancing in Greece and in other Balkan countries, and Apollo's patronage of music probably has its origin in this. The shepherd, too, must be able to care for his flocks, and Apollo was not only a healer himself, both of body and soul, a god who kept away plagues and pests, but he was also the father of the god of medicine, Asclepios.

The Asian cults which were absorbed into the worship of Apollo were as likely as not introduced into the Greek world during the period of overseas colonization which began in the 8th century BC, and from an early period Apollo took up the role of divine founder of colonies. Intending colonizers usually consulted the Oracle at Delphi, and Apollo was often accorded the honourary title of 'Found-

er' in acknowledgement of the usually enigmatic advice his oracle had given. It was believed by some that he guided emigrants to their new settlements in the form of a sea-bird. Perhaps this is the origin of one of his more mysterious cult names—Opsophagos, 'fish-eater'.

In most of his remarkably numerous love affairs, Apollo was curiously unlucky. Deceit and disdain are the constant themes of these myths, and most of Apollo's affairs had a fatal ending.

One very unlucky love of Apollo's was Cassandra, daughter of King Priam of Troy. She resisted the god's advances strenuously, and he wooed her with gifts, including the power of prophecy. When Apollo saw that she would not yield to him, he could not, as a god, recall his gifts, but he turned his blessing into a curse by making sure that while Cassandra always foretold truly what would happen, none of her prophecies would ever be believed by those they most concerned, her own people, the Trojans.

The Ears of Midas

Although Apollo was a god of protection and patronage, he was also, like all the Greek gods, a deadly enemy on occasion. The story of Niobe, told by Homer, illustrates this side of Apollo's character. She had seven sons and seven daughters, and in an ill-fated moment, boasted that she was superior to Leto, who had only two children. At this, Apollo and Artemis drew their bows, and Apollo slew the boys, while Artemis slew the girls. Niobe in her grief wept until she was turned into a pillar of stone, from which the tears still flowed, as visitors to Mt. Sipylon could see for themselves.

In another cruel legend, Marsyas the satyr challenged Apollo to a contest on the flute. Apollo agreed, on the condition that whoever won might have his will with the loser. Having won by his divine skill, he flayed Marsyas alive. In another contest, this time with the god Pan, King Midas of Phrygia, who judged it, decided against Apollo. Apollo then turned Midas's ears into those of an ass, and Midas had to wear a special head-covering, so that only his barber knew about the ears. The barber had to tell someone, and he dug a hole in the ground and whispered the story into it. Rushes grew up on the spot, and still whisper about Midas's asses ears to this day.

Apollo was adopted by the Romans as a god of healing, and later as a patron of oracles and prophecy, but although his cult was developed by the Emperor Augustus, who put up a great temple to him on the Palatine Hill, the Roman Apollo was not such a vivid figure as the great Greek god.

In the early centuries of our era, a number of new religions and cults, imported from the east, were rivals for the allegiance of the people in the Greek and Roman world. From this religious struggle Christianity, of course, eventually emerged victorious. But Apollo, the god so widely respected and adored, was throughout these centuries a force to be reckoned with. The early Christian leaders had to make a special effort to dislodge him from his place in the imagination and regard of the pagan masses they were trying to convert. It is possible that some of the later and more scurrilous stories put about concerning the god owed their inspiration to this Christian religious campaign.

DAVID PHILLIPS

FURTHER READING: Robert Graves. The Greek Myths. (Braziller, 1959); Alexander Duthie. Greek Mythology. (Greenwood, 1979); Charles Seltman. The Twelve Olympians: Gods and Goddesses of Greece. (Apollo Editions).

Ariadne

Ariadne was the mythological daughter of Minos, King of Crete who built the Minotaur's labyrinth, and Queen Pasiphae. She is said to be the actual daughter of the Sun-Titan Helios, who allows Minos to assume paternity. Accounts of her actions and relationships vary widely according to the source. By some accounts, Theseus arrives in Crete to slay the Minotaur, and Ariadne promptly falls in love with him, providing him a weapon to fight the monster and a magic ball of thread with which he finds his way into and out of the labyrinth. After Theseus' success, she runs away with him to be his wife. According to Homer, 'Theseus took her aboard with him from Crete for the terraced land of ancient Athens . . . ' (*Odyssey* XI.373–375) Subsequently, Theseus abandons or is otherwise separated from Ariadne, and Ariadne either dies and is immortalized by a devoted cult following, or marries Dionysus, god of wine. To the contrary, Homer claims that 'Artemis killed [Ariadne] on the Isle of Dia at a word from Dionysus' (*Odyssey* XI.376–377) suggesting a conflict between Dionysus and Ariadne; perhaps they were already wed and the god disapproved of her union with Theseus. She has twin sons by Theseus, Oenopion and Staphylus. Or else her twins are by Dionysus, with whom she also bears Thoas and Peparethos. In Hesiod's version, Dionysus loves Ariadne and makes her immortal. Ariadne is sometimes associated with weaving and thread, and the constellation Corona Borealis is said to be Dionysus' memorial of Ariadne's wedding crown.

FURTHER READING: Homer, Robert Fagles, and Bernard Knox. The Odyssey. (New York: Viking, 1996); Graves, Robert. The Greek Myths. (Baltimore: Penguin, 1955); Hesiod, and M. L.

West. Hesiod: Theogony. (Oxford: Clarendon, 1966); Plutarch, John Dryden, and Arthur Hugh Clough. Plutarch's Lives of Illustrious Men. (Philadelphia: J. C. Winston, 1908).

Ate

Greek word for 'ruin, disaster': personified as a power which so disorders a man's mind that he cannot tell right from wrong; in the *Iliad* she is the daughter of Zeus, an early example of the problem of how far Gods are responsible for evil; some later European writers thought of her as a demoness.

Athene

The greek goddess Athene (or Athena) was closely associated with the city of Athens, whose name in Greek is the plural form of the goddess's name; she was also called 'the Athenian', *Athenaie*. These names are not of Greek origin and the goddess was probably taken over from the earlier non-Greek population by Hellene invaders who entered the country about 2000 BC.

In the Mycenaean period (before 1200 BC) Athene seems to have been a palace goddess, who protected kings in different districts. She was especially their protectress in war and there are artistic representations of an armed goddess who may be Athene. Direct evidence is hard to come by but this much can be inferred from her status in Homer and in classical Greek religion.

The Homeric poems (8th century BC), which look back to the heroic age of the Mycenaean civilization, preserve many memories from the centuries before Homer, and Athene is one of the most important deities in them. Her antiquity is indicated by a number of her titles which were of unknown or uncertain meaning to the Greeks themselves: Pallas, Tritogeneia, Atrytone. She is the daughter of Zeus, and he pays her markedly more love and respect than he shows to his wife Hera. She is the city goddess of Troy, but at the same time the helper of Greek heroes in battle. Other gods and goddesses have favourites whom they are prepared to whisk away from danger, but only Athene will stand beside a warrior in his chariot. Besides her spear and helmet, she carries a magic goatskin (aegis), with which she flaps terror into opposing forces or courage into her own.

The more intelligible of her epithets in Homer almost all refer to her warlike qualities: agestratos or ageleie 'leader of the war-host', egrekydoimos 'rouser of battle', laossoos 'driving armies before her', leitis 'goddess of booty'. But she had other aspects. She was patron goddess of arts and crafts, including carpentry and weaving, and was noted for wisdom and resource.

The connections between these various functions are obscure. Wisdom and help in war probably reflect what the princelings of the Mycenaean age hoped for from her; perhaps she became the goddess of joiners and weaving-women because they looked to the palace for employment. But she remained their goddess long after the palaces fell and the princes were overthrown.

Born in Armour

According to mythology the goddess was born in full armour from the head of Zeus, which Hephaestus helpfully split with an axe. She thus had no real mother, though one was supplied by the story that Zeus married Metis, 'Resource', and swallowed her before she gave birth (a motif borrowed from Zeus' own birth. She had no husband either. Hephaestus, the other god of craftsmen, who was worshipped with her at Athens, might have been the obvious mate for her, but that would

have implied divine children.

Athene's warlike qualities made it natural that she should be given a leading part in the overthrow of the Giants, the earth born rebels who piled up mountains in their attempt to storm Olympus. But as she was responsible for warriors' successes, their disasters were attributed to her anger. Because Ajax the Locrian assaulted her priestess at Troy, she roused a tempest as the Greek fleet sailed home, and Ajax was drowned.

Goddess of Cities

Holy places are very tenacious of the respect in which they are held by the people. The old palaces fell but Athene remained on the citadels where they had stood. From being the goddess of the ruler she became the goddess of the city, and was given this express title in a number of places besides Athens. She was often associated in this function with a 'Zeus of the city'. Already in Homer she is the city goddess of Troy with her temple on the Acropolis. So long as her wooden image, given by Zeus to the first king, remained there, the city's safety was assured; the Greeks had to steal it before their victory.

The goddess developed some secondary characteristics in different localities; at Elis, for example, she had the title Mother, and apparently a connection with childbirth. But what appears in many places, and is therefore likely to be an ancient feature, is her association with the crafts, expressed in the title Ergane, 'craftswoman'. At Athens, where ceramics was a major industry, the potters particularly enjoyed her supervision, though she was also the goddess of the whole community. Another important item in the Athenian economy was the production and sale of olive oil, and so the olive too came under the goddess's special care.

This public aspect became more and more dominant as time went on. In

A Manly Goddess

On Olympus the gods were altogether superior to the goddesses, considered collectively—superior not only in their power but also in their appeal, in the feelings they inspired among men. The chief exception to the rule was Athena, and the significant quality of Athena as a goddess was manliness. She was the virgin goddess in a world that knew no original sin, no sinfulness of sex, no Vestal Virgins. She was not even born of woman, having sprung from the head of Zeus—an insult to the whole race—of women for which Hera never forgave her husband, Hera who was the complete female and whom the Greeks feared a little and did not like at all, from the days of Odysseus to the twilight of the gods.

M. I. Finley, *The World of Odysseus*

the 6th century BC the dictator Pisistratus made a stylish return from exile by getting a strapping girl to dress up as Athene and lead the way. Nobody can have believed it was the goddess in person, but the spectacle must have had its effect. As ruler of Athens, Pisistratus put Athene's head on the city's coins, built her a new temple on the Acropolis, and made her four-yearly festival, the Great Panathenea, more splendid. This was all politics rather than piety, but it was politically worthwhile because piety was still common. For the ordinary people it represented a visible expression of the increased glory of Athens. Pisistratus was succeeded in 528 by his sons, who continued his policies. Athene's face on the coins developed a merry smile, which remained there into the following century.

The Owls of Athene

Animals that appear in holy places are liable to be taken for manifestations of divinity, and the owls of the Athenian Acropolis were associated with the goddess from early times. Her epithet glaukopis may mean 'owl-faced'. In 480 BC the Persian invaders destroyed the sacred buildings, but the appearance of an owl put heart into the defenders, and the tables were turned in the naval battle at Salamis.

In the following decades, Athens became the most powerful city in Greece and its intellectual centre. In Aeschylus and other authors of the fifth century, Athene appears as a noble figure, embodying the city's highest ideals of justice, wisdom, and moderation. At the same time rebuilding was proceeding on the Acropolis in magnificent style. A huge bronze statue of the warrior goddess was set up where it could be seen miles away at sea. The old temple was replaced by a larger and finer one higher up on the crest of the hill, the incomparable Parthenon. It contained another great statue of the goddess, clad in a golden robe and holding a figure of Victory in her palm. The outside was decorated with sculptures representing Athene's birth, her dispute with the god Poseidon for control of the city, battles among gods and men, and the ceremonial procession of the Panathenea.

These proud and liberal works still proceeded after Athens became engaged in her long war with Sparta (431–404). But the aspirations that they expressed were disappointed, for

Owl, the symbol of Athena, standing on amphora, all surrounded by a wreath of olive leaves. Silver tetradrachm from Athens (c. 200–150 BC), reverse.

this war ended in defeat and disillusion. The goddess maintained her public position to the end of paganism, honoured with priestesses, shrines, and sacrifices, entitled 'Bringer of Victory'. But these municipal pieties had less and less to do with religious feeling. Already in fifth century art Athene's face had taken on an impersonal expression. The subsequent decline of the city's industries struck at the roots of her popular support; the number of private dedications to her fell off sharply after the 4th century BC.

An Intellectual Rebirth

At the same time, the traditional gods were suffering from a general loss of respect, due to the rise of scientific rationalism. But far from killing the gods, the intellectuals gave them a new lease of life, by identifying them with physical or mental realities for which divinity could be claimed. For example, Zeus the hurler of thunderbolts was for them not a sturdy male figure, but the sky.

This line of thought began in the 6th century BC, and was being applied systematically by the fourth at the latest. In Plato's time, Athene was being identified with 'mind'. The same method was embraced by Stoicism, the philosophy which exercised more

Temple of Athena Nike, Acropolis of Athens, Greece

influence on educated men than any other from the 3rd century BC to the 3rd century AD. For the Stoics, Athene was wisdom, or virtue, or the moon.

The aim in making these identifications was to find something which could be related to the name of a god as well as to his traditional titles and myths. So Chrysippus in the 3rd century BC explained that Athene was called Athene because the mind considers (athrein), and Tritogeneia because wisdom is tripartite; she was born from the head with the help of Hephaestus, the craftsman god, because wisdom comes to light by way of the voice, and arises from technical skills.

Through such devices the Greek gods remained alive, and preserved their ancient attributes. In the Orphic Hymns (probably of the 2nd to 3rd centuries AD), Athene is laden with the accumulated attributes of 1,500 years; goddess of war, destroyer of Giants, mother of arts, bringer of victory and health, personified wisdom. In a later hymn, addressed to her by the philosopher Proclus in the 5th century AD, she retains all these facets, and is accommodated to the highly abstract theological system of the Neoplatonists as well; and this artificial creature, formed as it were by sedimentation, served Proclus as a focus for his genuine piety and devotion.

The Roman Minerva

As early as the 6th century BC, a native Italian goddess Minerva was identified with Athene. In Etruscan artistic copies of Greek mythological scenes her name is written for Athene's; in Latin literature Minerva is the ordinary name for the Greek goddess.

Because this identification was so early, it is hardly possible to determine Minerva's original character, though it must have resembled Athene's in some important respect. Many scholars regard her patronage of arts and crafts,

which is conspicuous in historical times, as a basic attribute and the Latin proverbial phrase 'unwilling Minerva', indicating lack of inspiration, shows that she was established in the popular mind as goddess of wit and resource. Other functions of Athene were transferred to her by literary men and in official cult. The Etruscans set her up as a protecting goddess of cities, in company with Jupiter and Juno, and the Romans, when they took the south Etruscan town of Falerii in 241 BC, removed her image to Rome as the Greeks had removed Athene's from Troy. Little religious sentiment can have been involved. Roman religion was, after all, largely a mass of formalities, preserved from a pre-urban past by priestly conservatism and later by cultured antiquarianism, modified at intervals from political motives by the state.

M. L. WEST

FURTHER READING: H. J. Rose. A Handbook of Greek Mythology *(Dutton, 1959) gives an excellent brief survey of gods and myths. For the early period, M. P. Nilsson,* The Minoan-Mycenaean Religion *(Lund, Sweden, 1950) is the standard work. For the classical period there is much material in volume 1 of L. R. Farnell,* The Cults of the Greek States. *(Caratzas Bros., 1977, first published in Britain 1896–1909), though the discussion of the gods' natures is outdated. See also F. Altheim,* A History of Roman Religion *(Dutton, 1938).*

Atlas

In Greek mythology, the giant who held up the sky to prevent it from falling on the earth; he was identified with the Atlas Mountains in Africa and legend said that he was turned to stone when Perseus showed him the Gorgon's head; his name was first used for a collection of maps by

Statue of Minerva. Roman artwork of the Imperial era

Mercator in 1595, with a picture of him holding up the globe of the earth on his shoulders.

Bacchus

A name of Dionysus, the Greek god of fertility, wine, and ecstatic frenzy, whose worshippers were called Bacchae or Bacchantes; Bacchanalia was the Latin name for the mysteries celebrated in the god's honour, originally confined to women, banned at Rome in 186 BC but reintroduced during the 1st century AD.

Caduceus

Latin word for a herald's staff of office, associated with the Greek god Hermes, the messenger of the gods: in its oldest form possibly an olive branch with two prongs at the top, entwined with ribbons; later it was a wand with two snakes twined round it, and sometimes with wings at the top of the staff; in alchemy a symbol of the uniting of opposites: more generally, it has been interpreted as an emblem of power (the wand) combined with wisdom (the snakes); also used as a symbol of healing.

Carthage

Ancient city located on the site of modern day Tunis, Tunisia. Carthage was the capital of an empire that ruled over the Western Mediterranean coastal region from 650 BC to 146 BC, when it was defeated and occupied by the Roman Republic. It was a culture of Phoenician peoples who spoke Punic, Phoenician, and Berber. Carthage established its independence from ancestral Phoenicia, and in colonizing coastal Africa, Iberia, and Sicily, engaged in continual conflicts with Greek and Roman forces for control of Mediterranean trade and influence. Carthage was a monarchy until 308 BC, at which point it lost the First Sicilian War against Greek Syracuse and re-established itself as a republic. The Roman Republic finally subdued Carthage decisively in 146 BC when it besieged and burned the city at the end of the Third Punic War. Carthage's colonies were taken over by Roman forces.

FURTHER READING: Goldsworthy, Adrian Keith. The Punic Wars. (London: Cassell, 2001); Prevas, John. Hannibal Crosses the Alps: The Invasion of Italy and the Punic Wars. (Cambridge, MA: Da Capo, 2001); Caven, Brian. The Punic Wars. (New York: St. Martin's, 1980); Livy, John Yardley, and B. D. Hoyos. Hannibal's War. (Oxford: Oxford UP, 2006).

Cassandra

Princess of Troy, daughter of King Priam and Queen Hecuba, Cassandra is best known for the curse placed on her by Apollo. Due to Cassandra's extraordinary beauty, Apollo granted her the gift of prophecy (in some versions, by spitting in her mouth). Apollo proceeded to make romantic gestures toward Cassandra, who rebuffed the god, leading him to curse her: while she will be able to see the future, no one will believe her prophecies. Cassandra appears in Aeschylus' play *Agamemnon* as the captured concubine of the eponymous king returning from victory in Troy. Cassandra foretells her own death as well as the murder of Agamemnon at the hands of his wife Clytemnestra and her lover Aegisthus. No one believes Cassandra's prophecy, as is her curse, and so the murders play out tragically. She is described in the *Iliad* as a 'peer of golden Aphrodite' (Book XXIV:699). Cassandra's siblings include Helenus (her fraternal twin brother) and Paris.

FURTHER READING: Graves, Robert. The Greek Myths. (Baltimore: Penguin, 1955); Hamilton, Edith, and Steele Savage. Mythology. (New York: Penguin, 1969); Homer, and Robert Fitzgerald. The Iliad. (London: Collins Harvill, 1985); Homer, Robert Fagles, and Bernard Knox. The Odyssey. (New York: Viking, 1996).

Ceres

Roman goddess of corn and of the creative powers of the earth, the equivalent of the Greek Demeter; guardian of marriage, and associated with the dead under the earth and with the wine god; her name survives in our word 'cereal'.

Charon

This aged and irascible boatman was believed by the Greeks to ferry the souls of the dead across the infernal river (the Acheron or Styx) which separated the land of the living from that of the dead. Charon is thus associated with Hermes Psychopompos, who summoned those appointed to die and led them to Hades. It has been thought that he was originally a death god, as was his Etruscan counterpart Charun. He is mentioned in Greek literature as early as the 5th century BC and is frequently depicted in art, particularly on the white-ground vases called lecythi.

Charon had to be paid for performing his sombre office of ferryman of the dead. It was customary to place an obolus, a silver coin, under the tongue or between the teeth of the corpse, to pay the fare. The shades of the dead who had not been properly buried, and thus not equipped to cross into Hades, were refused passage by Charon and so left to haunt the living, seeking their release. The Roman poet Virgil draws a grim picture of the grisly ferryman in his *Aeneid* (Book 6). 'Charon, on whose chin lies a mass of unkempt, hoary hair; his eyes are staring orbs of flame; his squalid garb hangs by a knot from his shoulders. Unaided, he poles the boat, tends the sails, and in his murky craft convoys the dead.'

Though a pagan concept, the image of the grim boatman and his load of souls deeply affected the minds of many medieval and Renaissance Christians. Dante tells, in his *Divine Comedy*, of his encounter with Charon when he descends, with Virgil as his guide, into the Inferno. 'Charon, demonic form with eyes of burning coal, collects them all, beckoning, and each that lingers, with his oar strikes.' And Michelangelo, in the stupendous vision of the *Last Judgment* which he painted above the altar of the Sistine Chapel, depicts Charon and his fatal boat with a realism both terrifying and unforgettable.

The memory of the mythological Charon has now passed into modern Greek folklore where, under the related name of Charos, he carries off the young and old.

The Etruscans, the mysterious people who lived in central Italy and whose culture is known mainly from the evidence of their tombs, venerated a grisly deity called Charun. His demonic image appears on the walls of tombs, holding the hammer or mallet with which he dealt the death-blow to those whose destined time had come. This Etruscan Charun is clearly a death god; whether there was an original connection between him and the Greek Charon, as their names suggest, has not been proved.

The idea that the newly dead have to cross a river to reach the land of the dead is very ancient. It occurs in the Egyptian *Pyramid Texts* (c. 2400 BC) and many means of transport are devised. The most notable, in the present connection, is that of securing passage in a boat manned by one named 'He who looks behind'. The name is significant, for this Egyptian ferryman, like the Greek Charon, is a difficult character and has to be persuaded or threatened into taking the deceased to the next world. The vignette which illustrates Chapter XCIII of the Book of the Dead shows the deceased addressing a man or deity seated in a boat, whose head is turned backward. In the ancient Mesopotamian *Epic of Gilgamesh* a similar idea occurs: the hero is ferried over the 'water of death' by Urshanabi, the boatman.

Circe

The fair-haired sorceress Circe is described in the *Odyssey* as a goddess, although her reputation throughout mythology is rather that of a witch. She was the daughter of Helios, the sun god, and sister of Aeetes, the divine wizard and King of Colchis. Another celebrated witch, Medea, was her niece.

Circe was banished to the isle of Aeaea, after she poisoned her husband, the King of the Sarmatians, a nomadic people of Persia. Circe's island has been sited as lying at the head of the Adriatic, not far from the mouth of the river Po; according to Hesiod, however, Aeaea lay off the coast of Latium, now a part of Italy, in the promontory called Circaeum, which was at one time an island.

Circe lived in a marble palace surrounded by woods, practicing her magic arts, and singing as she sat by her loom. She was attended by nymphs and a troop of wild beasts, whom she had transformed from men she had ensnared. When Odysseus's men landed on her island, they cast lots to decide who should stay to guard the ship and who should go to reconnoitre the land. Odysseus's friend Eurylochus set out with a band of men and, attracted by Circe's singing, they were drawn to the palace. Wild beasts came out to meet them, but instead of attacking the men they fawned on them and made them welcome. Circe invited them to dine at her table and all entered unsuspecting, except Eurylochus who stayed behind, fearing a trap.

As soon as the sailors had drunk the goddess's drugged wine, she struck them with her wand and turned them into hogs. Eurylochus escaped and told Odysseus what had happened. He set off to rescue friends and on the way he met the god Hermes who gave him a magic herb named moly, to protect him against Circe's magic. When Circe attempted to transform Odysseus, her magic was useless. Odysseus forced her to restore his men to human shape.

Circe, who had become enamored of Odysseus, used her wiles to persuade him remain for a year on her island. At length Odysseus became restive and was determined to be on his way again. Circe advised him how to navigate the River of Ocean and descend into Hades, and how to deal with the ghosts. When Odysseus returned to Aeaea, having been advised about his own future by the ghost of Tiresias, Circe sent him off on his homeward voyage to Ithaca. She warned him against the Sirens and against Scylla and Charybdis, and also of the fatal consequences that would follow if any of his men were to kill and eat the cattle of the sun on the island of Thrinacia. Circe is

Circe, **John William Waterhouse (1849–1917)**

an important figure in the *Odyssey* and it is due to her warnings and advice that Odysseus finally reaches home.

She appears from time to time in later literature, always in connection with Odysseus. She bears him a son, Telegonus according to the Telegonia, the lost poem by the epic poet Eugammon of Cyrene, which has survived only in a prose summary. Telegonus comes to Ithaca, seeking his father. Arriving at night, he is mistakenly attacked as a raider and mortally wounds Odysseus with his poisoned spear. He then carries off Odysseus's body and also Penelope, Odysseus's wife, and their son Telemachus to Circe, who makes them immortal with her magic powers. Telemachus marries Circe and Penelope marries Circe's son, Telegonus.

In folk tales told from western Europe to Mongolia, Circe's story has many counterparts. It has been suggested that such folk tales spread from the Near East and originated in the Babylonian myth of Ishtar, who killed her lovers when she became tired of them. During the progress from myth to folklore, the slaughter of the goddess's lover became changed into transformation into beasts.

Circe, it has also been suggested, may be related to the powerful ancient Mediterranean goddess known as the 'Lady of the Beasts', and her image has been found engraved upon Minoan gems a millennium before Homer's day. Flanked by lions, she crowned the main gate of Mycenae at the time of the Trojan War. Around the year 1200 BC, invading Dorians drove the goddess's ancient worship from the shores of Greece, but it lingered for centuries in Italy and places further west.

Cornucopia

Literally in Latin, 'horn of plenty':

generally a twisted horn overflowing with fruit and flowers, a symbol of abundance and prosperity; often shown in the hands of Plutus, god of wealth; Fortuna, goddess of fortune; and other deities: in Greek mythology it was originally the horn of Amaltheia, the goat which suckled the infant Zeus; he rewarded her by putting her in the sky as the constellation Capricorn.

Corybantes

The whirlpool of Greek mythology not only mingled together a myriad of conflicting tales but sucked into itself many elements of foreign belief, especially from Asia Minor. The result, more often than not, is confused. The Corybantes provide a good example of this confusion. Their very name probably means 'whirlers', although even this is uncertain. In their various guises they usually appear as supernatural beings devoted to noisy, orgiastic dancing. But who they danced for and why is disputed—not only by modern scholars but also in the Greek stories themselves, where the Corybantes are frequently confused with another band of loud leapers, the Curetes (youths) of Crete.

The reason for this confusion is the interaction between Greek and Asiatic myths. Apart from their similar behaviour, both Corybantes and Curetes are presented as attendants on the Great Mother of the gods: Rhea in the Greek stories, Cybele in the Asiatic. As the cultures intermingled between the two sides of the Aegean Sea, Rhea and Cybele became identified with each other and so did their attendants.

Some authorities, attempting to make the matter clearer, tell us that the Corybantes are not Greek at all but purely Asiatic. They are ecstatic dancers in the train of the 'mountain mother' Cybele, playing the piercing

instruments of the uplands. These were cymbals, rattles, and 'bull-roarers', or stones with a hole in them which, when whirled round on a string, made a noise like a rushing wind; they were believed to invoke rain. As well as being dancers, the Corybantes are associated with magical cures, especially of mental disorders. They seem, in fact, to be an example of the ancient and still surviving concept of the medicineman, whipping his followers into a trancelike dance, purging them of evil and controlling the elements.

Such a precise attribution cannot get rid of the fact that the Greeks themselves muddled up the Corybantes and the Curetes and when they were describing the Cretan Curetes quite often called them Corybantes.

Yet another element arises in that the Corybantes, or Curetes, appear to be connected with the Dactyls, who also served Rhea, the Great Mother. Rhea's husband, Cronus, had the habit of devouring their children. After she had given birth to three daughters (Hera, Demeter, and Hestia), Rhea found that she was again with child. In order to cheat her husband, she decided to bear the infant secretly and went into hiding in a mountain cave in Crete. In which mountain the cave lay is, again, disputed: some say Aegeon, others Dicte, yet others Ida. It is interesting incidentally that Cybele was connected with another Mt. Ida, in Phrygian Asia Minor. When her labour began, Rhea pressed on the ground with her hands. From each of her fingerprints, spirits or divinities sprang up to assist at the birth and protect the infant Zeus. These beings are generally called the 'Idaean Dactyls', dactyl being the Greek for 'finger'. There are various accounts of their nature and characteristics but they are all, in a sense, children of the Great Mother.

The Corybantes (or Curetes) are sometimes identified with the Dactyls and sometimes said to be the latter's offspring. Whatever their name and parentage, they were armed with sword and shield which they clashed together as they danced round Zeus's cradle to prevent his father hearing his cries. (No scholar has yet suggested that the great god's later predilection for thunder dates from his earliest aural experiences.) The number of Corybantes or Curetes varies from account to account but they are often said to be three and it is thus that they are usually represented in art.

In other versions of the birth of Zeus, Hera persuaded her mother Rhea to allow her to take the newborn infant to the Cretan fastnesses, where she cared for her baby brother until he was old enough to marry her. In these accounts the Curetes are local youths assembled by Hera to dance and clash their weapons when the child cried. From a hymn discovered in Crete, it is evident that the Curetes were the object of a cult and were revered as attendants of 'Zeus Curos', the adolescent Zeus. The hymn is of the Hellenistic period but it has been plausibly suggested that the rite itself has far more ancient origins and that historical Curetes existed. These were Cretan youths who, in Minoan times, worshipped Zeus as a god of their own age.

In all these stories, whether they be of Greek or Asiatic origin, the same elements occur. In each there is a connection with the Mother of the gods, wild dancing, the warding-off of harm, and the clashing of metal on metal. The last point leads to further ramifications. Many of the ancient tales present the Dactyls as the earliest workers in metal and also as magicians, weavers of spells both good and bad. The same qualities are also attributed to the other beings associated with the Dactyls, including The Corybantes, the Telchines, semi-divine beings of Rhodes, and the Cabiri, Phrygian

Bronze shield depicting Zeus in the centre surrounded by Curetes with drums Discovered in Ideon Andron (Crete), Geometric period (7th–8th centuries BC)

deities associated with Samothrace and also with Asia Minor. In many versions there are dark stories of male fertility and mutilation, of three brothers, one of whom is murdered or revoltingly maimed by the other two.

This strand of fratricidal strife runs through all the accounts of the sons of the Great Mother. These artisan beings seem often to be thought of as dwarfs, echoing quite foreign myths such as that of the Niebelungen, the Teutonic smith-dwarfs who dwelt in caves beneath the earth.

Crete

An extraordinary civilization flowered in Crete after 2000 BC. Its geographical position made Crete a natural meeting-point for many of the cultural currents of the Mediterranean. It belonged to the Aegean world, making a link between Asia Minor and Greece,

yet at the same time commanded sea routes southward to Egypt and eastward to the rich trading ports of the Levant. The influence of such widespread contacts is particularly evident in the religious ideas by which Minoan civilization was so largely inspired.

Crete seems to have remained uninhabited until early Neolithic times when the beautiful and fertile island attracted settlers, presumably from the adjacent region of Asia Minor. The Anatolian peninsula is now recognized as one of the earliest centres of the development of the new farming economy and then of urban life. Already by 6000 BC a large settlement such as Catal Huyiik had many shrines devoted to fertility cults. A supreme goddess, a lesser male divinity, birds, lions, and bulls were represented in art. Actual bulls' horns were mounted as cult objects, while much later, in the Bronze Age of Beycesultan, in southwest Anatolia, these were architecturally formalized into horned altar—in one instance associated with a sacred wooden pillar.

These forms are strikingly similar to what was to emerge in Crete. Whether an important element of Cretan religion was directly derived from Anatolia, or whether it was only that both shared in a common inheritance is open to question. In spite of chronological and cultural difficulties, it is likely that there was a direct relationship. The initial settlement of Crete was followed by further immigration from the peninsula, and during Minoan times the two territories remained linked by ties of trade, and probably of language and of social custom as well.

Fashionably Dressed Goddess

For the Cretans the supreme embodiment of the divine power in the world was feminine. The Great Goddess or Mother Goddess, whose worship was common to the early agricultural peoples of the Mediterranean and southwest Asia, was probably immediately introduced into Crete by the Anatolian settlers. She kept her supremacy, although in appropriately changing forms, with the rise of high civilization. She was at once the one and the many. In the words that Apuleius put into the mouth of Isis herself in *The Golden Ass*, she was one 'whose godhead, single in essence but of many forms, with varied rites and under many names, the whole earth reveres'. In Minoan times the emphasis on pregnancy, maternal amplitude, and nakedness found in the prehistoric idols was left behind and the goddess was usually portrayed in the same elegant fashion as the ladies of the court.

Among the 'many forms' of the Great Goddess some, indeed, were domestic. One was as guardian of the house, and particularly of the royal palace, where the prince may have ruled as her servitor and consort. At the same time her wilder aspects, more

The Great Goddess in a swing

directly related to the old fertility cults, were no less important. She was the divinity of vegetation, mistress of animals, at home in forest, cave, and mountain peak. In rites concerned with the death and rebirth of vegetation and seed, the goddess was associated with a young male divinity, probably both son and consort. She represented the continuity of the vegetation cycle, he its discontinuity. He died and was born again.

The various aspects of the goddess can be seen emerging in the divinities of historic times. As guardian she is best represented by Athene—already worshipped at Cnossus in late Minoan times. Demeter, with her other-self Persephone, was recognized as Cretan, as also was Hera. An association with doves seems to evoke Aphrodite, while Artemis best expresses her role as mistress of animals and virgin goddess of the wild places. Artemis was identi-

fied with Britomartis (the name means 'sweet virgin') who was worshipped in eastern and central Crete, and with Diktynna (Lady of Dikte), who was her western counterpart.

As for the young god, he too has local Cretan manifestations in Hyacinthus and probably also in the leader, or single embodiment, of the Curetes. Under the influence of the Achaean Greeks, the Indo-European Zeus was identified with the Cretan god, and the story of his concealment (or birth) in a Cretan cave, and of the Curetes dancing and beating their shields to save the infant from his devouring father, was an accepted part of Greek mythology. While the Greeks thus allowed their supreme god to have been born in Crete, they denied the inevitable Cretan heresy that he also died there.

Opposite page:
Minoan Palace, Cnossos, Crete, Greece

Frenzied Dancing

The rites centred on the household goddess of the palaces and involving the princely families must have been formally ceremonious. Those enacted out of doors in the fertility and vegetation cults were ecstatic and mystic. The Greeks came to associate the island with mystical religion, and the Cretans themselves claimed, probably with justification, that they had enacted in public those Mysteries which at Eleusis were veiled in utter secrecy.

Scenes engraved on gold signet rings and seal stones may represent rites celebrating the cycle of the seasons. The goddess is shown sitting below a tree, dancing in flowery meadows or occasionally perhaps lamenting at a shrine or over ritual jars. In these scenes the goddess is attended by female votaries, including young girls. In others, especially where boughs and trees are being plucked, she is accompanied by the young god. In these vegetation rites the dancing, especially of the god, is often ecstatic or frenzied.

Ritual meaning was expressed in positions of the arms. The goddess is often shown with arms bent and raised above the head, or extended before her. A common position of worship was with the right hand clenched and pressed against the forehead. Conch shells were blown, perhaps in order to summon the goddess.

Funerary rites were related to the general conception of rebirth through the goddess. The elite were buried in unpretentious chamber tombs, dressed, ornamented, and accompanied by pots, bronze vessels, or other grave goods. It can be supposed that a happy Cretan view of the afterworld survived in the Elysian Fields of Greek mythology, associated as they were with the Cretan Prince Rhadamanthus, who was renowned as a just ruler. Frescoes on a sarcophagus from Hagia Triada in southern Crete illustrate funerary rites of the late Minoan period, c. 14th

Archaeological Museum in Herakleion; Minoan rhyton in form of a bull

century BC. They include the pouring of a libation, to the accompaniment of a lyre; the dedication of what look like fruits and wine at an altar; the blood sacrifice of a bull, to the accompaniment of a double flute, and apparently the carrying of offerings to the dead noble's tomb. The principal officiants are women wearing skirts of fur or fleece that may be priestly garments. Others, however, wear ordinary courtly dress and may have been royal ladies who were also priestesses. It seems to have been a princess of this kind who had been buried at Arkhanes near Cnossus. Among her rich grave furniture were gold amulets and a gold ring engraved with a ritual scene. She had been buried in a dress similar to that worn by the goddess on her ring.

The number and richness of ritual vessels are proof of the important place of libations and perhaps of ceremonial

purificatory sprinkling in Minoan ritual. These vessels were often in the shape of the heads of sacred animals, particularly of the bull and lion. In one of the Hagia Triada funerary scenes libations are being poured from a large two-handled vase into another vessel that may have carried them into the earth. On a seal stone strange composite figures referred to as 'demons' are represented bearing elegant beakers, the contents of which are to be poured into a conical vessel held by the enthroned goddess. Little narrow-necked jars of exquisite workmanship may have served to sprinkle holy water.

Serious Play

Minoan society had reached a stage of sophistication at which activities which were originally religious had become partly secularized. For the peaceful, conservative island society this led to a kind of serious playing characteristic of Minoan culture. Crete was later said to be the home of the dance, and dancing—sometimes graceful, sometimes frenzied—was among the rites of the goddess. Less purely religious dancing formed an important part of both court and country life, probably often associated with seasonal festivals. The sacred nature of some ring dances appears in a model where naked dancers, arms clasped, are circling within an area enclosed by horns of consecration (formalized horns, indicating sacredness). Dancing in line in an altogether more stately fashion was practiced by court ladies.

The most remarkable manifestation of serious play was in the famous Cretan bull games. Young men and girls, both wearing men's dress of tight-fitting belt and loincloth, performed athletic feats with the beasts, including vaults and somersaults between the horns. The bull, symbol of male potency in relation to the goddess, was here encountered in actuality, possibly to celebrate life's renewal, or as an initiatory test of skill and courage. These games were, however, watched by light-hearted audiences. The palaces were provided with sacred ways and theatres that must have made a setting for processions and other performances.

Snakes in the Palace

The goddess of many names was also identified by a variety of symbols and manifestations. The most used were the horns, the pillar, the double axe, the tree, the dove and other birds, the snake, and the shield. Horns of consecration were placed on palace buildings, on shrines, on the head of the goddess, and in many other settings. Freestanding or sculptured pillars were part of the sacred furnishings of palaces, villas, shrines, and tombs. They

were anointed and offerings were made on, or to, them. Their primary meaning was probably phallic, but some authorities believe that they stood for the Great Goddess herself. In 'pillar crypts' such as the one in the palace of Cnossus, functional pillars seem also to have been anointed and held sacred.

The double axe, perhaps originally a sacrificial symbol like the cross, came to represent the goddess. It may often, as in the scenes on the Hagia Triada sarcophagus, have been set on the apex of the sacred pillar; it was represented between the horns of a sculptured motif representing an ox's skull or within horns of consecration. For votive use, double axes were made in

The more ecstatic rites of the goddess were celebrated out of doors, in localities where there might be shrines for a sacred tree, or an enclosure with a sacred grove.

gold or bronze and in a variety of sizes. Trees appear in many ritual scenes, often growing in shrines or small enclosures. They were not formalized in the usual manner of symbols, but shown naturalistically, usually in leaf but occasionally bare.

The snake was principally an attribute of the goddess in her role as guardian of the household, although it may also have had chthonic and sexual meanings. The two 'snake goddesses' of Cnossus are well known. In the town shrine at Gournia, a crude goddess figure was twined with a snake, and there were snake tubes among the utensils; these were terra-cotta cylinders with snakes represented twining round them, the purpose of which is not known. Real snakes were probably kept in the palaces, and rooms were set aside for them in private houses.

The goddess was sometimes portrayed between a pair of lions (as

long before in Anatolia) or between birds and fabulous griffins, of oriental origin. The god was similarly shown as a master of beasts. Among the least understood figures of Minoan art are those known as demons—strange hybrid creatures, which often have the head of a lion or an ass. They attended upon the goddess, sometimes in procession and bearing libation ewers; demons appear to have been particularly concerned with the growth of crops.

A figure eight oxhide shield, a recurring motif, gave rise to a religious symbol. It was occasionally personified in male or female form, presumably god and goddess. Its significance may partly have derived from the shields of the Curetes, but it must also have stood for the protective power of the goddess. Not only the shield but also the snake, the bird, and the tree all survived as attributes of the Athene of the classical world.

Spirals, including linked and running forms, were among the most popular motifs in Minoan art. They were often used decoratively, but possessed symbolic meaning, perhaps of eternal continuance. They appear on altars, shrines, and ritual vessels. Among minor symbols were a sacred knot and a human ear and eye. The lily was the most sacred flower of Crete, and three poppy seeds might be worn or carried by the goddess.

Ecstasy in the Open Air

Unlike most of their contemporaries in the Bronze Age world, the Cretans had no large temples or temple figures. There were shrines of modest size in the palaces. At Cnossus there was a pillar shrine in the main court, and nearby the low, dimly lit throne room with stone basins and a sunken tank, suggesting use for purification ceremonies. The throne, with its flanking griffins, may have seated a divine prince, a

Small statue of Great Goddess, Cnossos, Crete

culture of the Achaeans in the late Bronze Age is nowhere more dominant than in its religious forms. The goddess appeared on the mainland with all her familiar attributes. The pillar between lions stood above the great gate of Mycene itself. Yet even by this time nearly all of the gods of the Olympian pantheon were already being worshipped. Dionysus also had his place, and at Cnossus there was a shrine to the legendary craftsman Daedalus. The goddess still held a high place but the male divinities, and particularly Poseidon, were now perhaps held in at least equal honour.

Directly, and through Mycenean civilization, Minoan religion gave much to that of Hellenic Greece. In addition to the relationship between the Cretan goddess and her classical descendants, there was the powerful Cretan element in the Eleusinian Mysteries, and a traditional Cretan founder at Delphi, later to be presided over by Apollo. All the main centres of Greek mythology were of Mycenean origin. The connection between the cult of Dionysus and the ecstatic rituals of the goddess is evident. In their stories of Theseus and the Minotaur, the Greeks embodied their sense of the strangeness of ancient Crete and memories of its former power.

JACQUETTA HAWKES

FURTHER READING: J. Hawkes. Dawn of the Gods. *(Random House, 1968); R. F. Willetts.* Cretan Cults and Festivals. *(Greenwood, 1980); G. R. Levy.* The Gate of Horn. *(Humanities, 1968); D. MacKenzie.* Myths of Crete and Pre-Hellenic Europe. *(Longwood Press, 1976, cl. 918); Arthur Cotterell.* Minoan World. *(Scribner, 1980); A. C. Vaughan.* The House of the Double Axe. *(Doubleday, 1959); T. B. L. Webster.* From Mycenae to Homer. *(Praeger, 1959).*

high priestess, or even a queen. Houses had their small shrines for private worship, and probably most towns and villages, like Gournia, had public shrines where little images and symbols of the goddess were ranged on a shelf in an inner sanctum.

More characteristic of Minoan Nature worship were sanctuaries in the countryside. Caves, often associated with the birthplace of the god, were among the most ancient and most popular. Some were walled and

provided with chapels, altars, and offering-tables. Very many generations of islanders visited them to worship and leave their offerings. The counterpart of the caves were the peak sanctuaries, of which there were about a dozen in the island.

The more ecstatic rites of the goddess were celebrated out of doors, in localities where there might be shrines for a sacred tree, or an enclosure with a sacred grove.

Minoan influence on the Mycenean

Cronus

More important in myth than in cult, Cronus was chief among the Titans, the 12 'former gods', according to the Greek writer Hesiod (c 700 BC). The Titans were the children of Heaven and Earth, together with the Cyclopes and the hundred-handed monsters, but they were not able to reach the light until Cronus, the youngest Titan, castrated his father with a sickle and so separated heaven from earth. As king of the gods, Cronus married his sister Rhea, who bore him six children: Hestia, Demeter, Hera, Hades, Poseidon and Zeus. Earth and Heaven had prophesied that one of Cronus's children would overthrow him, and he tried to prevent this by swallowing them as they were born. But Rhea smuggled the last child away to Crete, delivering to Cronus a swaddled stone, which he duly swallowed. Zeus grew up safely, and somehow made Cronus regurgitate his other children; after a ten-year war between the older and younger gods, Zeus defeated Cronus and the other Titans and fettered them in Tartarus, where they remain.

It was formerly assumed that the myth reflected a historical displacement by the worship of Zeus of an earlier, no doubt pre-Greek cult of Cronus. Hittite tablets, however, have revealed that a curiously similar story was current in Asia Minor before 1200 BC. The counterpart of Cronus is Kumarbi, who becomes ruler of the gods by biting off and swallowing the genitals of Heaven (a combination of the castration and swallowing motifs). As a result, Kumarbi conceives a son; who becomes the weather god (the chief deity, corresponding to the Greek Zeus). Like Cronus, Kumarbi wishes to destroy his offspring, and probably swallows a stone in an attempt at abortion — the same action as in the Greek myth, but differently motivated. The attempt fails; the weather god is born, he fights a battle, and emerges triumphant.

It was probably in the period before 1200 BC, when eastern contacts were strong, that the Greeks took over the Asiatic myth, though some scholars put it shortly before Hesiod. We should like to know what Cronus was before he had oriental castrations and swallowings foisted on him, and why he was chosen for that role. Possibly he was already the father of Zeus, though his name indicates non-Greek (possibly pre-Greek) origin and the relationship cannot go back to Indo-European times. If he had special functions, they are obscure. For the Greeks of the historical period, he is fettered in the underworld; in other words, he plays no part in the world of men and has no influence there. (In fifth century Athens his name was used to mock the old, the stupid, and the passe.)

There is, however, an alternative version which says that Cronus's reign was the Golden Age and that he now rules over the fortunate heroes in the Isles of the Blessed. It was Zeus's accession that brought hardship and the necessity of tilling the soil. This may be connected with the annual Cronia, or Feast of Cronus, celebrated in Athens and certain other towns. Its date differed in different places, but so far as we can tell, it always fell in the idle period between harvest (May) and ploughing (October), and slaves joined their masters in merriment. If Cronus was a seasonal figure who played a part only at this celebration, the myth can be understood as a construction to go with it. 'We enjoy this feast and this leisure as a legacy from the time when Cronus ruled all the year round; but now Zeus is king, and we shall need our ploughs again.' This relationship between Cronus and Zeus would make a suitable basis for the adoption of the more complex oriental myth.

Child Sacrifice

Other traces of Cronus in cult or myth are scanty and of uncertain significance. Adopting the form of a horse, he mated with the nymph Philyra and became the father of the centaur Chiron. At Olympia there was a Cronus Hill, at the top of which priests known as the Kings made an annual sacrifice to Cronus at about the spring equinox; this may be a pre-Greek survival. Here, before the foundation of the Olympic Games, Cronus and Zeus were said to have wrestled.

Cronus Hills existed also in Laconia in Greece, and in Sicily. Carthaginian influence had been strong in Sicily and it has been suspected that there 'Cronus' may represent the Phoenician El or Moloch. Cronus was identified with this god at least as early as the 5th century BC, probably because of the Phoenician reputation for sacrificing children to him. The identification affected interpretation of the myth of Zeus's birth, child sacrifice becoming attributed to the early Cretans. The Romans identified Cronus with their Saturn for a different but equally superficial reason: the Saturnalia, though held at a different season (December) from the Cronia, had the same character of egalitarian merrymaking.

Like all the main Greek gods, Cronus was affected by attempts at etymology. From at least the 5th century BC the obvious (but false) equation was made with chronos, meaning 'time'. This fused with the idea of Time as a divine progenitor, which reached Greece independently from Iran, to give an allegorical sense to the story that he swallowed his children: Time consumes us all, his progeny.

FURTHER READING: Hesiod & Theognis, *trans. by D. Wender, (Penguin, 1976), Hesiodic myth and its oriental counterparts are fully discussed.*

Opposite page:
Cronus, Francisco de Goya (1746–1828)

Cupid

The Roman god of love, identified with the Greek Eros: son of Venus or Aphrodite, the love goddess; frequently depicted as a beautiful winged boy with his bow and arrows, which arouse love in those they strike: like love itself, he is erratic and mischievous: the delightful story of how Cupid woos the mortal Psyche is told in *The Golden Ass of Apuleius.*

Cynicism

Cynicism was an ascetic philosophy that originated in the 5th century BC with Antisthenes, a student of Socrates, and died out fully in the 4th or 5th centuries BC. The word 'cynic' derives from the Greek Κυνικός (kynikos), or 'doglike'. While the exact origin of this label is uncertain, many classical authors associated the Cynics with dogs first because of their name, but then for their shamelessness, poor hygiene, and blatant disregard for norms of civilized society. The Cynic philosophy focuses on the desire to live a life of eudaimonia, or happiness and flourishing, by adhering to virtue and eschewing false desires such as wealth, power, fame and the pleasures of flesh. Cynicism has often been compared to Stoicism, another more formalized philosophy that was popular in the several hundred years surrounding the turn of the millennium in Greece and Rome. Cynicism may have influenced the teaching of Jesus as well as the thought and practice of early Christians, although this in dispute.

While Cynicism was not the first ascetic philosophy to emerge from the ancient West, Diogenes Laertes lists Antisthenes, the close friend and student of Socrates, as the founder of the school of the Cynics. Antisthenes expanded a number of key components of Socrates' teachings, including the rejection of wealth, the necessity of critiquing and undermining social conventions, and the primacy of virtue in living a good, happy life. According to Diogenes Laertes, Antisthenes insisted on the importance of being indifferent to the difficulties and painful experiences of life, a philosophy and life-style that he passed on to his most famous student, Diogenes of Sinope. He also taught the value of self-sufficiency, wisdom, accepting insults, and bad reputations. Diogenes Laertes recounts an exchange between Antisthenes and an Athenian: 'Many men praise you,' said one. "Why, what wrong have I done?" was his rejoinder.'

Diogenes of Sinope is perhaps the most famous Cynic for his perfect embodiment of Cynic principles. Ragged, dirty and living in a tub on a street corner of Athens, Diogenes was the most visible example of Cynicism as both an attractive philosophy of virtue and happiness as well as a life-style that reveled in flouting conventions and norms. A student of Antisthenes, Diogenes firmly rejected Plato's teachings as 'a waste of time', and called the Dionysian theatre, one of the central artistic features of Athenian life, a 'peep-show for fools'. By thoroughly ridding himself of current social norms and embracing the outsider position, Diogenes tried to force Athenians to confront and question the conventional paths to happiness: wealth, power, fame, reputation, and sensual pleasure.

Cynicism flourished for several centuries after it became a recognizable philosophy, from the 5th to 3rd centuries BC, then went into decline, replaced in the popular consciousness by Stoicism, which drew many of its central principles from Cynicism. With the rise of Imperial Rome at the turn of the millennium, the increase in population living in poverty may have encouraged a resurgence of Cynic rejection of authoritarian rules and conventions. Some scholars link the resurgence of Cynicism with the advent of Christianity, in particular the asceticism and revolutionary adherence to 'higher law' for which Jesus spoke in favour. The actual extent of influence of Cynicism on early Christian thought is difficult or impossible to document, but the philosophical similarities between the two schools as well as their physical and temporal proximity are evident, nonetheless.

Contemporary uses of the word 'cynicism' have drifted away from their original connotations; the modern sense of someone who distrusts the motives of others, assuming selfish or dishonourable desires, emerged in the nineteenth century. While this attitude is a recognizable feature of the ancient Cynicism, the modern understanding ignores the positive philosophical teaching that Cynicism espoused.

FURTHER READING: Diogenes, and Robert Drew Hicks. Lives of Eminent Philosophers. *(Cambridge, MA: Harvard Univ., 1925); Desmond, William D.* The Greek Praise of Poverty: Origins of Ancient Cynicism. *(Notre Dame, IN: University of Notre Dame, 2006); Navia, Luis E.* Diogenes the Cynic: The War against the World. *(Amherst, NY: Humanity, 2005); Cutler, Ian.* Cynicism from Diogenes to Dilbert. *(Jefferson, NC: McFarland &, 2005).*

Daedalus

Father of Icarus and Iapyx, Daedalus was a mythological inventor, architect, and craftsman. Daedalus is best known as the cause of the birth of the Minotaur on Crete, and then as the architect of the Labyrinth King Minos

Daedalus and Icarus, Anthony van Dyck (1599–1641)

subsequently uses to imprison it. His escape from Crete, along with his son Icarus, is a later tale from Ovid that is also well known.

Poseidon offers a magnificent white bull to King Minos of Crete to be used as a sacrifice to the god. But Minos goes back on his word and keeps the bull, enraging Poseidon who arranges for Minos' wife Pasiphae to lust after the bull. Daedalus, ever the innovative inventor, is said to have designed a wooden cow to facilitate Pasiphae's love-making with the animal. Pasiphae gives birth to the Minotaur, a bull-headed monster who eats human flesh. Minos has Daedalus construct a labyrinth to imprison the beast, a complex of passages so twisted that Daedalus himself has difficulty getting out. These stories show Daedalus' association with craftsmanship, complex design and invention.

When Minos keeps Daedalus and his son Icarus locked up to avoid him sharing the secret of the Labyrinth, Daedalus decides to escape. He constructs wings for himself and his son, much of which are kept together by wax. As they prepare to fly off the island of Crete, Daedalus warns Icarus not to fly too high or the sun will melt the wax of his wings. Icarus ignores this warning, flies too close to the sun, melts his wings, and plunges to his death in the ocean. Daedalus buries his son and escapes to Sicily.

Minos searches high and low for Daedalus and finds him by baiting him with a problem only Daedalus would solve: he asks each host to thread a string through a spiral seashell. Daedalus solves the problem (tying the string to an ant, luring the ant through the shell with a drop of honey), and Minos demands to take him from King Cocalus of Kamikos, Daedalus' host. But before Minos can leave with the inventor, the King's daughters murder Minos in a bath by pouring boiling water on him.

In popular culture, Daedalus is famously used to depict a semiauto-biographical portrayal of James Joyce in *Portrait of the Artist as a Young Man* and *Ulysses*.

FURTHER READING: *Ovid, A. D. Melville, and E. J. Kenney.* Metamorphoses. *(Oxford: Oxford UP, 2008); Hamilton, Edith, and Steele Savage.* Mythology. *(New York: Penguin, 1969); Graves, Robert.* The Greek Myths. *Baltimore: Penguin, 1955.*

Delphi

Site of the most influential oracle of the ancient world, at the temple of Apollo on Mt. Parnassus, north of the Gulf of Corinth: the oracles were delivered by Apollo's priestess, the Pythia, seated on a tripod and speaking in trance, and were transmitted to inquirers by the priests.

Demeter

Demeter was the ancient Greek goddess of corn, agriculture, and fertility. The second part of her name, meter, means 'mother' in Greek and De (or Da) was in ancient times thought to be a word for the earth. The Greeks in historical times had a separate goddess of the earth (Ge) and Demeter came later in the genealogy of deities, being a granddaughter of Ge and sister of Zeus. But in origin she is certainly an earth goddess and as such the author of all crops and vegetation, and so the sustainer of the life of animals and men. Her daughter by Zeus, Persephone, was also called simply Kore, 'the Maiden'. She represented more directly the fruits of the field, but the two were so closely linked that they were often known as 'the Twin Goddesses', and even sometimes as 'the Demeters', a title which demonstrates

Sculpture of Demeter, who as goddess of crops, life, and the growth of children, was central to the day-to-day of Greek families.

their original identity.

Because the life of plants between autumn and spring is one of hidden growth under the ground, a story was how Persephone was carried off by Zeus's brother Hades, lord of the underworld, and compelled to spend each winter with him as his wife. In spring, when the earth was covered in flowers, she would reappear, bringing men joy. So, as Kore, she was a deity of youth and gaiety, the leader of the nymphs, with whom she was gathering flowers

when she was carried off and with whom she looked after the growth of children and young men and women. But as the wife of Hades, she was also queen of the underworld, governing men's fate after death, and an awesome and dreaded goddess.

The Mysteries
As deities of the crops, and also as patrons of the life and growth of children, Demeter and her daughter were regarded as important civilizing

influences, drawing men toward a settled life of agriculture and domestic happiness. Since agriculture was the most important source of prosperity in early Greece, the favour of Demeter was essential to all men, and especially to the peasant and the common man. To her, and to the god of the underworld, the farmer would sacrifice at the beginning of his seasonal tasks, and to her he offered his thanks and first-fruits after the harvest. Hence, many of Demeter's festivals coincide with these seasonal activities, ploughing, sowing, reaping, threshing, and the storing of the harvest. One of the most important, the Thesmophoria, took place in late October, the time of sowing, and included ceremonies designed to ensure the fruitfulness of the seed, and also the fertility of mankind. It was celebrated only by women, who as the bearers of children were more suited for such ritual, and much of it was secret. Many of Demeter's festivals included secret ceremonies, and these were often restricted to women. The main reason for this secrecy was perhaps the sense of awe and fear which was aroused by the contemplation of the hidden powers of the earth, the powers governing birth, growth, and death, and also the life after death, below the earth.

The most important festivals of Demeter and Persephone were those ceremonies of initiation known as 'Mysteries', and of these the most influential in historical times were the Mysteries of Eleusis in Attica. These were open to both sexes. They guaranteed to initiates, above all, the promise of a happier fate after death. But the favour of the goddesses was also promised in this life, in terms of prosperity, especially agricultural. This was personified as a god Plutus (Wealth), who was the child of Demeter, born from her marriage to the Cretan Iasion, with whom she lay 'in a thrice-ploughed field'. The generation of the earth's

fruits is thus represented by the union of the goddess with a mortal in a field that has been prepared for sowing. Plutus is sometimes shown as a little child seated on a cornucopia, which is being handed by Ge to Demeter. The setting of the myth, in Crete, perhaps supports the view of some scholars that Demeter's Mysteries have a Cretan origin.

The Rape of Persephone

The most famous of the myths relating to Demeter is that of the rape of Persephone. This is closely associated with the story of the origins of crops and the art of agriculture, and of the Mysteries. Many legends told how, when Demeter was searching for her daughter, after Hades had carried her off, she received information about the rape from the local inhabitants of different parts of Greece and was offered their hospitality. In gratitude she gave them her gifts of agriculture and the Mysteries.

The chief claimants for this honour were Eleusis and Sicily, the most important centres of her cult. The earliest and best-known version of the myth, the so-called Homeric Hymn to Demeter, tells how Demeter came to Eleusis, disguised as an old woman, and was there welcomed by the family of King Celeus. She became the nurse of his baby son, Demophon, and attempted to make him immortal by anointing him with ambrosia, and hiding him in the fire to burn away his mortality. His mother detected her, and Demeter was thus thwarted, but she promised to teach the Eleusinians her mystic rites. She then caused a universal famine, which threatened mankind with starvation and the gods with the loss of their sacrifices. Zeus was forced to order Hades to release Persephone. But Persephone had eaten six seeds of pomegranate, and because she had tasted food in the underworld she was compelled to spend

part of every year there, returning to the upper world in spring. Demeter, however, restored the fertility of the fields and revealed her Mysteries to the rulers of Eleusis. The poem closes with the promise of happiness after death for the initiated, and of prosperity on earth for those whom the goddesses love.

The famine, in this version of the myth, reflects another form of the belief that the death of vegetation has a divine cause. When Persephone is absent, the earth is naturally barren, but here it is Demeter's anger and grief at the loss of her daughter which causes the death of the crops, and thus endangers the life of men and gods alike.

The Homeric Hymn does not refer to Demeter's gift of agriculture to man after her daughter's restoration, but another version told how she made Triptolemus, another of the Eleusinian rulers, the recipient of this gift, and gave him a winged chariot with which he travelled over the whole world, teaching men the art of agriculture and giving them the corn. Triptolemus was a very popular figure in Athens in the classical period, and his mission was often depicted in art.

Corn and Earth

Ceres, the Roman goddess of corn and of the creative powers of the earth, was in her indigenous worship closely associated with Tellus, the Earth. As a deity of fertility, she was also a guardian of marriage, and as an earth-goddess, she was connected with the cult of the dead. Her chief festival, the Cerialia, took place in April and was

Opposite page:
Fragments of the Great Eleusinian Relief with Demeter (left), Persephone (right), and Triptolemos (centre). Roman copy of the Augustan period after a Greek original of c. 450–425 BC found at Eleusis and now in the National Archaeological Museum in Athens

essentially agricultural in character. At an early date she became identified with Demeter, and her most important cult, on the Aventine at Rome, was introduced at the beginning of the 5th century BC under Greek influence. She shared this with Liber, god of wine, and Libera, who was sometimes identified with Persephone. Here, still more than in Greece, her associations were popular. The temple was supervised by the plebeian aediles, magistrates who represented the common people of Rome. As the provider of bread for the populace, and as guardian of the 'sacred laws' (*Ceres legifera*), she became a protectress of the common people in their early struggles for liberty.

Later, with the growing urban development of Rome, her original importance as a goddess of country life faded, and in the literature and art of the later Republic and Empire she is for the most part a pale copy of Demeter, inheriting with her daughter Proserpina (Persephone) the Greek myths already related. An annual festival centred on the myth of the rape and return of Proserpina was introduced, probably in the 3rd century BC, from the Greek cities of southern Italy. This was celebrated by women only, and included secret, initiatory rites. It thus resembled to some extent the Greek Thesmophoria but differed from this festival in that it was celebrated in midsummer, probably at harvest time. The Cerialia, in spring, were also extended in the course of time to include dramatic performances on the Greek pattern. Because these coincided with the time of Persephone's return, they too came to be connected with the Greek myth.

The story of the rape is a popular one in Latin literature. Ovid relates it on two occasions, in his *Fasti* and *Metamorphoses*, and the late Latin poet Claudian wrote a long epic on the subject entitled *The Rape of Proserpina*. It thus passed into the literature of the Middle Ages. Because of its funerary significance it also became a favourite subject for the artists of sarcophagi. This popularity is perhaps connected with the great proliferation of mystery cults and religions concerned with life after death, which arose in the 1st century AD.

N. J. RICHARDSON

FURTHER READING: The Homeric hymn is included in the Loeb edition of Hesiod (Harvard Univ. Press); see also M. P. Nilsson, Greek Popular Religion *(Harper and Row, 1940) and* History of Greek Religion *(Norton, 1964).*

Diana

Of all the great goddesses of the classical pantheon, the Latin Diana (and even more her Greek counterpart Artemis) is the most truly female. Compared, for instance, with Aphrodite (the vamp), Athene (the bluestocking) or Hestia (the trapped housewife), Diana or Artemis is woman as woman, not woman the mate of man nor woman the personification of an intellectual or social ideal. She has the basic feminine characteristics of directness, aloofness, and cruelty, in contrast to the masculine characteristics of romanticism, gregariousness, and brutality.

Indeed, to modern eyes, in an age when woman is gradually winning (or maybe regaining) her independence, many of the traits of this ancient goddess, however trapped out they may be in the apparatus of antiquity, appear oddly contemporary. Lithe and leggy, in tall boots and short skirt, a huntress, scornful of men, she holds her own in the wilds of the earth. A comforter of mortal women, she brings them the techniques of painless childbirth. Filling the night with brilliance, she rides

The goddess Isis-Sothis-Demeter bust; each goddesses embodies the attributes of fertility and the cyclical nature of life.

the clouds, mistress of the moon, mutable, cool, untouched. Hid in reeking fumes of incense, baring her huge and multiple breasts, hung about with symbols of fertility, she exists in a darkness shot through with oriental richness and wizardry. One feels that James Bond, intrigued and very wary, would have known what he was up against.

It is already clear that there is perhaps even more confusion attaching to Diana (Artemis) than to the other divinities of European antiquity. One reason for this is that while she was a comparative latecomer to the pantheon and had less 'mythology' than many of her peers, she became a favourite character, in her various aspects, in poetry and folklore. But the fact that she is the prime representative of the female (a subject on which everyone has personal opinions) made her capable of many varying interpretations and particularly susceptible to identification with foreign aspects of the feminine principle, as these were encountered by the ancients on their geographical borders, or on the frontiers of their own 'rational' minds.

The Grove of Diana

The Latin Diana might almost be thought of as the patron saint of this compendium, since it was an urge to explain the strange nature of her cult and priesthood at Nemi that led Frazer, some 80 years ago, to begin *The Golden Bough*, the book that lies behind all later comparative studies of *Man, Myth, and Magic*. The cult of Diana was popular in ancient Italy but her oldest and most famous place of worship was at Aricia, near the modern Nemi. Here is a volcanic lake known as the 'Mirror of Diana', surrounded on all sides but one by precipitous, densely wooded slopes, vividly described in the first chapter of *The Golden Bough*. In a grove (nemus) on the only accessible shore was the sanctuary of Diana, said to have been

Diana and Actaeon, Titian (1490–1576)

founded around 500 BC, although the cult itself had undoubtedly far older origins.

Diana was worshipped in this mysterious place (as elsewhere) as goddess of fertility and childbirth, of hunting, and of wild and domestic animals. Associated with her was a shadowy male divinity called Virbius, later identified with Hippolytus, the favourite of Artemis, who was said to have been restored to life by Aesculapius (the healing god) and brought by the goddess to Aricia, where he would be hidden from the wrath of Aphrodite.

In historical times, the priesthood of Diana at Nemi was without parallel. The priest was known as the 'King of the Grove' (*Rex Nemorensis*); he was always a runaway slave who, coming to Nemi, had to pluck a bough from a certain tree and engage the incumbent priest in single, and mortal, combat; having fought (and killed) his way to office, he then lived in perpetual expectancy of challengers, one of whom

in due time would overcome him and succeed him in his priestly duties and terrors. (Frazer's conclusion—in a nutshell—was that this barbaric ordination, this ghastly laying on of hands, was an echo of ancient human sacrifices to Diana).

Aricia had a political importance, too, as a religious centre of the Latin League. The foundation in Rome of the temple of Diana on the Aventine Hill was probably an attempt to transfer the most important cult centre of the League, and hence its political leadership, to Rome. It is noteworthy that the Aventine was the headquarters of the Roman plebeians and that Diana was regarded as the protectress of the lower social orders in general and of slaves in particular—a clear connection with the 'King of the Grove'. Slaves had a holiday on Diana's principal festival in mid-August, a date transformed by the Christian Church into the feast of the Assumption of the Virgin Mary, who also, in certain places, was venerated as patroness of outlaws and thieves. Moreover, Diana (Artemis) was, at least in historical times, thought of as a virgin, and no man could enter the temple on the Aventine.

Mistress of Wild Beasts

The classical mythology of Artemis tells that she was the daughter of Zeus and Leto and the sister of Apollo. In some of the stories Artemis was born first, with no pain, and immediately acted as midwife to her mother for the birth of Apollo, thus prefiguring her later care for mortal women. The evolution of her character is a good example of the transition from the pre-Hellenic to the Hellenic world in Greek mythology and of the resulting confusion. Artemis's name is apparently not Greek. In Homer she is a rather ineffective partisan of the Trojans and is called *agrotera* (she of the wild) and *potnia theron* (mistress of wild beasts). She is the huntress, leading the life (as remarked by Charles Seltman in *The Twelve Olympians*) of an unmarried daughter of Homer's 'gay and brilliant feudal families', the goddess of 'energetic women' such as Atalanta, the better of men in hunting and wrestling yet 'unwilling to wed any of them'. The analogy with the huntin', shootin', and fishin' young ladies of the English shires is not too far-fetched, given the change in space, temperament and time.

Although the later Greeks and the Romans certainly regarded Artemis as a virgin, this was not the view of the earlier Greeks. To them, she was celibate but above all independent—if she wanted a man, she would have one but she would not be bound to him. However, as the comparatively uncomplicated, guilt-free Homeric past slid away, Artemis changed from the attractively open-air girl, perhaps some-

times accompanied by an attendant lover, to the more forbidding character of the austerely chaste huntress. It is in this role that she is most familiar. This is the Artemis of Hippolytus, her virgin and, to most contemporary minds, priggish acolyte who repulsed the advances of his stepmother Phaedra and was destroyed (as was she) by Aphrodite; of Actaeon who, having by no fault of his own seen the goddess bathing naked in a spring, was by her changed into a stag and done to death by his own hounds; and of the later European imagination.

In the oldest, pre-Hellenic stage and particularly in Asia, Artemis, though concerned with the wild, was one of the many manifestations of the mother-goddess, the source of life and fertility. In the mainstream of the purely

> . . . *Hera, enraged (yet again), turned Kallisto into a bear and tricked Artemis into killing her . . .*

Greek tradition, this maternal aspect was transmuted into a role almost that of the maiden aunt, the busy attendant at births, a companion of the young. On the periphery, and especially in the cult at Ephesus, the more overtly female, life-generating aspect remains to the fore.

Tomboy Goddess

But this concern and love for young things may also be connected with the boisterous side of Artemis's character. In the famous hymn by the Greek poet Callimachus (c. 305–240 BC) the goddess asks Zeus, her father, to give her only nine-year-old girls as her companions: she appears as a kind of tomboy goddess. In Athens, for instance, girls of this age were dressed in bearskins

to take part in a festival of Artemis.

The image of the bear (like that of the stag) runs through several of the Artemis legends. One of the best known concerns Kallisto (the name means 'loveliest'), originally a Minoan forerunner of Artemis but in classical mythology a nymph in her train. There are many versions of the story. In one, Zeus seduced her in the form of a bear; in another, Hera, enraged (yet again), turned Kallisto into a bear and tricked Artemis into killing her; in a third, Artemis discovered Kallisto to be pregnant and turned her into a bear and shot her. The victim was transported to the skies as the constellation of the Great Bear (the Plough) and her son was Arkas, the ancestor of the Arcadians. Some say Arkas had a twin brother, none other than Pan.

In one of the stranger versions of the Kallisto story, Zeus had his way with her after assuming the form of Artemis herself. This is an example of the strand of what we would call lesbianism in the legends of Artemis. It would be a mistake to put too much emphasis on this; but her liking for exclusively female society, her savagery toward certain men and toward her female attendants if they involved themselves with men, all point in this direction. Some of her folk cults, indeed, were decidedly ambivalent, with male dancers impersonating women and girls sporting phalluses.

The link between Artemis and the moon, so evocative to later generations, did not emerge until the 5th century BC. It probably sprang from her concern with women and from her brother Apollo's identification with the sun; but the connection is nowhere recognized in any cult, as far as we know. Much the same goes for her frequent confusion with the witch-goddess Hecate who, like her

Artemis (Diana) of Ephesus. Marble and bronze, Roman copy of a Hellenistic original of the 2nd century BC

cousin Artemis, was also connected with the guardianship of women and the young. Nonetheless, these identifications gave rise to the eerily romantic image of the triple goddess, potent in the night sky, in the wilds of the earth and at accursed crossroads, where Hecate was worshipped and grim happenings occurred. On this darker side, Artemis was also credited with the power (and inclination) to send plagues and sudden death.

Diana of the Ephesians

Although essentially a goddess of hill and heath, Artemis was revered as the chief divinity in three famous Greek maritime cities—Syracuse, Marseilles, and Ephesus. It was in the last of these that her cult became particularly renowned. Tradition has it that the city of Ephesus was founded about 900 BC by Ionian Greeks who brought with them the worship of Artemis. These Ionians mingled freely with the local inhabitants and assimilated many Asiatic customs. Tradition also relates that the Amazons built a temple at Ephesus to house a primitive image of a goddess (later identified with Artemis), probably made of a palm trunk. This temple was destroyed by barbarians around the middle of the seventh century. About 100 years later the great king Croesus erected a magnificent temple which in time became one of the Seven Wonders of the World. The chief object of veneration, mentioned in the Acts of the Apostles, was a wooden statue of Artemis.

The temple was the recipient, over a very long period, of rich gifts, which often took the strange form of gold and silver panoplies and garments for the statue. These would be changed at intervals, rather as a child dresses a doll. The most curious of these accoutrements were vestments to which were attached large golden representations of dates, giving the appearance of clusters of ample breasts. But oddest of all, on the head of the goddess was set a small shrine which probably contained the diopet, the most ancient and sacred thing in the temple. This was a small stone (possibly, in fact, a neolithic implement) which had been venerated in Ephesus since long before the Ionians came and which was believed to have fallen from Zeus in heaven. (This belief enabled the Ephesians to retort to their tiresome Christian critics that they did not worship an idol but something fashioned by the hand of God himself.)

The temple continued in fame and splendour for many centuries and did not go into a decline until the second half of the 3rd century AD. Finally, about the year 400, the statue was smashed by a Christian who boasted on an inscription that he had torn down 'the demon Artemis'. But it is said that the diopet was saved and hidden; and it is quite possible that an object now in the Liverpool City Museum is the very 'Zeus-fallen thing'.

It is curious that the Diana of the Ephesians, the exuberantly rich symbol of fertility and splendour, surrounded by oriental pomp, yet bearing on her head a relic of neolithic man, should be the longest surviving historical manifestation of the goddess Artemis. For she has lived on in the European imagination as something very different; the pure huntress goddess of the moon invoked by Ben Jonson in the words 'Queen and huntress, chaste and fair . . . Goddess, excellently bright.'

Witch Goddess

Greek and Roman authors connected witches with darkness and night, and so with Diana as goddess of the moon. In a poem by the Roman writer Horace (1st century BC), the witch Canidia appeals to 'Night and Diana, you faithful witnesses of all my enterprises.' As a pagan goddess and patroness of witches, to the early Christians Diana was a demon, and traces of her in this capacity survived into the Middle Ages. In 1318 Pope John XXII accused some of his court at Avignon of copulating with demonesses called 'Dianas'.

The most famous survival, however, was the belief that witches flew through the night with Diana. An ecclesiastical regulation called the Canon Episcopi, which has been traced back to the ninth century, says that some deluded women falsely believe that during the night they 'ride upon certain beasts with Diana, the goddess of pagans, and an innumerable multitude of women.' In other versions of this belief different pagan goddesses are named but it was natural to connect Diana, the moon, and the huntress, with night-flying. Margaret Murray (in The Witch-Cult in Western Europe) called the witch religion of Europe 'The Dianic cult', a hint that has been taken up by those modern witches who worship a Queen of Heaven. But although there are occasional references to a goddess in the history of witchcraft—among the Basques and some of the Scottish witches, for example—traces of her are rare, and witches were mainly concerned with a male god, the Devil.

CHARLES DE HOGHTON

FURTHER READING: M. Grant. Myths of the Greeks and Romans. *(Weidenfeld, 1962); W. K. C. Guthrie.* The Greeks and their Gods. *(Methuen, 1950); C. S. Seltman.* The Twelve Olympians. *(MaxParrish, 1956).*

Dionysus

The thirteenth god of the Greeks, Dionysus was a son of Zeus, according to Hesiod, although his paternity has been disputed. He was a stranger in Hellas, coming from wild uplands, mystic, the object of both frenzied devotion and hostility. After many

Lady of Light

When the hounds of spring are on winter's traces,
The mother of months in meadow or plain
Fills the shadows and windy places
With lisp of leaves and ripple of rain;
And the brown bright nightingale amorous
Is half assuaged for Itylus,
For the Thracian ships and the foreign faces,
The tongueless vigil, and all the pain.
Come with bows bent and with emptying of quivers,
Maiden most perfect, lady of light,
With a noise of winds and many rivers,
With a clamor of waters, and with might;
Bind on thy sandals, O thou most fleet,

Over the splendour and speed of thy feet;
For the faint east quickens, the wan west shivers,
Round the feet of the day and the feet of the night.
Where shall we find her, how shall we sing to her,
Fold our hands round her knees, and cling?
O that man's heart were as fire and could spring to her.
Fire, or the strength of the streams that spring!
For the stars and the winds are unto her
As raiment, as songs of the harp-player;
For the risen stars and the fallen cling to her,
And the southwest-wind and the west-wind sing.

Swinburne, *Atalanta in Calydon*

wanderings and much trouble, he came to sit at the High Table of Olympus as one of the great gods, taking the place surrendered to him by Hestia, the goddess of hearth and housework. This bare account contains nearly all the clues we need for as much understanding as we are ever likely to achieve, rationally, of the mythology and cult of Dionysus, the god of far more than wine.

The difficulty in writing about Dionysus is not that he is distant but that he is so close: indeed, he is always with us. But he is often denied and, when this happens, he wreaks a terrible vengeance. He is the god of the wilds—not the wilds of visible nature where Artemis reigns, but the wilds that extend so far and smile so deep in the secret regions of the human personality. He is the god of the irresistible but often resisted urge to 'let oneself go', to throw off the trammels of custom and respectability, to abandon, indeed, the Greek ideal of moderation in all things. He represents a permanent human force and yet a force that every age and culture seeks, if not to suppress, to channel and contain. Every age will reinterpret him according to its own attitudes and beliefs, its own restraints and permitted releases. This is no bad thing, so long as we are aware of it: it makes us (because he is so strange and fascinating, so known and yet so unknown) think about him more deeply than about Ares or Hera, or perhaps even Zeus or Athene. We can learn more about ourselves from Dionysus and how his cult revered him than we can from any other Greek deity—except Apollo, the god of order and reason, with whom Dionysus is curiously and significantly linked.

Born from the Thigh

The mythological stories told of Dionysus's birth and his adventurous progressions through the lands of men will of themselves lead us on to the nature of his cult and the historical background of its introduction and acceptance in classical Greece. In origin, Dionysus is no Greek. He plays, for instance, no partisan role in Homer's account of the Trojan War—not even on the side of the Asiatic Trojans. He figures only occasionally, in passing. Homer had heard of his wild rites but clearly knew little about him. Dionysus hails, in fact, from Phrygia and later moves to Thrace, the wild tracts on either side of the Hellespont. His mother, Semele, is associated with the Phrygian earth goddess Zemelo. The Greek mythologists, however, make Semele a mortal, the daughter

Semele, needless to say, was beautiful and attracted the attention of the ever-amorous Zeus, the father of the Gods.

of Cadmus, King of Thebes—that doom-laden site of so many products of the Greek imagination.

Semele, needless to say, was beautiful and attracted the attention of the ever-amorous Zeus, the father of the gods. Hera's jealousy, ever fertile of new ways to thwart Zeus, caused her to visit Semele in the guise of an old woman and suggest to the naive girl that she ask her divine lover to appear to her in his full immortal splendour not least to impress her sisters Agave, Ino, and Antonoe. Zeus, who had promised Semele any favour she might ask, reluctantly consented—whereupon Semele was annihilated by his lightning and thunderbolts. Her unborn son was rescued by Zeus and shut away by him in his own thigh, whence in due time he was born.

But Hera was not to be deceived, and on her orders Dionysus was seized by the Titans, who tore him limb from limb and began to cook him up for a meal. Having been restored to life by Rhea (his earth goddess grandmother), he was finally hidden, disguised as a girl, in the household of Athamas, King of Orchomenus in Greece. But Hera made the king demented and he killed his son Learchus, thinking he was hunting a stag. Dionysus was next fostered by nymphs on Mt. Nysa where, some say, he invented wine. Grown to manhood, he was himself driven mad by Hera and went wandering about the world, accompanied by Silenus, his tutor, and a rout of satyrs and wild women—the maenads or bacchantes—his former nymph nurses and others.

Strange tales are told of these followers and of their extraordinary powers. They caused fountains of milk and wine to spring from the earth; fire could do them no harm—they often carried it in their hands or on their heads; weapons left them unscathed; they had the strength to tear apart live bulls and other fierce beasts, the women no less than the men—yet the women showed great tenderness to young animals and suckled them at their own breasts. Armed with the thyrsos, an ivy-twined staff tipped with a pine cone, brandishing swords and enwreathed with serpents, they followed the god as far as India and then retraced their steps to Greece.

As he went, the god founded cities, so it is said, taught laws and the culture of the vine, and engaged in battles. But if he was victorious in the latter, he frequently met with opposition from stubborn folk who denied his divinity. These paid dearly for their blindness. Lycurgus, for instance, King of Thrace, was driven mad, killed his son Dryas with an axe thinking he was cutting down a vine, and mutilated his

Dionysus and Ariadne

corpse. Thrace was smitten with a great drought. Dionysus, who had taken refuge from Lycurgus's persecution at the bottom of the sea, reappeared and said relief would come only with the death of the king. Whereupon his subjects tied Lycurgus to wild horses and tore him apart. In Argos and Boeotia, both provinces of Greece, there was similar hostility to the god with similar results: the women went berserk and ripped their children to pieces.

The most famous account of the denial of the godhead of Dionysus and the frightful consequences was set in Thebes. The story is told in one of the most memorable of Greek tragedies, *The Bacchae of Euripides* (c. 487–407 BC). Dionysus, accompanied by his followers, came to the city, the place of his birth, and was angered to find that Agave and his mother's other sisters denied his divinity and that he was the son of Zeus; but old Cadmus and the blind seer Tiresias recognized him. Dionysus therefore sent a madness upon his aunts and the rest of the Theban women, who abandoned their household chores and went raving upon Mt. Cithaeron. Pentheus, son of Agave and now King of Thebes, a pillar of unimaginative authority and male supremacy, was outraged and tried to arrest Dionysus and his maenads, but they walked out of prison completely unharmed.

Meanwhile the women are out on a high mountain, at this stage in a comely trance, like flower-children of antiquity. But set upon by herdsmen, they go into a frenzy, tear the Theban cattle limb from limb, eat the flesh raw, plunder the neighbouring villages and steal the children. Nothing can avail against them. Then Pentheus begins himself to fall under the spell of Dionysus, who so far in the play has appeared as a mortal. He is persuaded to go and watch the women, hidden in a pine tree and disguised as a woman. But the possessed women discover him, uproot the tree, and dismember him alive. Agave, his mother, wrenches off his head, believing she has slaughtered a lion cub with her bare hands. The women return in ecstasy to the city but Cadmus manages to bring them back to their senses. As Agave and the others realize the full horror of what they have done and stumble off into hopeless exile, Dionysus reveals himself as the god.

A Wild and Frenzied Joy

By the account so far, Dionysus might well seem a bestial character and his deeds even more horrific than most of the cruel doings of the ancient Greek divinities. But the point is this: horrors occur when Dionysus is denied. If you surrender to him you will have joy—a wild and frenzied joy but not a joy destructive in itself; but if you resist, the joy becomes a foul and frenzied horror, a punishment for the refusal of joy.

The stories illustrate this point, particularly the Bacchae, in which one of the most striking elements is the contrast between the accounts of the women on Cithaeron. In the first, when they are left alone in communion with the god, all is peaceful and idyllic, in the second, after they have been startled by the herdsmen and think they are being hunted, they erupt into bloody madness; and in the third, when they discover Pentheus in their midst, there is a climax of unspeakable fearfulness.

The stories also reflect something unique in Greek religion and mythology: the historical fact of the introduction, by groups of foreign missionaries, of what was to all intents and purposes a new religion and a new ethos—and of the inevitable resistance they met. The Dionysiac cult is totally different from the mainstream of Greek, Olympian religion. The latter was founded upon the immortality of the gods and the mortality of men and upon the gulf between the two. It was man's duty to revere the gods, from a distance, and to avoid their anger by decent and orderly behaviour—self-knowledge and no extremes. Dionysus offered the complete opposite. Within a ritual frame, his cult allowed, indeed encouraged, the release of irrational impulses which gave freedom, identification with the god, and thereby happiness. He is known as 'Lusios'— the liberator. Moreover his cult is open to all: to young and old, men and women, slaves and freedmen.

It is this which makes Dionysus the god of far more than wine. He is the god, says Plutarch, of the whole of 'moist nature'—sap and blood and sperm—or, in the words of Professor E. R. Dodds, of 'all the mysterious and uncontrollable tides that ebb and flow in the life of nature.' It was the later Greeks and the stolid Romans who looked to a degenerate Dionysus, the tipsy, merry Bacchus and his Saturday-night-out boys and girls: and modern Europe followed them until anthropology and psychology suggested different ideas. For the real devotees of Dionysus, wine was merely one means of union with the god. There

were others more potent—above all, the dance.

Dancing Madness
In many societies throughout the world dancing has had a profound religious significance. Everyone knows of savage dances and the states of 'ecstasy' —standing outside oneself— that they induce. Jalaluddin Rumi, the founder of the Mevlevi sect of dervishes noted for their dancing, taught that 'he who knows the power of the dance dwells in God'. There have, throughout the Christian era, been outbreaks

> *Dionysus . . . sent a madness upon his aunts and the rest of the Theban women, who abandoned their household chores and went raving upon Mt. Cithaeron.*

of 'dancing madness' in Europe; and their characteristics as described in the records are strikingly similar to those that we read of in Euripides. Even in our own time, the dance has become more of a cult. On the wilder shores of pop music, events may be observed that are strongly reminiscent of a Dionysiac 'orgy'. And be it noted that the word 'orgy' is not used here in its debased common sense. For a Dionysiac, and for many alive today, the 'orgy' is not a drunken revel but a means of seeking, by dance and music, a communion with something beyond the ordinary, in company with a band of like-minded people.

Apart from dance and music, there is evidence that the behaviour of the bacchae, the women inspired to ecstatic frenzy by Dionysus, is not a figment of the possibly warped imagination of an old and disappointed Athenian playwright. In many countries and in any number of modern clinical descriptions, the same elements recur.

The tossing back and around of the head and hair, the handling of snakes, insensitivity to pain, the tearing apart and eating raw of animals—all these are characteristic of hysteria and, very often, of hysteria channeled in the practice of religion.

In the Dionysiac cult, the rending and devouring of raw flesh is probably based on straightforward magic: you may become god by devouring god in one of his manifestations. This concept is not so far removed from that of the Christian who receives the wafer of consecrated bread during Holy Communion, not to mention that of Scandinavian tribes in the Dark Ages who, it is said, devoured their kings when times were bad in order to spread their royal strength throughout all the members of the band. Maybe the fate of Pentheus reflects this kind of human sacrament, behind the ostensible motive of revenge—an echo of ritual symbolism.

It seems probable that the actual cult of Dionysus was introduced into northern Greece about the beginning of the 7th century BC. Its coming, and its gradual penetration southward, are likely to have had the twin results of disturbing the settled routine of domestic and religious life, and of provoking violent opposition from the Pentheus figures of the time. About the start of the 6th century the problem may have reached crisis point and it appears to have been resolved in a thoroughly Greek, pragmatic way by incorporating the Dionysiac cult into the existing state cults—rather, to take a tame parallel, as British would-be revolutionaries are sometimes elevated to the House of Lords.

Night on a Bare Mountain
This unlikely marriage took place notably at Delphi, the seat of Apollo, the

ally, 'goat-singers') who gave performances before the statue in honour of the god. Many people believe that this is the origin of Greek tragedy and thus of Western theatre. It is interesting that this may at least partly explain why Greek actors wore masks: Dionysus had long been the god of masquerade—the Master of Illusions, as Professor Dodds calls him, capable of transforming himself into many shapes to avoid his enemies. In the Attic countryside, the Dionysia were less subtle and included, we may be sure, a good deal of rural jollification and drunkenness.

But the most extraordinary manifestation of the Dionysiac cult, which lasted until the age of Plutarch in the 2nd century AD, was the joint mountain dancing festival of the women of Athens and Delphi. This was held in midwinter every two years. A group of well-born Athenian women and girls were chosen to walk the 100 miles, barefoot across the mountains, to the shrine of Apollo, where they joined their Delphic sisters. After prayers and sacrifices to the god of license in the precincts of the god of reason they set off at night to scale Mt. Parnassus, more than 8,000 feet high. There, on the bitter heights, they held the oreibasia, the mountain dancing of Dionysus.

Nobody knows exactly what they did. The remarkable fact is that they did it at all—these cloistered women from upper-class homes upon the serene Attic coast, abandoning themselves in midwinter to the harsh night on the bare mountain. Other parts of Greece held similar rites, but nowhere were they in such dramatic surroundings. Wild they may have been but their timing in midwinter and the exclusion of men point to something very different from the popular idea of an 'orgy'. For these women, the orgia

god of law and order. Commenting on this remarkable outcome, Charles Seltman writes (in The Twelve Olympians): 'Law could be redeemed from mechanistic rote by the natural human contact of the anarchic god, while license could be put under control by complying with the god of self-knowledge and moderation. Order could learn about disorder, and disorder about order.' When one compares this solution with the earlier troubles and the sorry Christian history of persecution and sectarianism, one may yet

think the Greeks worthy of study and admiration.

Of particular interest is the establishment of Dionysiac religion in Athens. Peisistratus, ruler of Athens in the mid-sixth century, founded both the Panathenaic Games and the Great Dionysia. He invited the priest of Dionysus at Eleutherae—a village on the borders of Attica which claimed to be the god's birthplace—to set up his statue at the foot of the Acropolis. The priest was accompanied by a troupe of country players called tragodoi (liter-

were acts of devotion and communion, of release into the unknown, terrifying yet fulfilling.

Other Dionysiac festivals may have been more 'orgiastic'. In some, men were allowed to take part and these may have been characterized by sexual freedom. But it is well to remember a passage from the Bacchae: 'Dionysus compels no woman to be chaste. Chastity is a matter of character and she who is naturally chaste will partake of Bacchic rites without being touched.' As Seltman says, 'Their state of ecstasis left the Bacchae free to follow either the instincts or the restraints of nature. No inhibitions stopped the satisfaction of desire; no exhibitionist urge drove them toward promiscuous folly.'

Beyond Good and Evil

The Dionysiac cult recognizes the universal human need to fling off the fetters of habit, if only—willingly—to take them up again and soldier on to cope with the demands of an ordered social life. Dionysus allows us this release, this necessary respite from regime. And in spite of the frenzy, this does not free us from ultimate responsibility. As Professor Dodds observes 'Dionysus is beyond good and evil . . . he is what we make of him.' The god, in fact, is already within us: we have to seek him and allow him to escape, if we do not wish him to break out—as he did from Pentheus's prison—and drive us mad. In this sense, we are indeed one with Dionysus; and that is why he fascinates us.

CHARLES DE HOGHTON

FURTHER READING: E. R. Dodd's introduction to The Bacchae *(Oxford University Press, 1944); see also his* The Greeks and the Irrational *(University of California Press, 1951); W. F. Otto,* Dionysus: Myth and Cult*, transl. Robert B. Palmer (Spring Pubns., 1981); Philip Vellacott's translation of* The Bacchae *is in the Penguin Classics series.*

Dioscuri

'Sons of Zeus', the twin heroes Castor and Polydeuces of Greek myths (Castor and Pollux of Roman), they protected sailors and were believed to have come to the aid of the Roman army at the battle of Lake Regillus, c. 496 BC; they sailed on the voyage

Rug containing the image of the god Dionysys created sometime in the 3rd to 5th century.

Gold phaler (ornament worn by horses), one of a pair, representing Dionysos. Syria (3rd century BC)

with the Argonauts to fetch the Golden Fleece; they were worshipped in Sparta, where their symbol was two upright pieces of wood joined by two cross-pieces, hence the astrological symbol for Gemini, with which they were associated.

Dodona

Site of a famous oracle of Zeus, in the mountains of northwestern Greece: the priests 'of unwashed feet who couch upon the ground' and priestesses interpreted the rustling of the leaves of a sacred oak as the words of the god: they may also have drawn oracles from the sound of a sacred spring in the grove, the echoes of a gong, and the flight and calls of sacred pigeons; later, the god's answers were given through lots.

Echo

Repetition of sound which can often be heard in high mountains; in Greek mythology the name of a mountain nymph, vainly loved by the God Pan, who in his wrath had her torn to pieces by mad shepherds, only her voice remaining; in another story Echo was doomed by Hera to repeat only what others say because she had distracted Hera's attention from Zeus's amorous affairs with her idle chatter; she was, therefore, unable to declare her love for Narcissus and sadly pined away until only her voice was left.

Eleusis

Held in honour of Demeter and Persephone, the Eleusinian Mysteries were ceremonies of initiation, celebrated annually during antiquity at Eleusis in Attica. Their nature was a closely guarded secret, any breach

of which was liable to punishment by death. Originally they were a purely local cult, possibly restricted to a single family or clan; their secrecy has been sometimes explained as due to these original restrictions, but it is more probably due to the sense of awe and fear which was felt by those who took part in ceremonies which concerned the forces of life and death.

Like all other rituals of Demeter and Persephone, the Mysteries were in origin agricultural ceremonies, but comparison with similar rituals in other societies shows that the processes of agriculture tend to be associated in ceremonies of initiation with those which govern the life of men. It is therefore probable that already in their earliest stages a personal significance was attached to the Mysteries. Unlike other types of initiation, they were not restricted by age or sex, and their significance was thus potentially universal.

The incorporation of Eleusis into a unified Attica probably led to an expansion of membership. Legend dates this to the mythological period, but adds that Eleusis was allowed to keep control of the Mysteries, according to the Greek writer Pausanias (2nd century AD). Apparently Athens did not interfere much, if at all, with the cult in the early historical period. The Homeric Hymn to Demeter, which dates from the late 7th or early 6th century BC, does not refer to Athens or to Athenian elements of the cult. The management of the Mysteries appears to have been in the hands of the Eleusinian family of the Eumolpidae, from whom the Hierophant was drawn. His title indicates that he revealed the sacred objects, and he was the chief priest at Eleusis. At some stage, however, this management was shared with the family of the Kerykes, who had Athenian connections. They provided the daduchus (torch-bearer) and the keryx (herald) who were the

other chief officials of the cult. Athenian influence first becomes apparent in the sixth century, with the building of an enlarged telesterion (hall of initiation), and toward the end of the century there is evidence of the construction of a sanctuary of the Eleusinian deities at Athens. A procession from Athens to Eleusis was instituted and initiation into the rites of Demeter and Persephone at Agrae, on the outskirts of Athens, was made a necessary preliminary to initiation at Eleusis. This first stage was called the Lesser, the second the Greater Mysteries.

A further development was the opening of the Mysteries to all who could speak Greek, provided that they were free of pollution. The first definite evidence comes from an anecdote in Herodotus, the Greek writer of the 5th century BC, which is set at the time of the battle of Salamis in 480. This tells how a great cloud of dust like that of the procession to Eleusis was seen moving toward Salamis and a sound like the cry made during the procession was heard. The story was taken as a sign that the Eleusinian deities had come to the aid of Greece in her struggle against Persia.

This legend must have contributed to the popularity of the Mysteries, and Athenian propaganda during the 5th and 4th centuries BC also greatly increased their prestige. This remained undiminished down to the Roman period, and they survived in fact until the end of the pagan world, when the invader Alaric in 395 AD finally destroyed the sanctuary.

Dancing by Torch Light
Archeology shows evidence of a series of buildings on the site of the telesterion from prehistoric times onward, but the first literary evidence for the cult is found in the Homeric Hymn. This throws light on some of the preliminary rituals. One of these was a purification ceremony, in which the

initiate was seated on a stool with his head veiled and his foot resting on a ram's fleece, while a priest or priestess purified him. In the Hymn Demeter is portrayed performing a similar ritual on her arrival at the palace of the ruler of Eleusis. On later monuments Heracles is shown undergoing the same purification.

Fasting was also a preliminary to initiation, and the Hymn describes how Demeter fasted for nine days when looking for Persephone and how she would not accept food or wine in the palace at Eleusis. She also carried torches in her search, and these played an important part in the ritual. There were dances by torchlight around the well Callichoron ('of the fair dances') at Eleusis, and this well is mentioned in the Hymn. It is still visible at the entrance to the sanctuary. The dancing formed part of a panny-chis (all-night festival).

Demeter's fasting is broken when she is made to laugh by the jokes of a servant called Iambe. She then asks for a drink of barley and water, flavoured with the herb pennyroyal. In the cult fasting was also broken with this simple drink, and the making of coarse or obscene jokes (called aischrologia), which is common to many rituals of fertility, took place during the preliminaries to the Mysteries.

The Hymn goes on to describe Demeter's attempt to immortalize the king's son Demophon by placing him in the fire every night, her detection by the child's mother and the consequent failure of this project. There might be a reference here to the preliminary purification, in which fire was probably used. It has however been suggested that the story has a deeper significance, and that Demeter's nursing of the child reflects the 'adoption' of each initiate by the goddess in the Mysteries. As Demophon is reborn through his baptism of fire, so the initiate experiences a rebirth and the promise of a new life.

Demeter and Metanira (queen of Eleusis); Detail of the belly of an Apulian red-figure hydria (c. 340 BC)

After the takeover of the Mysteries by Athens the preliminary ceremonies increased in complexity. The first stages were purificatory. These were followed by the Lesser Mysteries, which took place in the month of anthesterion (February–March). Their purpose was also mainly that of purification, and they included washing in the river Ilissus. We are told that they had some kind of instructive content and prepared the initiates for the Greater Mysteries.

These took place in the month of boedromion (September—October), from the fifteenth to the twenty-third day. There were two grades of initiation, and a year had to elapse before one was admitted to the final grade, which was known as the epopteia, meaning 'spectacle' or 'vision'. Before the festival the hiera, sacred objects, were brought to Athens from Eleusis. Their nature is unknown, but it was presumably these which the Hierophant or chief priest revealed during the ceremonies. They were kept in sacred boxes which are often represented in art.

The festival began with a solemn assembly at Athens during which the proclamation was made, which stated those classes of people who were forbidden to take part in the initiation. This was followed on the sixteenth day by a journey to the sea, where the initiates again took a sacred bath. Each took with him a pig, which was sacred to Demeter, and washed this also in the sea, after which the pigs were probably sacrificed. An official sacrifice to Demeter and Persephone took place the next day, and on the eighteenth day the initiates rested.

The great procession to Eleusis took place either on the nineteenth or twentieth. This was called the Iacchus procession, after the deity who personified the cry which was made during it. The journey was a long one, some 14 miles, and it was interrupted by many

ceremonies and included dancing, singing of hymns, and sacrifices. There was also a form of obscene humour in which prominent citizens were abused. On arrival there was a night festival with further dancing. This is portrayed on a votive tablet found at Eleusis.

About the main ceremonies of the Mysteries, which took place on the following days inside the telesterion, much less is known. The various stages of the building itself have been excavated, and the one which dates from the time of Pericles, in the second half of the 5th century BC, was a vast structure of approximately 167 feet in length and width. Along the sides were tiers of steps, wide enough to accommodate an audience of almost 4,000 spectators. It is now thought that a small room stood in the centre of the hall, forming a Holy-of-Holies; from which the Hierophant would appear when he displayed the sacred objects.

The ritual took three forms, the 'things spoken', legomena; 'things performed', dromena; and 'things revealed', deiknymena. The first of these are thought to have been brief sentences, rather than a long exposition, and we are told by Aristotle that the initiates did not go to Eleusis to learn, but to have an experience and to be put in a receptive state of mind. Other authors emphasize the emotional experience of initiates to the Mysteries, whose reactions are said to be religious awe and fear, and at the close of the ceremonies joy, encouragement, and hope. The story of Demeter's 'passion', her search for Persephone, and joy at her return, were central to the Mysteries, but it is not known how this was represented or referred to. Any form of dramatic representation appears to be ruled out by the nature of the telesterion. There were however important

Female torch carrier, taking part in the worship of Demeter and Persephone. Terracotta figurine, Attic artwork (c.140–130 BC), from Eleusis

dramatic effects from the interchange of darkness and light, and the sudden blaze of torches at the climax of the Mysteries is often mentioned.

Supreme Revelation

The Phrygians also say, however, that he is a 'green ear of corn reaped'; and following the Phrygians, the Athenians when initiating (anyone) into the Eleusinian (Mysteries) also show to those who have been made epopts the mighty and wonderful and most perfect mystery for an epopt there—a green ear of corn reaped in silence. And this ear of corn is also for the Athenians the great and perfect spark of light from the Unportrayable One; just as the hierophant himself, not indeed castrated like Attis, but rendered a eunuch by hemlock, and cut off from all fleshy generation, celebrating by night at Eleusis the great and ineffable mysteries beside a huge fire, cries aloud, and makes proclamation, saying: 'August Brimo has brought forth a holy son, Bromios,' that is, the strong has given birth to the strong.

> *For august is, he says, the generation which is spiritual or heavenly or sublime, and strong is that which is thus generated.*
>
> Hippolytus, *Philosophumena* (trans. F. Legge)

A Single Ear of Corn

Most of the evidence for what happened inside the telesterion comes from Christian writers, and is suspect on the grounds of prejudice and also of confusion with other pagan cults. Several authors refer to a 'sacred marriage' between Zeus and Demeter in relation to the Mysteries, and the Christian writer Asterius accuses Eleusis of celebrating 'a union between the Hierophant and the priestess' in an underground chamber. The Eleusinian myths do not refer to a marriage of Zeus and Demeter, but to that of Hades and Persephone. Originally the divine couple appear to have been anonymous, and they are sometimes referred to simply as 'the God and the Goddess'. If however a ritual union was enacted at Eleusis it cannot have taken place in the telesterion, where there was no underground chamber. Another Christian writer, Hippolytus, implies some form of sacred marriage, and he adds that during the Mysteries the Hierophant announced the birth of a sacred child to the goddess.

The Mysteries were celebrated near the season of the autumn sowing, and their foundation is linked to the myth of the rape and return of Persephone . . .

A second valuable testimony is given by Hippolytus about the epopteia, the name of which indicates that its essential nature was some form of revelation; references to the Mysteries throughout antiquity stress the fact that it was the vision of them that gave the initiates their hopes for the future. According to this writer, the 'supreme revelation' of the epopteia was simply the showing of a single ear of corn. This may seem hard to believe, and Hippolytus is eager to suggest the primitive nature of such a revelation. But if the agricultural basis of Demeter's worship is remembered, and the analogy that was felt between the life of the corn and that of men, one may be less inclined to question this testimony. The Mysteries were celebrated near the season of the autumn sowing, and their foundation is linked to the myth of the rape and return of Persephone, who personified the corn which was sown in the earth and 'came to life' again in the spring. In the symbol of the ear of corn the initiates may likewise have seen the promise of a new life beyond the grave, and the announcement of the birth of a divine child may also have symbolized this promise. At the same time, the child of the goddess of the earth is sometimes named as Plutus, the god of wealth, who in the Homeric Hymn is sent by Demeter and Persephone 'to the house of the man whom they love', and the divine birth and revelation of the corn must also have represented for the initiates the hope of prosperity in their present life.

We do not know much about the closing stages of the festival, but many authors speak of the encouragement and expectation of a better life which visitors to the Mysteries carried away with them. How far this involved moral resolutions it is hard to determine, although it seems that there was a kind of rudimentary ethical code at Eleusis which encouraged respect for family, fellow-citizens, and foreigners alike. But the influence and prestige of the Mysteries throughout antiquity is rather to be explained as a result of the optimistic view of life and death which they offered, in contrast to the more pessimistic attitude of traditional Greek religion. Their influence on philosophy was strong, and through Pythagorean and Platonic circles they came to have an important effect on the philosophical and religious thought of the 1st century AD and also to some extent on the development of early Christian theology.

N. J. RICHARDSON

FURTHER READING: G. E. Mylona. Eleusis and the Eleusinian Mysteries. *(Princeton University Press, 1961); M. P. Nilsson.* Greek Popular Religion. *(Harper and Row, 1940);* History of Greek Religion. *(Greenwood, 1980).*

Elysian Fields

A paradise for dead souls, this location in the afterlife was reserved for certain heroes, relatives of the gods, and virtuous people. The Elysian Fields are distinct from Hades (the generic location of the ancient Greek afterlife) and Tartarus (a special abyss in Hades saved for torture and torment.) The Elysian Fields are first mentioned in Homer's *Odyssey* as a place where there is 'no snow, no winter onslaught' but instead 'singing winds of the West refreshing all mankind.' [IV:637-639] Homer indicates that 'gold-haired Rhadamanthys' [IV:635] dwells in the fields. Later, writers such as Hesiod and Virgil develop the myth of the Elysian Fields by referring to 'Elysium' or 'The Isle of the Blessed.' 'Elysium' has become synonymous with 'paradise' in literary parlance. Most ancient writers located Elysium in the extreme West, at the edge of the world.

FURTHER READING: Homer, and Robert Fagles. The Odyssey, Book IV. *(Penguin, 1997); E. Hamilton.* Mythology Ch. 1 and Ch. 16. *(Warner, 1942); Virgil, and Robert Fagles.* Aeneid Book VI. *(Penguin, 2010).*

Epicureanism

Greek philosophy of restrained hedonism espoused by Epicurus (341–270 BC) in Athens. Epicureanism teaches that pleasure, defined as the absence of physical pain combined with a tranquil state of mind, is the greatest good toward which we should aspire. Typically, hedonism advocates a selfish revelry in sensual pleasures. Epicureanism, while hedonic in its advocacy of pleasure as goodness, is much more restrained in practice given that sensual pleasure is not the highest pleasure per se.

Portrait of Epicurus, founder of the Epicurean school; Roman copy after a lost Hellenistic original

Epicurus established 'The Garden', a small group of friends and thinkers, controversially including women and slaves, which met at his home in the garden. His philosophy, like many Hellenic schools of thought, confronted questions of physics and ethics in its quest for the good, happy life. Lasting happiness could be achieved by seeking pleasure, which meant physical health, lack of pain, freedom from oppression and fear, communion with companions or friends, and peace of mind. These kinds of pleasures, what he called 'higher' pleasures, are distinct from momentary, or 'lower' pleasures of the flesh. Higher pleasures, according to Epicurus, need to be cultivated over time. Tranquility would be achieved through the use of reason, as well as by avoiding the pitfalls of public life.

Epicurus' theories of physics followed from Democritus' materialism, which held that the universe was made of infinitely small atoms of matter, and that these atoms were the only type of material. In other words, Epicurus rejected spiritualisms and dualisms, which included Plato's idealism.

The Epicurean materialism led to a kind of peace of mind in its own right: the universe and the gods were indifferent to the lives and actions of humans, and by accepting this state of affairs we can avoid the discord and worry that comes from the possibility of divine interventions or fortune.

FURTHER READING: Annas, Julia. The Morality of Happiness. *(New York:*

Oxford UP, 1993); Mitsis, Phillip. *Epicurus' Ethical Theory: The Pleasures of Invulnerability. (Ithaca: Cornell UP, 1988); Long, A. A., and D. N. Sedley.* The Hellenistic Philosophers. *(Cambridge UP, 1987); Epicurus, Brad Inwood, and Lloyd P. Gerson.* The Epicurus Reader: Selected Writings and Testimonia. *(Indianapolis: Hackett, 1994).*

Eros

The chubby cherub with his bow and quiver, favourite device of Victorian valentines and rococo art, bears little resemblance to the earliest conceptions of Eros, the Greek god of love. His origins are obscure; some say that he was hatched from a silver egg laid in the womb of darkness, emerging as a monstrous being, four-headed, golden-winged, and uttering animal cries. Others hold that he was the son of Iris or of Ilithyia, the goddess of childbirth; while later mythology makes him the son of Aphrodite by Zeus, her father, or by Ares, the god of war, or by Hermes. The Greek writer Hesiod (8th century BC) makes Eros, together with Earth and Tartarus, the oldest of the gods. He represents him as the powerful creative force that attracts together and unites the cosmic couples who created the universe, 'bringing harmony to chaos' and making it possible for life to develop.

Long before Aphrodite appeared among the gods, the ancient Greeks worshipped a god of sexual potency named Eros. That Eros was not only a creative agent but also on occasions a destructive one was already understood: an implicit acceptance of the power of passion to wreck society and threaten law and order. The Latin writer Apuleius (2nd century AD) in later times makes the same point when he speaks of the god 'running from building to building all night long with his torch and his arrows, breaking up respectable homes.' But it is as a cosmic principle that Eros first makes his appearance in Greek myth, a far cry from the petulant boy archer of later tradition.

Although there is no mention of the god in Homer, the passages in which the word eros occur illustrate clearly its early meaning. In the *Iliad* and the *Odyssey* eros stands for irresistible physical desire; it is the force which attracts Zeus to Hera, Paris to Helen, an affliction which causes the limbs of Penelope's suitors to tremble uncontrollably. In the later lyric poets of the 6th and 7th centuries BC the conception of this force is broadened to include mind as well as body.

From his birth, Eros's variously imputed parentage signifies several different aspects of his role as the god of passionate love. As the son of Hermes, god of fertility, who was worshipped with phallic images, Eros represents sexual potency and is himself a god of fertility: at his cult centre at Thespiae in Boeotia he was represented by a simple phallic figure. From the devious god Hermes, too, he draws his cunning and his penchant for trickery. With Ares the warrior for his father, Eros reminds us of the fighting man's immemorial attraction for women and the often ambivalent—or, as we would say, 'love-hate'—nature of sexual relationships. As the son of Aphrodite by Zeus, according to Hesiod and the most widely held view, the contrary and perverse element of Eros is symbolized; his parents' union is an incestuous one, signifying that erotic love knows no boundaries and trespasses on forbidden relationships.

God Who Never Grew Up

The changing conception of the god is reflected in art, in which Eros remains perpetually youthful, even growing steadily younger. He is represented as a youth in archaic times, as a young boy in the Classical period and as a baby boy in the Hellenistic age. He is shown winged to represent the fleeting nature of passion, blindfolded to suggest the inconsequence and unpredictability of his attacks, and carrying a torch to symbolize the flame which he kindles in others. He has power over gods and men—even Zeus himself is frightened of him—and no one is immune to his cruel darts.

Indulged by Aphrodite, he is half god, half spoilt, undisciplined boy. His bow and arrows, first mentioned by Euripides (484–407 BC), are his favourite playthings; the sharp arrows from his quiver producing sometimes love and sometimes disdain in their victims. He takes a malicious pleasure in choosing unlikely targets and delights in the misery he causes. Sometimes Aphrodite, who herself suffers from his archery and is led into all sorts of

Eros, Parmigianino (1503–1540)

Woman and Eros; Attic red-figured skyphos (c. 420–410 BC, from Athens

undignified liaisons in consequence, loses patience with him and confiscates his weapons. The poet Anacreon (6th century BC), while dwelling on Eros's playful side refers also to his cruelty. The god is shown (as also on vase paintings) striking the lovelorn with an axe or wielding a whip. At the same time Eros is the embodiment of the sweetness of youth. He is associated with all beautiful things, he walks on a carpet of flowers and wears a crown of roses. Yet it is not for nothing that the rose is his special emblem, for the rose, though sweetly perfumed, has a sharp thorn. The poet Sappho describes his contradictory qualities as 'bitter sweet'.

The playmates of the god in Aphrodite's train are Pothos and Himeros, representing longing and desire. Eros has a brother, the son of Ares and Aphrodite, named Anteros. Earlier writers show Anteros in opposition to Eros, as the god who avenges slighted love; it is only later that he becomes the brother of Eros, standing for mutual affection and tenderness, yet still constantly at odds with the selfish god of love. Anteros was the younger brother and was conceived on the advice of Themis, Zeus's first wife, when Aphrodite complained to her that Eros remained perpetually a child and never seemed

to grow any older. Themis suggested that the remedy was for Eros to have a brother, who would spur him on to outstrip him. As soon as Anteros was born Eros grew stronger and the span of his wings increased. If ever he was separated from Anteros, however, he found himself reduced to his former size. The story seems to suggest that passion that is mutual rather than one-sided makes love grow stronger and more mature.

There was not one Eros but many,

according to Euripides and a number of later writers, and he was worshipped in many places: notably in Parion in Mysia and in Thespiae with phallic images, as the god of both passion and fertility. A festival in his honour, the Erotidia, was celebrated at Thespiae in the spring, every fifth year, with sports and games in which musicians and others took part. If any strife or sedition had arisen among the people, prayers and sacrifices would be offered to the god to resolve the disagreement.

Cupid, that Very Wicked Boy

Known to the Romans as Cupido or Amor, the Latin counterpart of Eros has strongly marked human characteristics, due to the influence of the Alexandrian poets and artists. He is less of a god and more of a mischievous child: he is the 'knavish lad' referred to by Shakespeare (*A Midsummer Night's Dream*), 'this wimpled, whining, purblind, wayward boy'. The word cupido means desire but it is an emotion on a different scale from Hesiod's power 'that loosens the limbs and damages the mind.' Apuleius describes him as 'that very wicked boy, with neither manners nor respect for the decencies.'

Statue of Cupid and Psyche kissing, 2nd century AD; Room E of the House of Cupid and Psyche (regio I, insula XIV), Ostia Antica, Latium, Italy

In earlier times, however, he was a more powerful god, accorded the same honour as his mother. It was believed that his influence extended not only over the heavens and the sea but even to the underworld. His godhead was widely venerated and prayers and sacrifices were offered to him daily.

According to some authorities, there were two Cupids, one of whom, the son of Jupiter and Venus, was a lively and pleasant youth, while the other, the offspring of Night and Erebus, was given to debauchery and riotous living. Cicero indeed mentions three Cupids, their parentage being ascribed to Mercury and Diana, Mercury, and Venus, and Mars and Venus. In common with other immortals, Cupid had the power of changing his shape at will: in the *Aeneid* of Virgil, he assumed the form of Ascanius at the request of his mother Venus and went to the court of Dido, where he inspired the queen with love.

In art, Cupid is usually shown amusing himself with some childish pursuit. He chases a butterfly, plays with dice, drives a hoop or throws a quoit. Sometimes he plays upon a horn to entertain his mother; sometimes he marches like a warrior, a spear on his shoulder and a buckler on his arm, signifying that love conquers all. Occasionally he is shown riding on the back of a lion or a dolphin, or engaged in breaking up the thunderbolts of Jupiter.

The Taming of Love

Like Eros, Cupid is vain and cruel, and the Latin poet Ovid speaks of his 'savage spite'. A story in his *Metamorphoses* illustrates the vindictive side of the god of love. Cupid's arrows, he explains, were of two kinds: one golden, shining and sharp, the other leaden and blunt. The first inspired the victim with love and the second produced fear and repulsion. Once Phoebus Apollo teased Cupid for carrying weapons

Eros and Psyche

which were better suited to a warrior than a naughty boy. Determined to get his own back on Apollo, Cupid shot an arrow of desire at his tormentor, who promptly fell in love with the nymph Daphne—only to be repulsed, for Cupid had wounded her too, but with a leaden arrow. Refusing Apollo's advances, she fled terrified, but the god pursued her relentlessly. Finally she implored her father Peneus to efface her beauty by turning her into a tree to escape the god.

It is in the legend of Cupid and Psyche, as told by Apuleius, that the god of love is shown at his most tender and human. For once he is made to experience the suffering which he has inflicted on others. Psyche is an earthly maiden of such extraordinary beauty that she arouses the jealousy of Venus, who orders Cupid to cause her to fall in love with the vilest and most degraded of men. Cupid, however, himself falls in love with her and has her carried off to a marvelous palace, where he visits her nightly in darkness but conceals his identity from her

and tells her that she must never see his face. Lonely during the daytime, Psyche begs to be allowed to invite her sisters and Cupid agrees, though warning her that they will try to set her against him. Out of jealousy at her wealth and good fortune, the sisters persuade her that her husband must be a repulsive monster since he will never permit his face to be seen.

The following night, when the god is asleep, she lights a lamp to look at him. Instead of a horrible serpent, as her sisters had described, she sees a beautiful youth, winged and golden haired. In her ecstasy, she lets fall a drop of scalding oil on his shoulder. Cupid awakes and tells her that for her disobedience she will never see him again. Psyche searches the earth for Cupid, hounded relentlessly by Venus, who has discovered the lovers' secret and has locked up Cupid in his bedroom. Cupid, unable to bear separation from Psyche, flies out of the window to enlist the aid of Jupiter, who puts an end to their troubles by raising Psyche to the level of the gods and making her immortal. Venus is reconciled and accepts Psyche as her daughter-in-law and the lovers are reunited.

Psyche is held to be the personification of the human soul and is often shown in art winged, like her lover, following an ancient belief that the human soul took the form of a butterfly or other winged insect. In Platonic philosophy love, in the most elevated sense, is an agent of the soul's progress and from the 4th century BC Psyche and the god of love were often depicted together in allegorical representations.

ISABEL SUTHERLAND

FURTHER READING: Apuleius, Cupid and Psyche, *eds. M. G. Balme and J. H. Morwood (Oxford Univ. Press, 1976); and* The Golden Ass of Apuleius, *trans. Robert Graves.*

Euhemerism

The theory that mythology has its origins in history; propounded by the Greek scholar Euhemerus in the 3rd century BC, who tried to prove that the gods were in fact ancient kings who had been deified: in an account of a fabulous journey to islands in the Indian Ocean, he claimed to have discovered inscriptions commemorating great kings and heroes, whose names corresponded with those of the Greek gods: Christians later used the theory to discredit the pagan gods.

Founding of Rome

The name of Aeneas, the Trojan warrior who is first mentioned in Homer's *Iliad*, is linked in legend with the foundation of Rome. In the *Iliad* Aeneas's mother, the goddess Aphrodite, and the god Poseidon predicted that his heirs would rule over the Trojans in great glory; thus of all the Trojans only Aeneas was assured of survival after the Greek conquest. The figure of Aeneas also belonged to the series of legends on the wanderings of heroic warriors after the Trojan War. Because of the incidence of towns and other coastal landmarks, which anciently bore names similar to his, Aeneas became the archetype of the wandering refugee who founded cities. The most remarkable of his postwar exploits were his visit to Carthage and a contribution to the beginnings of Rome, whose Italian empire was destined to fulfill Aphrodite's prophecy of the Trojan's enduring dominion. The legend of Aeneas's activities in the western Mediterranean is far older than Virgil's epic poem the

Aeneas carrying Anchises, Attic black-figure *oinochoe* **(c. 520–510 BC)**

Lupa capitolina: she-wolf with Romulus and Remus

Aeneid, which was published after the poet's death in 19 BC.

In this poem, Aeneas flees from the sacked city of Troy in the company of his son Ascanius and his aged father Anchises. After many adventures Aeneas reached Italy where various sites were connected with his visits and dedications. Aeneas strengthened his band of Trojan followers by a dynastic marriage with the native princess Lavinia, whose father Latinus offered land to the Trojan and shared his kingship with Aeneas.

In some accounts Aeneas is represented visiting the place that would later hold the city of Rome founded by his descendants. However, Aeneas himself never played an actual role in the foundation. Before the Romans began to investigate and record their origins there already existed two reports of the relationship between Aeneas and his descendant Romulus, who according to the older reckoning was the grandson of Aeneas. The accepted date of the destruction of Troy as around 1200 BC, and the tradition of the foundation of Rome as c. 753

BC involved both Greek and Roman scholars in a chronological discrepancy. This they solved by creating a dynasty of kings, usually named Silvii, who ruled over the people of the ancient Latian city of Alba Longa.

According to the literary tradition of the Silvian dynasty, Amulius deposed his brother, the rightful king Numitor, and consecrated his niece, Rhea Silvia, to the goddess Vesta so that she would remain forever childless. The maiden was loved by Mars and she conceived and gave birth to twins who were exposed to die. They were borne along by the Tiber and brought to land near the site of an archaic Roman shrine, the Lupercal and its neighbouring holy fig tree, the Ficus ruminalis: both landmarks play an important role in the legend of the twins. Although the literary devices of the tale bear the marks of a Greek legend, it also bears unmistakable traces of Roman invention by its attention to well-known local landmarks. The names of both Romulus and Remus refer to places: Rome itself and Remoria or Remona, evidently an old name

of the Aventine Hill. Indeed Romulus itself means no more than 'Roman'.

Wolf-Mother or Wanton?

The Lupercal was a grotto at the foot of the Palatine Hill attached to the cult and ceremonies of the two old religious fraternities of Luperci, the Fabiani and Quinctiales, who annually purified persons and places during the festival of Lupercalia on 15 February. In consequence of the linguistic derivation of Lupercus from lupus, 'wolf,' the Romans believed that a she-wolf had suckled the newborn twins. The suckling itself was suggested by the Ficus ruminalis, the name of which was thought to have come from an obsolete word for teat and the verb ruminare, 'to chew'. In fact, the manifest sense of the fig tree's variant names, Romula and Romularis, and the obsolete name of the Tiber river, Rumo, demonstrate that the sense of ruminalis was 'Roman'. In any event, the story of the wolf and the twins was already well established in 296 BC when two Roman magistrates dedicated a statue group of the three at the Lupercal.

Romulus and Remus, Peter Paul Rubens (1577–1640)

A later rationalization of the tale attempted to suppress the unlikely animal by reinterpreting the wolf as a lupa, the common Latin designation of a whore. In this account the twins are discovered by the shepherd Faustulus who entrusted them to his wanton wife, Acca Larentia. A minor goddess, she was worshipped at her shrine in the place called Velabrum, also situated at the foot of the Palatine Hill.

Marking the Boundary

Reaching manhood among Faustulus and his fellow shepherds, Romulus and Remus assumed the leadership of a band of cattle-rustlers who plundered the territory of the usurper Amulius. Caught and brought before the deposed Numitor, Romulus and Remus pleaded so eloquently and regally that their identity became known to their own grandfather. Thus reunited and aware of their rightful inheritance, the twins overthrew the usurper and restored their grandfather. Yearning for their old haunts and impatient of waiting their turn at the Alban kingship, they returned to the place where the waters of the Tiber had once set them down. In the tradition of Alba Longa as the mother-city of Latian towns, they led a proper Alban colony to found a new city on the site. The brothers quarrelled over the colony's location and name and decided to seek a sign from the gods to settle the matter. Remus took his place upon the Aventine Hill and Romulus upon the Palatine, and both watched the heavens for a sign. To Remus first appeared six vultures, but twelve vultures flew into Romulus's line of vision. In this fashion the god Jupiter indicated to the colonists the site and name of Rome.

Romulus himself drew the sacred boundary of the city which the Ro-

mans called a pomerium. The manner of marking the boundary was to plough a furrow with a team of a cow and a bullock. The plough had to be lifted over the place of each gate. The cow was yoked on the inside of the boundary, apparently to invite fertility within the city, and the bullock on the outside, to keep sterility beyond the town's boundary. Romulus forbade his brother to leap the boundary, a magical act evidently bringing ill-luck and in the most frequent version, and he slew Remus who taunted the founder by leaping over it.

Romulus's foundation was Roma Quadrata, 'squared Rome', a formal colonial settlement on the Palatine Hill which does in fact yield the oldest traces of continuous habitation at Rome. Romulus divided his colonists into three major divisions called tribes and these again into 30 subdivisions, the curiae. Traditionally, the three tribes represented the ethnic constituencies of Latins, Sabines, and Etruscans, while the 30 curiae served the gods of the common people and were also military units of the primitive army. The usual treatment of the foundation relates that the first Romans numbered 300 cavalrymen and 3,000 foot soldiers. The features of the foundation legend are entirely drawn from the Romans' experience of later colonization in Italy.

Romulus reigned long and well, leaving a much larger kingdom than he had founded. One day while performing some public act in the Campus Martius—the field of Mars—he ascended into heaven and joined the gods. Later a certain Julius Proculus announced that he had seen Romulus, who told him that he had become the god Quirinus. This apotheosis of Romulus is closely connected with the cult of Mars.

It was Mars who fathered the twins of the Vestal Virgin and it was from the Campus Martius that Romulus ascended to heaven. In addition the name of Numitor seems cognate with a title of Mars, 'Numisius'. The word Quirinus was commonly a cult-title of at least two Roman gods, Mars and Janus. It probably comes from curia and thus means 'of the (Roman) curiae'. Apparently in no case did a founder who had given his name to the city enjoy an actual cult at Rome. Rather, the Romans chose to see in Mars Quirinus the figure of their founding father. The festival of Quirinus (Quirinalia) fell on 17 February, just two days after the festival of Lupercalia.

Romulus's divine appearance to Julius Proculus belongs to the ancestral pretensions of Rome's Julian clan. The surname Proculus is related to the fiction of the Silvian dynasty of Alba which had a king Proca or Procas. The Julii clan claimed that through their ancestor Iullus, another name of Aeneas's son Ascanius, they were directly descended from Aeneas and Venus. The clan, though patrician, had not maintained a continuously dominant position among the vigorous and long-lived Roman aristocracy which for centuries controlled Roman politics. Hence their pretensions to divine and heroic ancestry complemented the Julii's eclipsed history and family position. In this framework Gaius Julius Caesar created a third confraternity of Luperci called after himself, since the other two archaic ones bore designations related to other patrician families. On the occasion of the Lupercalia in 44 BC, Mark Antony, serving as a Julian Luperus, offered Caesar the diadem of a king. It is this event which Shakespeare portrays in his *Julius Caesar*. Finally, both Caesar and his adopted son Octavian fostered the cult of Venus Genetrix, Venus the Ancestress. Indeed when Octavian became emperor he adopted the preferred honourific title 'Augustus' rather than 'Romulus'. Augustus also restored the architectural embellishments of the Lupercal. Both Caesar and Augustus proudly bore the title Father of the Fatherland which had a significance peculiar to their clan alone.

R. E. A. PALMER

FURTHER READING: Livy, History of Rome *(in the Loeb edn);* Plutarch, Lives *trans. by E. Cary; vol I contains a chapter on Romulus (Heinemann, 1914); Virgil,* Aeneid *trans. C. Day Lewis (Hogarth Press, 1952).*

Furies

In their original and best remembered form the Furies are among the most fearsome products of the Greek imagination. They are the avengers, three loathsome and implacable female beings, fulfillers of curses and especially of curses called down upon those who murder their elder kith and kin. Born of blood, roused from hell by the shedding of blood, they are satisfied only by the blood of their quarry.

In the dreadful beginnings of the gods, Uranus, lord of the sky, fathered the Titans upon Gaia, the earth. Uranus was afraid of his children and hid them away in the body of their mother. At length she could bear it no longer and persuaded Cronus, her youngest son, to attack her husband. Cronus took a sickle and castrated his father, and when the blood from Uranus's genitals fell upon the earth, his wife, she conceived and bore the Furies. It seems strange that they, whose chief task was to hunt down the betrayers of blood kinship, should themselves have been born of their father's blood, shed by their brother. But they came into being out of an act of revenge that was done in defence of their mother, and it is the rights of mothers, even when they are unjust, that they uphold with particular ferocity.

Representation of the Furies

The ancient authors describe the Furies with relish. They are horrifying in appearance and they stink. With snakes in their hair, they brandish torches and metal-studded whips. They bark like bitches, virgin hellhounds. They have suitably ominous names: Alecto, 'the Endless'; Tisiphone, 'the Retaliator'; Megaera, 'the Envious Rager'. Although their main duty was to avenge those murdered by their kin, they also sometimes took it upon themselves to right the established order in other ways.

The Greek word for Furies was Erinyes, and they were also called Maniai 'raging women', and, more interestingly, Eumenides, 'the kindly ones'. This last name may have been given them by prudence and, almost, wish-fulfilment, rather as the Black Sea, noted for its violent storms, was called the Euxine or 'the Calm'. Robert Graves, writing of the Furies, says it was 'unwise to mention their (real) name in conversation'. But it is perhaps more likely that the name, at least in historical times, is a sign of a typically Greek habit; the taming of

86 Oreste tourmenté par les furies

Orestes pursued by the Furies

something wild not by weakening it but by finding a place for it in an existing ordered system.

The classical Greeks, heirs to a fierce and ancient myth like that of the Furies, emphasized the positive and preserving, rather than the negative and destructive, aspect of these savage beings. They dwelt on their role as guardians of the social order more than on their being avengers of crime. And as guardians the Furies were kindly. Moreover, an educated fifth century Athenian would be quite prepared to accept the Erinyes, the avengers, as credible inhabitants of a mythical, heroic past, as doubtless did those who lived in that past, but as a citizen of his time he would more readily believe in the Eumenides, the guardians proprieties and values of his urban society.

Ancient, Mindless Fiends

This transformation of Furies, in nature and role as well as in name, is vividly portrayed in the *Eumenides* of Aeschylus, which is concerned not only with the Furies' most famous pursuit, but also with their being tamed,

and established as Athenian divinities.

The drama opens in the precinct of the temple of Apollo at Delphi. Orestes has come there in the hope of throwing off the Furies who are, quite literally, after his blood. For he has killed his mother, Clytemnestra, and also her lover, Aegisthus, for their murder of Agamemnon, his father. Orestes did this terrible deed out of duty, his inescapable duty to avenge his father at any cost; and he did it after much agonized self-questioning, and having sought the guidance of Apollo. But the Furies, more ancient beings than Apollo, know nothing of this duty. Their fate-appointed task is to track and destroy all those who slay their elder kin, and particularly those who kill their mothers. Mitigating circumstances or the code of the younger gods mean nothing to them.

At the beginning of the play, the Furies are lying senseless on the ground, put to sleep by Apollo. It is possible to see that they are female but they are too loathsome to be called women. Their skin is black, they are dressed in foul rags. Their breath is hot as they snort in their disgusting sleep and a noisome ooze drips from their eyes. Apollo gazes at them in horror, for they are hated by both gods and men. He is of a younger more gracious generation of divinities dwelling in the bright sunlight and, god though he is, he has far more in common with the man Orestes, trapped in the toils of conflicting duty, than with these ancient, mindless fiends from the gloom of Tartarus.

Clytemnestra, however, thinks differently. Her ghost appears and rebukes the Furies for sleeping. They begin to whine and moan. As they writhe awake they spit out their first words, a ferocious string of sounds: 'Labe, labe, labe, labe, phradzou!' 'Seize him, seize him, seize him, seize him, mark him!' They revile Apollo who, a younger god, has broken the

ancient laws by harbouring a doomed transgressor of these laws. He turns them out of the sanctuary. They are eager to go, for Orestes has fled to Athens to throw himself upon the mercy of Athene. During his flight Orestes has tried to expunge his guilt by ritual purifications but the Furies remain unplacated.

We see them in pursuit and then, having reached Athens in their 'wingless flight', performing a horrific *danse macabre*. They shriek of human blood, the scent of which fills them with delight. They intend to suck the living blood from Orestes and take him alive to hell to torture him there. They boast that their song drives their victim mad, binds his soul and withers his life. The gods may not touch or impede them in the inexorable task set them by fate. They do not care if they are dishonoured and despised. Nothing can hinder them, although they are separated from the gods by a light 'not of the sun'.

Respectable Matrons

Athene enters and is amazed at the extraordinary and revolting spectacle. But when the Furies explain them-

Lekythos depicting Orestes in the sanctuary in Delphi with Apollo and the Erinyes (furies), from the workshop of Assteas, red-figure pottery from Paestum, Campania, Italy; Ancient Greek civilization, Magna Graecia (4th century BC)

selves she says she knows their lineage and name. They, somewhat surprisingly, say they are willing to let her judge Orestes, since they reverence her and her birth. This the beginning of their transformation, though at this point they probably trust Athene more than Apollo simply because she is female, and they expect her to side with the mother rather than the son; they are soon to be disappointed by Athene's championing of the rights of the male over the female.

Orestes puts his case to the goddess. She is sympathetic but is afraid that if the Furies are cheated of their prey the venom of their resentment will fall on the ground and afflict the land with 'intolerable and perpetual pestilence'. Athene therefore decides to have the issue tried by her court of citizens, the Areopagus.

The Furies accept this decision but declare, in effect, that if Orestes is acquitted all the ancient virtues will be subverted by a new permissiveness. They call themselves 'the Furious Ones that keep watch upon mortals', particularly concerned to guard parents from impious children. Some fear, they say, is good and should 'abide enthroned as guardian of the heart'. Although the content of the Furies' speech, the sacredness of the ties of kinship and filial reverence, is similar to their earlier ragings, the tone is now very different. There is a stern and lofty conservatism, an almost matronly respectability, which contrasts very strongly with the savagery and odiousness of the first scenes of the play. One feels the Furies have had a bath and changed their clothes. But when Orestes is acquitted, by the casting vote of Athene, their rage breaks out anew. The younger gods 'have ridden down the ancient laws', they cry in Athene's face, and, quite forgetful of their acceptance of her arbitration, they threaten to poison and pollute the land.

The final scene of the play depicts Athene's difficult struggle to placate the Furies. She offers them a temple and a home in Athens, and a role as guardians of the city and its virtues. For a long time the Furies refuse, enraged at the decision of the court. But although they are furious, it is now only because they believe ancient justice has been violated; they no longer shriek for blood. They are outraged but they are no longer hounds from hell. Gradually, in a dying fall, they succumb to Athene's pleadings and promises and move off in a solemn procession to dwell in a cave beneath the Acropolis, and to watch over the well-being of the city.

In the surrender of the Furies, these ghastly yet magnificent fiends, and their acceptance of a tamer role as guardians rather than avengers, we may see the triumph of reason over unreason; 'the furious ones' have become 'the kindly ones', a characteristically Greek transformation.

CHARLES DE HOGHTON

Golden Fleece

In Greek mythology, the object of the voyage of Jason and the Argonauts who, helped by the enchantress Medea, stole it from Colchis on the Black Sea, where it hung on a tree guarded by a dragon; it was the fleece of a ram which could think, speak, and fly, sent by Hermes to save two children whose lives were threatened by their cruel stepmother.

Graces

The three Charites (plural of charis) of Greek mythology, Aglaia (the radiant), Thalia (the flowering), and Euphrosyne (joy), personifications of grace and charm, companions of the love goddess; originally there were more than three of them and they stood for the joy and beauty of fertile Nature; associated with flowers, especially the rose and the myrtle; later, they conferred on human beings not only beauty and charm but also wisdom, intellectual power, and artistic ability.

Greece

The history of Greek religion reflects an uneven, halting but recognizable development from magic to officially sponsored religion; from an epoch when men had not clearly separated

The temple of Athena in Aegina, Greece, is one of Greece's oldest surviving temples.

themselves from Nature and natural forces to a time when gods and goddesses were worshipped in human shape. However, the uniformity of this process should not be overestimated. For magic continued to be inseparably associated with religion, especially in the realms of popular cult, just as birds, beasts, and flowers continued to be identified with particular gods and goddesses.

The traditional polytheistic religion of classical times incorporated, in varying forms and with varying emphasis, many survivals from earlier periods, including the Minoan and Mycenean periods of the Bronze Age, especially in nature religion and fertility cults. Broadly speaking, the Greek religion of classical antiquity was an amalgamation of early Aegean with later Indo-European elements, the latter having been contributed by people who spoke Greek as one of the Indo-European family of languages.

However, realization of this is comparatively recent. A hundred years ago there were no accepted objective criteria, in the form of buildings, pottery, jewellery, and armour, which were relied upon to form an independent witness of the realities of the world which emerges in the Homeric poems. The history of Greece was thought to have begun with the first Olympiad in 776 BC, and everything that went before including the Homeric Age, was legend or myth.

Now, however, what is sometimes described as the Aegean civilization has been discovered by archeologists. In consequence, the objective criteria of Greek pre-history reach back to the beginning of the Iron Age (roughly 1000 BC), and through the two millennia of the preceding Bronze Age into the earlier Neolithic period.

This vast change in outlook is mainly the result of the work of two men, Heinrich Schliemann and Sir Arthur Evans. Schliemann's excavations at

A statue of Zeus, found at Kameiros, late Hellenistic period

Troy, Mycene, and Tiryns proved that there was some historical reality behind the Homeric epics. Sir Arthur Evans began to excavate the Bronze Age palace of Minos at Cnossus seventy years ago. Now, no one can ignore the Cretan (or Minoan) background.

This background, complex though it may be, is shown by a variety of evidence collected from many different sites that date from the earliest periods to the later Bronze Age, when the Minoan and mainland Mycenean traditions became increasingly interfused.

There is now a mass of symbols, representations on seals and frescoes, cult paraphernalia, and idols and stat-

ues collected from tombs, cemeteries, cult rooms, altars, shrines, sanctuaries, and temples, which have to be set beside the mythology, poetry, and general literature of the period. There are also numerous inscribed documents which, although they are often fragmentary, sometimes throw light upon religious beliefs and practices.

The abiding mystical concepts derived from Cretan religion are significantly marked by the influence of a mother goddess and a dying god, associated with the bull, who later became worshipped as 'Cretan-born Zeus'. This Zeus, who died and was born again, was different from the Olympian Zeus of the familiar Greek pantheon. He was much more comparable with the Greek Dionysus, also a bull god and a dying god. These two different concepts help us to establish distinctions between the Minoan and the Mycenean phases of earlier Greek religion.

The historian Herodotus records that the poets Homer and Hesiod were the first to compose theogonies, poems dealing with the origin of the gods, and gave the deities their epithets, allotted them their offices and occupations, and described their forms. It is probable that these traditional Greek theogonies derived from the Greek epics which were rooted in the Mycenean period of the late Bronze Age.

Traditional mythology recorded legends about conditions before the Mycenean pantheon of the Olympic gods became paramount. Before this time, the Titans, the children of Uranus and Gaia (Heaven and Earth) held sway. To prevent Cronus, the youngest Titan, from swallowing his baby son Zeus, his wife Rhea bore him secretly in Crete and substituted a stone wrapped in swaddling clothes for the infant, who was reared in hiding. The legends about the birth of Zeus in Crete were responsible for the specific epithet of the supreme god as 'Cretan-born'.

Funeral mask also known as 'Agamemnon Mask'; Gold, found in Tomb V in Mycenae by Heinrich Schliemann (1876)

This epithet and the oriental connections of his mother Rhea, indicate that he was an old Minoan god, involved in the same basic pattern of oriental ritual which prompted the myths of Ishtar and Tammuz, Isis and Osiris, Venus and Adonis. It is probable that Greek-speaking people who arrived in Crete gave the name of their sky god to an old Minoan deity whose ritual and character can be guessed from the evidence of later times.

The Olympian Zeus was the leader of the traditional Greek pantheon. There is reason to suppose that the hierarchical organization of the gods and goddesses as portrayed in the Homeric epics reflects the actual social conditions of the Mycenean period. The Homeric Greeks (the Achaeans) burst the bonds of their own ancestral tribal organization and adapted their control of Bronze Age techniques to warfare. The martial character of the Myceneans of the later Bronze Age is exemplified in their fortification of their urban centres, in marked contrast with the unfortified cities of Minoan Crete. Similarly, the Achaean chieftains of the Homeric poems dominate the battlefield.

The heroic age of ancient Greece, as it is portrayed in Homer, represents the violent and ruthless conquest of an older, sophisticated, peaceful, and refined civilization by warlike adventurers. Its richest and most important centres were away from the mainland, especially on the island of Crete; so the greatest prizes were out of reach until the Achaeans became sailors.

After 1400 BC the leadership of the Aegean world passed to mainland Mycene; and the Mycenaean pantheon presumably spread its influence as the Mycenaean social and economic system penetrated widely from its mainland centres. The ensuing social conflict, and fusion of peoples and customs, was paralleled by increasing complexity in cults and in mythology, and in the composition and organization of the pantheon. The most dramatic form of this process was a struggle, never quite resolved, between the old concept of a mother goddess and the newer concept of a dominating male god, Zeus.

Under the monarchical leadership of Olympian Zeus, the gods and goddesses were gathered together in a sin-

Olympian assembly, from left to right: Apollo, Zeus, and Hera

gle heavenly stronghold. Their dwelling places, built by Hephaestus, surrounded the central palace of Zeus. Although the authority of the supreme male god had become fairly stable, it was not unchallenged. In fact Hera, wife of Zeus, was amongst those who intrigued against his authority.

This Homeric picture of the Olympian hierarchy is paralleled by the Homeric picture of earthly conditions. Even in the midst of war, Agamemnon, the leader of the Greek expedition to Troy, could claim only a loose kind of authority: his control was often disputed by his fellow chieftains. This instability has its analogy in the inability of the Achaeans to establish a centralized, enduring Bronze Age economy similar to the older oriental type.

There is, too, a lack of uniformity in the Homeric accounts of the Olympian system. In two passages of the *Iliad* Zeus is living alone on Olympus. In one passage he hurls a thunderbolt, in the other he sends a storm. It is highly probable that Olympus itself was a kind of generic term for mountain. However, in a well-known evocative passage of the *Odyssey*, the heavenly Olympus is described in a way that is more appropriate to the Minoan Fields of the Blest than to a lofty, mountainous seat of storms, rain, and lightning.

The growth of the Olympian pantheon was a process of tribal federation which led to military kingship. The mortal prototype of the weather god who was lord of storms, rain, lightning, and thunder, and reigned in a mountain fortress, was the Mycenean overlord. The companions of the god, with their differing functions, at first lived apart from him but eventually, although they kept their traditional functions, they went to live with the Olympian overlord in his stronghold and were subject to his will.

Dying God from Crete

The traditional function, or privileges, or spheres of influence of the gods were the outcome of heavenly tribal warfare. Legend tells how Zeus made a promise to his supporters before he went to war against the old order represented by Cronus and the Titans. He swore that if he won he would guarantee the rights they already had, and would apportion rights to those who had none; when the conflict was over he became the supreme overlord and bestowed the honours. The traditional province of Hephaestus, for instance, was fire; Atlas held up the skies; Apollo was concerned with music and dancing; Hades with lamentation; the nymphs cared for mortals in the time of their youth, and so on.

The Twelve Gods who were early united into a sort of official Olympian society were normally Zeus, Hera,

Poseidon, Demeter, Apollo, Artemis, Ares, Aphrodite, Hermes, Athene, Hephaestus, and Hestia. There were sometimes modifications to the list, as when Dionysus replaced Hestia in the representation of the Twelve on the east frieze of the Parthenon in Athens.

Dionysus has a place of special importance in Greek religion, essentially popular and non-Olympian. However, the cults which he personified and which played such a major role in historical times, had their counterparts elsewhere in much earlier times. Explaining why the cult of Dionysus was conspicuously absent in Crete, M. P. Nilsson observed in Minoan-Mycenaean Religion: 'The reason why Dionysus does not appear in Crete can only be that he was not needed there, the religious ideas of which he was the herald having already been applied to the Cretan Zeus.'

The copious amount of legendary material regarding the birth of Zeus in Crete emphasizes its pre-eminence compared with other birth stories of Zeus. However, the very existence of such a remarkable birth story, and the cults associated with it, inevitably meant that places other than Crete were also credited with being the site of Zeus's birth. These included Messenia where Zeus was reputed to have been reared by nymphs on Mt. Ithome; Arcadia which, apart from Crete, made the strongest claims, with a legend that Cronus had swallowed the stone on Mt. Thaumasius and that Zeus was born and reared on Mt. Lycaeus; and Olympia, which was said to be Zeus's birthplace in a legend of the founding of the Olympic Games.

It was quite consistent that the dying god, Zeus of Crete, should not only have had his sacred marriage to Hera commemorated in an annual ceremony during which sacrifices were offered with traditional wedding rites but that his death also should have been mourned. This explains why

the legend of Zeus's tomb, supposedly located at various places in Crete including Cnossus, Mt. Ida, and Mt. Dicte, has endured from ancient to recent times.

There are a number of versions of the inscription on this legendary tomb, which suggests that 'Zan', the old name for Zeus, was certainly well known in Crete, and also that the cult of Cretan Zeus was involved with, if it did not actually develop from, an earlier cult of Minos. A common link was an annual festival celebrating a god such as Adonis or Tammuz, at which this god was eaten in the form of a bull. The evidence for the tomb, relatively late though it may be, indicates that Cretan Zeus was looked upon as a dying god, with the implication that he died annually and was born again.

Initiation, which may well have originated in the Bronze Age,

continued to play a major part in various Greek cults and in social life generally. The death and rebirth of an initiate tended to be dramatically represented, often with a contest and some kind of ordeal. It was not only the god, or his animal symbol, who continually died and was born again. A similar pattern persisted in the training of the youth of the Greek city-states in classical times.

The late appearance and subordinate status of a male Minoan deity served to emphasize the overriding importance of the Minoan goddess. In Neolithic times there seems to have been no concept of a male divinity in human form. He emerged later, as a secondary deity, but the tendency to raise him to a superior status was clear by the end of Minoan times. With the decline of the mother goddess, the bull became associated with the

Zeus with a laurel crown, gold stater (ancient coin) from Lampsacus, Mysia (c. 360–340 BC), obverse

Minoan kingship, which perhaps had important functions in relation to the governing of the calendar. Hence the bull became a symbol of the sun, and both were fertility symbols. Bull-worship and snake-worship remained associated with traditions of the prehistoric Bronze Age kingship.

The Minoan goddess is a central feature of Minoan religion, just as the palace was a central feature of Minoan social life. In surviving monuments and artefacts she is shown in association with animals, birds, and snakes; with the sacred pillar and the sacred tree; with poppies and with lilies; with the sword and the double axe. She appears to have been huntress and goddess of sports, she was armed and also presided over ritual dances; she had male and female attendants, and she held sway over mountain, earth, sky and sea, over life and death. She was household goddess, vegetation goddess, Mother and also Maid.

There are many examples of figurines from Minoan Crete, including votive images from sanctuaries, cult idols from shrines, and statuettes which have been recovered from graves and tombs. The various attitudes assumed by these figurines, which include the 'gesture of benediction' familiar in portrayals of the mother goddess, sometimes recall the postures of a sacred dance. The sitting or squatting position of early specimens could well represent the attitude actually assumed for childbirth. Hence the differing gestures depicted by later statuettes could also have been supposed to have had a beneficial influence on childbirth and on the growth of crops.

As puppets, the images had clear associations with birth and with death, accounting for their presence in graves and tombs. As votive offerings, they represented worshippers appealing for the protection of the goddess in sickness or childbirth, an initiation,

marriage or bereavement; or the statuettes could represent the goddess herself. Figurines dating from the earliest times onward have been discovered in Greece, showing that the ancestral idols of magic did not easily yield to the deities of religion.

By Minoan times the bull, the dove, and the snake had already acquired special prominence. Large numbers of votive offerings included figurines of oxen, goats, rams, swine, and dogs. There is no doubt that the birds that are so often portrayed in Minoan religious contexts, perched upon double axes, columns, trees, or idols represent divine manifestations. In fact, the birds of the domestic shrines are not mere votive offerings but real representations of deity; and the idea of birds as manifest forms of the spirits of the dead was persistent in later Greek religion.

The most conspicuous Minoan domestic cult was that of the snake, especially in connection with the so-called snake goddess. Snake cults are worldwide, and are associated with the belief that snakes are incarnations of the dead. They also signify immortality because they cast their skins and renew themselves, personifying the ability to be reborn. Both dreaded and revered, snakes became beneficent, guardians of the house. Snake-worship was common in later Greek religion and indeed plays a part in modern Greek folklore.

All these powerful traditions seem to have played their part in the formulation of the mother goddess as an abstract and unifying principle, both one and many. It was perhaps in the Cretan palaces of the Bronze Age that the Neolithic figurine developed most rapidly into a female deity in human form, still attended by magical and totemistic symbols, in the form of trees and stones, animals, birds, and flowers. The most sacred Minoan flower was the lily.

Hero and God of Health

Some goddesses of the later conventional pantheon markedly perpetuate the role of the old Minoan mother goddess. Demeter was said to have reached Greece from Crete; she was regarded as divine protectress of agriculture and the fruits of the earth. The myth of Demeter and Persephone recalls the Minoan concept of the mother goddess as both Mother and Maid. The famous Eleusinian Mysteries performed at Eleusis near Athens, were in their honour. These mysteries may have originated in the East, but there is little doubt that they were brought to Greece from Crete.

The cult of Apollo and his mother Leto originated in Asia Minor. Their association with Crete has long been recognized, together with evidence that the cult of this goddess survived more markedly in Crete than in mainland Greece, where her cults are few and of uncertain age. Other deities and semi-divine heroes were loosely connected with the official Greek pantheon and with traditional Greek mythology. They include Eros ('Love'), Selene ('the Moon'), Hercules, and Asclepius.

The hero of physicians, elevated to divine status, Asclepius had a cult and temple at Lebena in Crete in historical times. The snake, his constant companion and symbol, indicates his association with earlier phases of religion, recalling the prominence of the snake cult in Minoan belief. He did not really become a god until the end of the 6th century BC; excavations at Epidaurus, the most famous centre of his cult, revealed that the buildings dedicated to him cannot be dated earlier. But the cult, with its combination of superstition, miracle cures, and genuine medical lore, enjoyed an increasing respect in the Greek world in later antiquity, which has rightly been contrasted with the growth of scepticism toward the traditional Olympian hierarchy.

By the Christian era the worship of Asclepius had spread widely and was a potent force while other cults had lost ground. In fact, Asclepius was looked upon as the chief opponent of Christ in the late pagan period: he was firmly entrenched in his position as one of the great, and one of the most popular, ancient gods when the final struggle between Christianity and paganism ensued. The Christians did not deny that he possessed real power, just as they had to acknowledge the reality and strength of the other heathen deities. They admitted that he was able to heal but as with other gods and goddesses whom they opposed, they believed that Asclepius was weaker than their own Lord.

R. F. WILLETTS

FURTHER READING: W. Burkert. Greek Religions. (Harvard 1985); W.K.C. Guthrie. Orpheus and Greek Religion and The Greeks and Their Gods. (Methuen, 1952 and 1950 respectively); M. P. Nilsson. Minoan-Mycenaean Religion. (Lund, 1927); The Mycenaen Origins of Greek Mythology. (University of California Press, 1983); R. F. Willetts. Ancient Crete: A Social History. (Routledge, 1965); Cretan Cults and Festivals. (Routledge, 1962).

Hades

'The unseen', the Greek god of death: later the name of the underworld which he ruled, the home of the dead: later still, another word for hell: feared as pitiless and unyielding, Hades had little cult and was not often represented in art; his queen was Persephone, who spent the winter with him in the underworld.

Halcyon

Fabulous bird, supposed to breed at midwinter in a nest which floats on the sea; the wind and waves remain calm for seven 'halcyon days' to make this possible; from the Greek word for 'kingfisher'.

Hecate

A minor goddess of the Greek pantheon, Hecate was not a true Olympian. But she was the most important representative of the uncanny, a powerful figure in the kind of popular and private belief that is ignored in Homer. Indeed she is not mentioned in the *Iliad* or in the *Odyssey* or in fragments of heroic epic. If her name is Greek, it is the feminine form of the epithet hekatos, which as applied to Apollo means 'far shooting' but might in her case mean merely 'distant' or 'remote'. She has connections with Apollo's sister Artemis, also an archer, and she may share with Artemis a common origin in Asia Minor.

The earliest full account of her is in Hesiod's *Theogony* (eighth century). Most scholars consider this an interpolation, though an early one, interesting in its own right. Most recently it has been argued by M. L. West that it is on the contrary a personal confession of faith by Hesiod, who was less interested in his other deities. In this passage Hecate is said to be daughter of the Titan Perses by Asteria who was sister of Leto, the mother of Apollo and Artemis. 'Zeus honoured Hecate above all and gave her glorious gifts, to have a portion in the earth and in the unharvested sea'; she thus has a portion or a footing in earth, in heaven and in the sea, and is invoked by any who make sacrifices to the gods. Those whose prayers she receives favourably achieve great honour and wealth. Though she had been among the Titans defeated by the gods, Zeus did her no violence and she continued to be honoured on Olympus. She sits by kings in judgement, helps speak-

Triple-formed representation of Hecate

ers in the assembly and gives victory and glory in war to those whom she favours. She is a helper in games, in sea-fishing and in cattle-breeding. She is appointed by Zeus to be nurse of the young.

In strong contrast to this dignified, universal and wholly anthropomorphic goddess stands the figure presented in nearly all the other references. Her special connection with the underworld appears in the Homeric *Hymn to Demeter* where she alone, except for the sun god Helios, hears the cry of Persephone as she is carried off by Pluto to Hades. By the end of the 5th century BC literature presents her in her usual character, which must have been much older in common belief, as the mistress of ghosts and specters and of everything dark and uncanny. She appears sometimes with the title of antaia (she who meets), since travelers or walkers by night might meet her in lonely places as a terrifying apparition. In this aspect she was also called einodia (the goddess who appears on the way), once apparently a name for a goddess in her own right, and triodos or trioditis (the goddess of parting ways). She is in many scattered references connected with the ghosts of suicides or of those who had died untimely, who could join her host of uncanny followers at night. Her favourite animal was the dog, which was often sacrificed to her. She was even reckoned the mother of the monster Scylla with her many dogs' heads; she could send up ghosts from Hades, drive people mad, and cause epilepsy by her assaults. She is associated with sorcery and black magic, and in the *Argonautica* of Apollonius, the sorceress Medea shows her beloved Jason how to win Hecate's aid by a sacrifice.

Medea instructs Jason to bathe in the river and then, alone and clothed

A triform of the goddess Hecate

in dusky raiment, to dig a round pit. In the pit he is to kill a ewe and sacrifice it whole and to propitiate Hecate he must pour on honey from a goblet. He must then retreat from the pyre and not turn back when he hears the sound of feet or the baying of hounds, or he will spoil the rites and may even not return to his comrades. Jason carries out these instructions, wearing a robe given to him by his former lover, queen Hypsipyle of Lemnos. He pours mixed libations on the victim as it lies on the pyre, calling on Hecate under the name of Brimo (Mighty One) to be his helper in the ordeal which faces him, of yoking the fire-breathing bulls of Aeetes. When he steps back, Hecate, who has heard the invocation in her cave, comes to receive the offering. Round her head is a garland of oak leaves, among which are fearful snakes. There is a gleam of innumerable torches and shrill howling from her infernal hounds. The ground trembles at her tread and the river nymphs cry shrill.

She Who Makes Dogs Shiver

In Theocritus Simaetha weaves a love spell to win back her faithless lover, in the course of which she prays to Hecate of the underworld 'before whom even the dogs stand shivering as she comes over the graves of the dead and the dark blood' to make her drugs potent. In Lycophron's *Alexandra* Cassandra prophesies that Hecuba will be turned to a dog, stoned to death, and then become one of the hounds of Hecate, terrifying with her baying all who will not worship the image of the goddess. Ulysses, who will lead the stoning, will later on his wanderings be forced to build a cenotaph to Hecuba in Sicily, fearing the anger of the three-necked goddess.

So too in Virgil's *Aeneid* Aeneas is instructed by the Sibyl to invoke Hecate for her necessary help if he is to be admitted to the underworld, and Hecate's coming is attended

by the howling of wolves and the trembling of the ground. In Ovid's *Metamorphoses* Hecate is one of the powers invoked by Medea to help in rejuvenating Aeson by magical rites. In Lucian's *Philopseudes* (The Liar) Hecate is raised to bring with her Chrysis, who had been the lover of Glaucias. But she disappears at dawn with Chrysis and all her infernal spectres. From these passages it is clear that Hecate's help was needed in many forms of magic, particularly of black magic, including necromancy.

Hecate seems to have originated in Caria, in the southwest corner of Asia Minor, where Greek personal names based on hers, such as Hecataeus, were most common. The boundary between her and Artemis is not always easy to define, particularly because both have some connection with the moon, but in Homer and in the more accepted mythology the two goddesses have different places in the divine genealogies. The explanation of this affinity between dark and infernal Hecate and bright Artemis, who may not stay in the presence of death, is no doubt historical. Artemis herself in some cults was savage and in Ephesus had many breasts, like a mother goddess. The Greek imagination, so productive of myths like later philosophical thought, was increasingly given to clear distinctions and definitions. Natural forces and phenomena which even for us have contrasted aspects, were personified in ancient myth in deities that had often contradictory natures. In Greek myth the contradictory aspects of a great Nature goddess were developed into distinct goddesses, rather as white light is broken into component coloured rays by the spectroscope. One of these aspects was Hecate, who retained primitive characteristics. Thus in the *Orphic Argonautica* of the 3rd century AD she still appears with three heads, on the left that of a maned horse, in the middle that of a savage snake, on the right that of a frenzied bitch.

Statues or other representations of her with three heads or three bodies joined back to back, facing three ways, appear only late in Greek art, but must represent an ancient conception. The threefold aspect of Hecate, however represented, is clearly an antique notion, recalling that of savage idols as depicted in other mythologies and traditions of art.

E. D. PHILLIPS

FURTHER READING: M. P. Nilsson. History of Greek Religion. *(Greenwood, 1980).*

Hecate Detail of the Pergamon Altar, a monumental construction built in the 2nd century BC on one of the terraces of the acropolis of the ancient city of Pergamon in Asia Minor.

Helios

Greek god of the sun, also called Hyperion. Some myths identify Helios as a Titan, with Apollo replacing him as the sun god in the Olympian pantheon. In that case Apollo and Helios are two distinct gods. Later myths and cults suggest that the two gods were interchangeable or identical. Helios was said to drive his fiery chariot across the sky each day and through the waters of Oceanus each night, re-emerging in the morning. Ovid tells the story of Phaeton, Helios' son, who attempts to drive the sun-chariot but loses control and crashes into the earth. Another famous tale involving Helios is an interaction between Odysseus and his men and the sacred cattle of the sun in Book XII of the *Odyssey*. Odysseus warns his men to abstain from killing the cattle, but they slaughter and eat them anyway. Helios persuades Zeus to take revenge by killing all of Odysseus' men. Helios is referred to as 'all-seeing': Odysseus warns that 'no man avoids his eye' (*Odyssey* XII:413), and in another myth Helios sees Aphrodite and Mars engaging in a clandestine affair. The Colossus of Rhodes, one of the Seven Wonders of the Ancient World, was a gigantic statue of Helios.

FURTHER READING: Ovid, A. D. Melville, and E. J. Kenney. Metamorphoses. *(Oxford: Oxford UP, 2008);* Homer, Robert Fagles, and Bernard Knox. The Odyssey. *(New York: Viking, 1996);* Hesiod, and M. L. West. Hesiod: Theogony. *(Oxford: Clarendon, 1966);* Athanassakis, Apostolos N. The Homeric Hymns. *(Baltimore: Johns Hopkins UP, 1976);* Graves, Robert. The Greek Myths. *(Baltimore: Penguin, 1955).*

Helen of Troy

According to Greek mythology, the most beautiful woman in the world: daughter of the mortal Leda and the god Zeus in the guise of a swan: her beauty attracted all the princes of Greece and to avoid strife her foster-father made the suitors vow to defend the chosen husband against anyone who resented his good fortune; she married Menelaus, and on her abduction by Paris, the former suitors stood by their oaths and besieged Troy: Helen reappears in some of the Faust stories of the Middle Ages.

Hephaestus

The uncouth god of smiths, who was himself a smith, Hephaestus (or Vulcan as he was known to the Romans) was originally a god of fire, in the aspect of flaming gas rising from the earth in certain places. It was only later that he came to be associated with volcanoes in Sicily and Italy. His name was used poetically as a synonym for fire from Homer down to poets who were familiar with Nature-philosophy. He was not in origin a Greek god, his name having no etymology in Greek, but his cult spread from Lycia in southwestern Anatolia to various parts

of Greece; there are frequent references to him in Greek literature.

In the *Iliad* he is the son of Hera, who threw him into the sea in shame at having borne such a weakly infant. He was rescued by the nymphs Thetis and Eurynome and remained with them in secret for nine years, making jewels and ornaments, until his talents were discovered by the gods and he was given a smithy on Olympus. Reconciled with his mother, he once tried to protect her from the anger of Zeus, but for this interference Zeus seized him by the foot and hurled him out of heaven. He fell for a whole day before finally striking the island of Lemnos, crushing his legs in the

The Forge of Hephaestus, Diego Velázquez (1599–1660)

fall: this is only one explanation for his lameness.

Hephaestus built the palaces of the gods on Olympus and Zeus's golden throne, but he is particularly famous as a maker of armour: of Diomedes' breastplate, of the sceptre and also of the aegis, or shield, held by Zeus, which when shaken produced storms and thunder, and of the arms made for Achilles to replace the armour lost with the slaying of Patroclus. Among his other wonders are mechanical handmaidens of gold, possessed of thought and speech, who support him as he moves, and assist him at his work. Sometimes he acts as cupbearer at the feasts of the gods, who laugh at him as he bustles round clumsily on his lame legs. In his elemental character he is called by Hera to drive back the river Xanthus because the river god, also called Xanthus, is furious at his stream being blocked with corpses slain by Achilles, and threatens to overwhelm him. Hephaestus spreads fire everywhere, burning the corpses and the vegetation by the river, and then begins to dry up the river until Xanthus entreats Hera to stop him.

A Net to Ensnare Lovers

In the *Odyssey* Hephaestus, with Athene, is called 'skilled in making gold flow round silver'. He is the maker of a silver mixing bowl with gold edges given by Phaedimus of Sidon to Menelaus, also of the gold and silver hounds that guard the palace of Alcinous, immortal and ageless animals. In a celebrated mythological scene, the lay of Demodocus, minstrel of Alcinous, Hephaestus takes revenge for the faithlessness of Aphrodite, his wife. While he is away on his favourite island of Lemnos, Aphrodite is joined by her lover, Ares, but at dawn they are trapped together by an invisible gossamer-light metal net which Hephaestus had forged for the purpose. While they are ensnared, the

Thetis at Hephaestus' forge waiting to receive Achilles' new weapons

gods are called in to laugh at them.

Hesiod in the *Theogony* states clearly that Hera bore Hephaestus without any union with Zeus because she had a bitter quarrel with him at the time. This could explain why Hephaestus was born lame: Hera on her own could not give birth to normal children. Hephaestus's wife here is Aglaia, the youngest of the Graces. Hesiod relates how Zeus, who wishes to punish men for having acquired fire through Prometheus, orders Hephaestus to create the beautiful Pandora to be a plague to them. She was fashioned of clay in the form of a beautiful maiden, like the immortal goddesses, and other deities

gave her other qualities including a deceitful nature and a shameless mind.

In the *Homeric Hymns* it is said that Hephaestus, like Athene, taught men on Earth to make glorious works. They had formerly lived in caves in the mountains like beasts, but now, having learned crafts through him, they live in safety and comfort all their lives in their own houses. Much the same claims are made by Aeschylus for Prometheus as teacher and benefactor.

Among the lyric poets, Simonides (c. 556–468 BC) said that Hephaestus made for Minos of Crete the bronze giant Talos who guarded his coasts. Pindar, following others, mentions

Hephaestus as maker of the bronze axe which split open the head of Zeus for the birth of Athene. In his *Pythian Odes* the expression 'fountains of Hephaestus' is used for the volcanic fires of Etna which are said to be the breath of the monster Typhon.

In Aeschylus's *Prometheus Bound* Hephaestus appears with the giants who drag Prometheus to the place where he is to be chained on the crag. They remind him that he has orders from Zeus to fasten Prometheus to the rock in bonds of adamant, impenetrably hard, with wedges driven through his body. He is most unwilling to do so and greatly pities Prometheus, a god of his own kin. The sound of his cosmic hammering disturbs the nymphs of Ocean in their caves so that they rise to lament with him.

The divine smith of Greek mythology, Hephaestus was cast into the sea at birth by his mother Hera, who wished to rid herself of such an ugly child. Found and reared by two nereids, his fame as a craftsman quickly reached the ears of the gods and he was summoned to assume his rightful place in heaven: the return of Hephaestus to Mt. Olympus, from the Clitias krater

In Sophocles's *Philoctetes* Hephaestus's fire on Lemnos is mentioned, and in his *Daedalus* the making of Talos by the smith god is prominent. In his satyr-play *Cedalion* it seems that the scene was Hephaestus's workshop on Lemnos, and that the god gave to the blinded giant Orion his servant, the dwarf Cedalion, as a guide to keep him walking eastward until the rising sun struck his face and restored his sight. In Plato's *Protagoras* Hephaestus works with Athene in a heavenly workshop from which Prometheus steals fire.

In Callimachus's *Hymn to Artemis* the goddess as an infant is taken by her mother Leto to visit Hephaestus on the island of Lipara, where he has his forge and the Cyclopes Arges and Steropes are working under his

direction on a golden horse-trough for Poseidon. In Apollonius's *Argonautica* the returning Argonauts pass the smith god's forge in the Aeolian islands. Iris swiftly brings word to him from Hera that he shall keep his fires quiet until the Argo has passed. Later Hephaestus drops his hammer to watch, like most of the other gods, the passage of the Argo through the Wandering Rocks.

God of Erupting Fire

The presence of Hephaestus in the volcanoes of Italy and Sicily becomes even more marked from the time of Aeschylus and Pindar onward, in the 6th century BC. By their day the Greek colonists who settled on these coasts, some of whom came from the eastern Aegean, had transferred to their new homeland the scene of Hephaestus's activities, as of other fiery manifestations. The god's first western home was apparently Lipara (now Vulcano) also called Hiera Hephaistos, the sacred isle of Hephaestus. He came only later to Etna, where the earlier established Cyclopes became his workmen.

The original seat of Hephaestus was in Lycia where the Lycian Olympus, as described by Maximus of Tyre, 'gives forth a flame from its summit, not like the fire of Etna, but peaceful and moderate. This fire is regarded by the Lycians as the temple of the god and his visible images.' The hot gas, as modern travelers have found, was in fact a small escape of burning petroleum. In the *Aegean* there was such an escape of gas on Hephaestus's mountain Mosychlus on Lemnos, his first foothold. The sudden spread of fire which Hephaestus was able to make is most like that of igniting gas over a wide area. The vents of gas were commonly regarded as the chimneys of his underground forge.

In Asia Minor Hephaestus had fifty shrines but far fewer in other Greek lands, though his cult as a craftsman god was well known in Athens. The

Greeks who arrived in the Sicilian and Italian volcanic belt attributed its much more devastating fires to the same god, no doubt fusing him with earlier native gods of fire and volcanic action.

The history of the Roman Volcanus (Vulcan) forms a rather puzzling epilogue to that of the Greek Hephaestus. In classical Latin literature Vulcan makes his appearance very much in the style of Hephaestus. The name Volcanus is of doubtful origin and meaning, but there appears to be an Etruscan deity Velchanos; scholars are inclined to think that Volcanus or Velchanos is an eastern deity, perhaps brought by the Etruscans, and perhaps having a common origin with Hephaestus. Volcanus is a god of fire, but usually of a more menacing or destructive fire than that of the original Hephaestus in his normal manifestations. Thus his name is the source of our word 'volcano'.

E. D. PHILLIPS

FURTHER READING: M. P. Nilsson. History of Greek Religion. *(Clarendon Press, Oxford, 1940); H. J. Rose.* A Handbook of Greek Mythology. *(Methuen, 1958).*

Hera

'Lady or mistress' was possibly the original meaning of the name Hera, which indicates a line of descent from the old Aegean mother goddess. She became a goddess of marriage and, especially in this capacity, she was worshipped in most areas of Greece in historical antiquity. Yet there can be no doubt that her principal cult centre was the Argive territory in the northeast of the Peloponnese. Tracing the origins of the cult back into Mycenean times, it becomes clearer that the Argolid peninsula was her real domain and that other genuine early centres are indeed rare. In fact these can be reduced to three: Euboea, the large island which lies adjacent to the coasts of Attica, Boeotia, and the southern part of Thessaly, whose inhabitants are called Abantes by Homer; Samos, another principal island of the Aegean, off the coast of Ionia; and Olympia, a small plain in Elis, in the west Peloponnese, where there was the sacred grave of Zeus and where the Olympic games were celebrated.

In Euboea, the myth and ritual of Hera were almost identical with the Argive. The name Euboea means the island 'of fair oxen'. Legend said that the Abantes settled there under the leadership of Abas, an early Argive king.

Hera's temple on Samos was very large and her cult there of considerable antiquity. Tradition said that her image came there from Argos, though the Samians disputed this and believed she had been born under the willow tree in the sanctuary. The confusion in the tradition may support the view that Hera had supplanted an even earlier cult of a goddess but again there is memory of a connection with the Argive.

Hera's temple at Olympia was the oldest and this would imply an association with the tradition that the games were founded by the Argive Hercules —the hero 'called after Hera.'

Here the chief centre of her cult was the Argive Heraion, 'Our Lady's Temple', built on the lower slopes of a mountain called Euboea and said to have been so called after Hera's nurse. As the principal goddess of the Argive plain, where Agamemnon's royal stronghold of Mycene was situated, she gave wholehearted support to the cause of the Achaeans in the Trojan War. 'The three towns I love best,' says Hera in the *Iliad*, 'are Argos, Sparta and Mycene.'

The Spartan cult of Argive Hera was brought from Argos. Hera's most northerly shrine was at Pharygai, on the Gulf of Malis, in south Thessaly,

Statue of Hera in the park at Versailles, Paris, France

and this was founded by settlers from the Argolid. She had cult centres in most cities of Boeotia; the oldest appears to have been on Mt. Cythaeron at the top of the Corinthian Gulf. Here she had cult centres too at Corinth, Heraia, and Sicyon, which are included in Agamemnon's domains as defined in the *Iliad*. It seems from excavation that her cult at Heraia derived from the Argive Heraion and, according to tradition, her cults at Sicyon derived from the same centre.

It has been argued by G. Thomson (in his Prehistoric Aegean) that, if the focus of Hera's worship on the mainland was the Argive Heraion, it follows that she must have reached the Argive plain from overseas. Her oldest image in the Heraion, made of pear wood, had been brought there from Tiryns, not far from Nauplia, with its fine harbour, which could well have been a main port of call for Minoan traders. At Nauplia there was a cult of Hera

Parthenos, 'the Maiden'. At Hermione there was another good harbour. Here also there was a cult of Hera Parthenos; and there was a tradition that Zeus and Hera landed at Hermione when they arrived in Greece from Crete.

Uneasy Marriage

Not the least contradictory aspect of the relationship of Zeus and Hera, traditional Olympian patrons of lawful marriage, is its lack of lawful offspring. Zeus is father of many children, but Hera is not their mother. Hera has fewer children, but Zeus is not their father. According to Hesiod, Hebe, Ares and Ilithyia were the children of Zeus and Hera, but it is doubtful if this can be supported. Ilithyia however, could well have been Hera's daughter. For her birthplace was a cave near Cnossus in Crete.

The evidence from inscriptions and from coins in historical times confirms the continuing importance of Hera in Cretan religious belief. Her early Cretan associations suggest that she was originally a manifestation of the Minoan mother goddess; and they equally support the inference that, despite the supremacy of Argive Hera on the mainland, the worship of Hera had been carried from Crete into Greece. Hence the uneasy marriage relationship of Zeus and Hera has been explained as the result of the intrusion of a Greek patriarchal deity, whose original partner may have been called Dione, into the province of the Minoan mother goddess. This goddess's partner, who was supplanted by Zeus, had once been the hero 'called after Hera', that is to say, none other than Hercules himself.

Certainly the Greek evidence for a sacred marriage of Zeus and Hera, though comparatively late, suggest that Zeus had an older partner who was not Hera. Alternatively, Hera may have had an older partner who was not Zeus. It should be explained that the sacred marriage (hieros gamos) is part of the Oriental ritual pattern underlying the concept of such relationships as the Great Mother-Attis, Ishtar-Tammuz, Aphrodite-Adonis. In our oldest literary source, Homer, there was a sacred marriage in Crete between Iasion and Demeter in a thrice-ploughed field, that is to say, in a field prepared for sowing. The sacred marriage was originally closely involved with the religious conception of a vegetation cycle of the death and rebirth of crops.

There are definite mythological grounds for the view, maintained by Sir James Frazer and A. B. Cook, that, at Cnossus in Crete there had once existed a ritual marriage of sun god and moon goddess in bovine form. In later cults, the ritual became a sacred marriage of Zeus and Hera, which reputedly occurred near the river Theren, where a sanctuary was built and yearly

Hera and Zeus Metope of the temple of Hera in Selinuntuma, Palermo, Sicily

sacrifices were offered with traditional wedding rites. Similarly, at Gortyna, also in Crete, the goddess Europa, who had originally been carried off by Zeus in the form of a bull, became identified with Hera.

Here mention should be made of the view that Hera, described by Homer on many occasions with the traditional epithet boopis ('cow-eyed', 'cow-faced') was originally a cow goddess. Her priestess at Argos was Io, who was ravished by Zeus when she had been transformed by him into a cow. The myth of Io also reflects a sacred marriage, the bride being the priestess of Hera, the bridegroom the priest of Zeus disguised as a bull. The ox-herd Argos who watched over Io was Panoptes ('all-seeing')—an epithet of Zeus and the sun; and Argos wore a bull's hide.

Mother of the Minotaur

According to the famous myth, Pasiphae ('She who shines on all', that is, the moon), wife of King Minos, conceived a passion for a bull, sent in answer to the prayers of Minos. Instead of sacrificing this bull, as he had promised, Minos sent it away among his herds and sacrificed another one. His punishment for this piece of deception was the unnatural passion of his wife. Daedalus made for Pasiphae a hollow wooden cow on wheels, sewed it up in the hide of a cow which he had skinned, and put it in the meadow where the bull grazed. Inside this image he put Pasiphae, and the bull coupled with it. In due course Pasiphae gave birth to Asterios ('Starry One'), who was called the Minotaur ('Minos bull'). The Minotaur had the head of a bull, but the rest of him was human. In obedience to certain oracles, Minos then shut him up under guard in the labyrinth, which had also been made by Daedalus, the Athenian architect. The labyrinth in the Greek tradition, was a building whose intricate windings led astray those who sought to escape from it.

The cow and bull became such integral factors in the life of the communities that they figure in mythology as guides in the founding of cities by those who followed the advice of the sun god. The story of Cadmus, who, in obedience to the Delphic oracle, followed a cow until it lay down on the site of Thebes, is familiar. Since the sun was conceived as a bull, it seems likely that the labyrinth at Cnossus was an actual arena of solar pattern

designed for the performance of a mimetic dance, in which a dancer may have masqueraded as a bull and represented the movement of the sun.

The labyrinth supposedly built by Daedalus was recognized in antiquity as an imitation of the Egyptian labyrinth, which, in turn, was generally believed to be sacred to the sun. The dances in the labyrinth were connected in antiquity with the Roman Game of Troy, performed by bands of armed youths on horseback.

Juno was identified by the Romans with Greek Hera, and she was worshipped as the queen of heaven, protectress over females, as was Jupiter over males. She was supposed to watch over women from birth to death and the month of June which was named

for her, was supposed to be most favourable for marrying.

The Etruscan Herkle and Unial and the Roman Hercules and Juno were in the same sort of mythological relationship as Greek Hercules and Hera. At Roman weddings the bride's girdle was consecrated to Juno and its knot, untied by the bridegroom on the marriage couch, was called the 'Herculean knot', which, as Cook concluded, indicates that, when the cult of Hercules spread to Italy, at a very early date, the acknowledged partner of Hercules was Hera.

R. F. WILLETS

FURTHER READING: M. P. Nilsson. Minoan-Mycenaean Religion. *(Lund, Sweden, 1950); G. Thomson.* The Prehistoric Aegean. *(Lawrence & Wishart, 1949); R. F. Willetts.* Cretan Cults and Festivals. *(Greenwood 1980).*

Hercules

The greatest hero of Greek legend, Hercules (in Greek, Herakles) was the only one to become an Olympian god. His legend is complex and widespread, being associated in Greece with Boeotia and the Peloponnese, while some of his exploits are set in eastern and western regions remote from Greece and imperfectly known. He was adopted by the Romans because of his doings in Italy.

Hercules is one of the great wanderers, like Perseus, the Argonauts, and Odysseus. His legend, like theirs, contains material of great vitality which comes from folktale and supernatural myth. Only with these more than human qualities could he have ended as not only a god but as one of the most important gods during the last years of paganism. His deeds, even though he sometimes leads an army, are individual feats of strength.

Heracles fighting the centaur Nessus

Attended usually by his squire, Iolaus, he faces perils and monsters too great for human valour. In this he is like the Mesopotamian Gilgamesh or the English Beowulf, whose greatest deeds were not done on human battlefields. Such primeval figures are but little modified by the conventional traditions of a heroic age. Yet his most famous deeds, the Labours, were not done by him as a free agent but by order of the unworthy ruler Eurystheus, whom the gods decreed that he should serve. In his own character Hercules was noble as well as valiant, but he was subject to fits of fury or madness, in which he committed terrible crimes.

His name is puzzling but evidently significant. There is no reason to disbelieve those ancient writers who interpreted it as 'glory of Hera'; yet Hera (the Latin Juno) queen of heaven, appears as his relentless enemy during all his earthly life. Some light on its original sense may perhaps be got from the myth of Gilgamesh, who was persecuted all his life by the Nature goddess and queen of heaven, Ishtar. She had first desired Gilgamesh for her lover, but he refused and so was punished. It appears that some Babylonian and Sumerian kings were regarded as official consorts of Ishtar. Does the name Hercules descend from a remote time when some Greek kings were regarded as Hera's consorts?

During the nineteenth century some scholars argued that Hercules, who was certainly in classical times a favourite of the Dorian Greeks, was originally a Dorian hero only, and was no more than an intruder in legends inherited from the Mycenean Greeks whom the Dorian invaders overthrew. But although Dorian chiefs claimed later to be descendants of the exiled children of Hercules (the Heraclidae) who departed northward, there is not sufficient reason to tear Hercules loose from his pre-Dorian setting,

which represents the actual Mycenean age of prehistory.

Early poetry dealing with Hercules has come down to us in fragments or in allusions only. A complete cycle of myth concerning him may be assumed with certainty, but it is not likely that this was well ordered or consistent. Nor can it be shown that there was a complete cycle of formed poetry about him. However, the distinction between legend and its literary embodiment is hard to draw for ages when literature itself was oral. Our material of all dates does make possible a general outline of Hercules's life through his Labours until his death or deification. But there is no definite relatior between his stray exploits and the well-known Labours which he carved out for Eurystheus. The clearest among continuous narratives are those of the late compilers of mythology, Diodorus (1st century AD), in a legendary part of his *Universal History* and Apollodorus (1st century BC) as representee in the summary *Library of Mythology* attributed to him.

Hercules was born at Thebes to Alcmena wife of Amphitryon who had come fron Tiryns to live at Thebes. His father was Zeus who took the form of Amphitryon, then absent, for a supernaturally prolonged embrace. At the same birth Alcmena bore Hercules's twin brother Iphicles, the son of Amphitryon. Hera in her jealousy sent two serpents to kill the infants as they lay cradled in a shield, but Hercules strangled them. As he grew up, he was taught chariot racing, wrestling, and the use of weapons, particularly the bow; Linus, brother of Orpheus, also taught him music. When Linus struck his pupil once to discipline him, Hercules in a fit of temper killed him with the lyre. He was sent to guard cattle, and while on watch killed the lion of Cythaeron, whose skin he afterward

A 2nd-centrury BC bronze statue of Hercules.

wore complete with the head as helmet or hood.

When Erginus, king of Orchomenus in Boeotia, sent envoys to demand tribute from the Thebans, Hercules outraged the envoys, so that Erginus made war. Hercules killed him and compelled the Minyan inhabitants of Orchomenus to pay double the tribute that they had exacted from the Thebans. As a prize for valour, Creon, king of Thebes, gave him his daughter Megara to be his wife. By her he had three sons but later, driven mad by Hera, he killed them.

When he recovered his reason, he went into exile and inquired of the Delphic oracle where he should live. He was ordered to settle in Tiryns, which was his family's original home, and to serve its overlord, Eurystheus of Mycene, for 12 years; in some accounts his servitude was decreed even before his birth. He was to perform the Labours that would be imposed on him, but after these had been accomplished he would be made immortal.

The number and details of the Labours vary in different sources, but eventually a canon of 12 was recognized. The earliest evidence for this total appears in the reliefs on the pediments of the temple of Zeus at Olympia carved during the 5th century BC. Firstly, Hercules was to bring back the skin of the invulnerable lion of Nemea in Argolis; on finding that his arrows had no effect, he stunned the lion with his club and then choked it. Next he had to kill the Hydra, the many-headed water-snake that infested the marshy plain of Lerna in Argolis; it had nine heads, the middle one being immortal, while the rest grew again whenever Hercules smashed them with his club, until Iolaus burned their roots. Hercules cut off and buried the immortal head, but this feat was not accepted by Eurystheus because of Iolaus's help.

Hercules capturing the Ceryneian Hind

Thirdly, Hercules was set the task of catching the Ceryneian hind and bringing it from the border of Arcadia to Mycene. It had golden horns and was sacred to Artemis (Diana). After hunting it for a year, Hercules shot it as it was crossing the River Ladon, and was eventually allowed by Apollo and Artemis to carry it alive to Eurystheus. His next Labour was to bring back alive the boar of Mt. Erymanthus in Arcadia. On his way Hercules was entertained by centaurs but later fell out with them, so that he had to disperse them with arrows and flaming brands; he caught the boar in deep snow and carried it to Mycene.

The fifth task was to carry out the cattle dung from the stables of Au-geas, king of Elis, in a single day; the stables had not been cleaned for many years. When Hercules arrived, Augeas promised him a tenth of the cattle if he accomplished this. He did so by diverting the rivers Alpheus and Peneus through the stables. But Augeas broke his promise and would not pay the reward; later Hercules made war on Augeas, killed him, and devastated the country. Hercules next had to rid the Stymphalian lake in Arcadia of a great flock of birds that used their feathers as darts; he did so by scaring them with castanets of bronze presented by Athene and shot some of them on the wing.

The seventh Labour was to bring to Mycene the bull given to Minos by Poseidon (Neptune) but not sacrificed as promised, so that Poseidon drove it wild. Hercules captured it and brought it to Mycene, but Eurystheus let it go. After this Hercules had to bring to Mycene the man-eating mares of Diomedes, king of the Bistones in Thrace. After fighting with the Bistones, Hercules succeeded in carrying off the mares to Eurystheus. The next task was to bring back the girdle of Hippolyta, the queen of the Amazons, who lived by the River Thermodon in Asia Minor. When Hercules's ship arrived at Themiscyra, her capital, Hippolyta promised to give him the girdle. But Hera, disguised as an Amazon persuaded the women that Hercules intended to carry off their queen. When the Amazons charged down on horseback to the ship, Hercules killed Hippolyta and set sail with the girdle to Mycene. On his way back he set free Hesione, princess of Troy, who had been chained on a rock as prey for a sea' monster. The monster had been sent to ravage the country by Poseidon and Apollo, who had fortified Troy for King Laomedon and had been cheated of their reward. Hercules killed the monster, but was also cheated; later he besieged and took Troy.

The tenth Labour was to fetch the cattle of Geryon from the island of Erytheia in the far west. Geryon had three heads and bodies joined at the waist, below which again he had three pairs of legs and feet. Hercules journeyed through Libya, destroying many wild beasts, until he came to the western end of the Mediterranean, where he erected two great rocks known as the Pillars of Hercules (Gibraltar and Ceuta on Mt. Hacho in Morocco) before going on to Tartessus and Erytheia. He crossed to Erytheia using the boat of the sun god, and killed Geryon, his servant and his hound. Return-

Hercules Suffocates Antaeus, Marco Marchetti (c. 1528–1588)

ing eastward with the cattle by Iberia and Liguria to Italy, he crossed to Sicily in pursuit of a bull stolen by Eryx, son of Poseidon, whom he killed. He then drove the cattle round the Ionian (Adriatic) sea, but lost many of them when a gadfly sent by Hera dispersed them about Thrace. When he brought them to Mycene, Eurystheus sacrificed them to Hera.

After this exploit, Hercules had to fetch the golden apples of the Hesperides, nymphs who lived in the far west of Libya, though sometimes they were thought to dwell in the far north of Europe. The apples were guarded by a gigantic many-headed serpent, usually said to have been immortal. According to some accounts Hercules persuaded the Titan Atlas, who held up the heavens on his shoulders, to approach and charm the serpent and so bring the

apples for him, while he supported the burden. The last of Hercules's Labours was to fetch the three-headed hound Cerberus from the entrance of Hades; Pluto allowed Cerberus to be carried off by Hercules provided he was brought back again.

On one of his journeys, Hercules was bringing home a new wife, Deianeira, when the centaur Nessus offered to carry her over a swollen river. Nessus attempted to rape Deianeira and was shot down by Hercules with his poisoned arrows. Before he died, Nessus told Deianeira to preserve his blood, saying that it would be a charm for reviving Hercules's love for her if it should fail. Sometime later Hercules came home from the wars with a captured girl, Iole, and Deianeira in her distress gave Hercules a garment stained with the blood of Nessus to wear. The tunic stuck to his skin and spread deadly poison through his body. Maddened with pain, Hercules had himself burned on a pyre on the top of Mt. Oeta. The myth held that after his death he became an Olympian god, was reconciled to Hera and married Hebe, daughter of Zeus and Hera. But a shadow of him went to Hades.

A number of well-known works, passages or fragments within surviving poetry and drama deal with Hercules. Homer says that Zeus swore irrevocably, when the birth of Hercules was expected, that on that day the next child born of his own blood would rule over all that dwelt about him. Hera, by delaying the arrival of Hercules, contrived that the first birth should be that of Eurystheus.

Hesiod's *Theogony* tells how Hercules killed the eagle that fed on Prometheus's liver, of his origin, of his killing of Geryon, and of his marriage to Hebe and immortal bliss. The poem *Shield of Hercules*, attributed to Hesiod, relates the battle between Hercules and Cycnus, son of Ares, and describes Hercules's elabourate shield.

Among lyric poets, Stesichorus of Himera in Sicily told of Hercules's expedition to fetch the cattle of Geryon. Pindar tells vividly the stories of his birth and killing of the serpents; of his expedition against Troy; of his journey through Libya and his wrestling with the giant Antaeus; and of his founding of the Isthmian and also the Olympic Games. He mentions his journey to the Ister (Danube) to get an olive spray to plant, so that he himself and later athletes might have shade. Other details given by Pindar include Hercules's gluttony, his eating of two oxen seized from the plough and, curiously, his short stature.

Among dramatists, the Trachiniae of Sophocles covers all the events leading up to the death of Hercules on the pyre on Mt. Oeta, but contains no mention of his deification, though he appears as a god at the end of Philoctetes. Euripides's *Mad Hercules* presents the insane frenzy of Hercules as he is struck by the demon Lyssa, sent by Hera, and tells of how he kills his children. His Alcestis shows Hercules first as a greedy, cheerful, and insensitive guest in the grief-stricken house of Admetus, after the death of his wife Alcestis, but later as the deliverer who restores Alcestis after defeating Death. The cruder aspects of Hercules are shown in Aristophanes's *Frogs*, where everyone in the underworld remembers his plundering gluttony.

Ambassador of Zeus

Among prose writers, the Sophist Prodicus, (c. 5th century BC) appears to have originated the idea of the Choice of Hercules, made between the lives offered to him by the seductive figure of Vice and the austere one of Virtue. This was the beginning of the long history of Hercules as a symbolical figure used by the philosophers. He was a useful subject for sermons because he was a famous folk hero everywhere in the Greek world and had ended in unique glory.

Hercules and the Nemean lion

The Strength of Ten

Hercules sighed gustily. 'The poor child is an orphan. I killed his father myself. This was what happened. I was wandering through western Thessaly on some expedition or other, and one day I happened to feel hungry. I came across a Dryopian farmer ploughing a fallow field in a sheltered valley, and uttering, for luck, the usual obscene imprecations. I saluted him with: 'My lucky ploughman, I am so hungry that I could eat an ox.' He answered, with a smile, but continuing to curse, that I should at any rate not eat his ox until the field had been ploughed and harrowed too. 'Holy Serpents,' I cried, losing patience, 'I will, if I like.' 'Hold hard,' said he. I am Theiodamas the Dryopian. I must ask you not to speak to me in that peremptory way.' I answered: 'To the crows with your "peremptory." I am Hercules of Tiryns and I always say, do, and get, just whatever I please. At Delphi the other day I told the Pythoness exactly what I have just told you; but she refused to believe me. I pulled the sacred tripod from under her and carried it out of the shrine. "Now," said I, "if needs must I will have an oracle of my own." Ho, ho! That soon brought her to her senses.' But Theiodamas either had never heard me or else could not believe that I was I. He threatened me with his ox-goad, so I gave him a friendly tap with my club and cracked his skull like an eggshell. Alas, I never meant to kill him. I never know my strength, that is my curse. The same thing happened to me when I was a boy learning to play the lyre, and my music-teacher, a pompous fool named Linus, rapped my knuckles and told me that my fingering was incorrect. I gave him a playful whack with the lyre and dashed out his brains. A pure accident, that I swear! I pleaded self-defence and the affair blew over, but I have never touched a lyre since.

Robert Graves,
Hercules, My Shipmate

Hercules's slow change of character from hero to something more was foreshadowed by the Athenian orator Isocrates (436–338 BC), who celebrates his intelligence. In Aristotle's *Problems*, in a discussion of the melancholic man, the ancient forerunner of our man of genius, Hercules in his greatness and in his fits of madness is quoted as a legendary example of the type. In Roman times the Stoic philosopher Dio of Prusa developed the idea of the Choice of Hercules as one between tyranny and kingship. Hercules was moving toward being a pagan saint. Among the Stoics he became a symbol of divine energy and order.

Meanwhile the Romans themselves had eagerly adopted Hercules. This is shown in literature by the litany of his exploits which appears in Virgil's *Aeneid*. A peculiarly Roman addition was his killing of the monster Cacus who had driven off the cattle of Geryon to his cave in the Aventine Hill. His sufferings and his death on the pyre as treated by Ovid and Seneca make explicit in another way his change to divine nature by telling how the pyre burned away only the mortal part of him.

Hercules continues to grow in stature and in wisdom in late philosophical and religious literature. Because he had fought and suffered as a man battling against beasts and monsters and hardship, he became a saviour who had much greater appeal than the traditional Olympians who had never endured the mortal state. He came to be regarded as the special representative of Zeus or Jupiter in dealing with mankind.

The development had gone far by the 4th century AD when Christianity was made the official faith of the Empire by Constantine. Scholars have noticed an affinity between the legendary Hercules, who had acquired a new religious and philosophical significance, and the Christ of Christian theology.

Though some have exaggerated this, there was certainly an analogy between the Herculean theology and Christian belief, which was influenced by Stoic modes of thought. In some writings of the apostate Emperor Julian, Hercules appears to be a figure maintained as a rival to Christ. But Hercules was not more than a legendary or mythical figure and no more than one of many gods. He could not really rival Christ, the historical saviour and manifestation of one God.

E. D. PHILLIPS

FURTHER READING: L. R. Farnell. Cults of the Greek States, 5 vols. (Caratzas Bros., 1977); Gilbert Murray. Greek Studies. (Clarendon Press, 1946).

Hermes

In many ways Hermes is the most sympathetic, the most baffling, the most confusing, the most complex and therefore the most Greek of all the Olympian gods. Like the Olympian goddesses, he had a prehistory; he is a very uneasy kind of Olympian, with deep popular roots.

There seems to be little doubt that Hermes signifies 'the god of the stone heap', the spirit immanent in stones set up as cairns or pillars to serve as boundaries, or as landmarks for the wayfarer. Truly a god of the countryside, he was associated with the Minoan pillar cult and there is evidence that the cult of Hermes existed in Crete in historical times.

Coins found at Cydonia and dated to about 250–267 BC, feature a nude Hermes with his wand and familiar broad-brimmed hat. It seems that at Cydonia Hermes could have had very special associations with the old Minoan population. According to the historian Ephorus (4th century BC) certain festivals were regularly celebrated for the serfs of this district, during which no free persons entered the city; the serfs were masters of everything and even had power to flog the freemen. It is tempting to connect this account with another old tradition that festivals of Hermes were celebrated in Crete, and that while the serfs were feasting their masters assisted in menial duties. On these occasions they would have been assuming temporarily the free status which their old Minoan ancestors had once enjoyed.

As W. K. C. Guthrie explains,

Heracles and Omphale; Ancient Roman fresco

Medaillon with Hermes

Hermes with Dionysus, Praxiteles

Hermes was named by the Greeks from herma or hermaion, a cairn or heap of stones. To explain this connection the Greeks characteristically invented a myth to account for it, that when Hermes killed the many-eyed monster Argus, he was brought to trial by the gods. They acquitted him and, in doing so, each threw his voting pebble at his feet and a heap of stones grew up around him. In fact Hermes must simply have been the daemon or spirit of the stone heaps themselves, about which there were several superstitious beliefs. Even now, in some parts of Britain, the wayfarer who wishes for good luck will add a stone to the cairn which he finds on the hilltop. This custom also prevailed in antiquity; and belief in the spirit of the cairn is still an occasional feature of northern European belief.

As the mythological explanation suggests, the herma consisted of an upright monumental stone with a heap of smaller stones around its base. Gradually the god, and the pillar which represented him, became more and more human in conception. He was given a phallus to promote fertility, and finally emerged as a fully human figure. Yet even in the 5th century the 'herma' which stood in front of Athenian houses had not thrown off all traces of their origin, and were no more than half-human in shape.

As Charles Seltman put the matter, it is now becoming apparent that, just as in Christian theology there are always two distinct influences, one Jewish and the other Greek, so in pagan theology there are two distinct influences, one pre-Hellenic, the other Hellenic, for all the most important Olympian deities. This is certainly true of Hermes, whose name is Greek but whose nature and functions are mainly derived from the beliefs of earlier peoples. He seems to emerge as a pastoral god and a guide to travelers because of his association, in remote antiquity, with cairns.

The later Greek-speaking peoples did not know the name that the pre-Hellenic inhabitants had given to the god of these stone heaps; and the name, as often in similar cases elsewhere, was doubtless withheld from them. Therefore they could only refer to him as 'Hermes' from their word for 'stone heap'. In the Laconian dialect which some of them spoke, he was known as 'Herman', 'He of the stone heap', or more familiarly, 'Old Heapy'.

It is true, as Seltman added, that recent research has provided a clearer perception of what the Greeks at different times thought and felt about Hermes, and more is known about him than about several other deities. The multiplicity of his titles and functions must not be allowed to disguise the fact that he is one of the earliest and most primitive of all the gods of Greece. In the prologue to the *Ion* of Euripides Hermes introduces himself in this way:

Atlas, who wears on back of bronze the ancient
Abode of gods in heaven, had a daughter
Whose name was Maia, born of a goddess:
She lay with Zeus and bore me, Hermes,
Servant of the immortals.

This introduction modestly stresses his prehistoric origin and his subordinate status in the Olympian hierarchy. Further insight into the varied functions of this truly popular god is given in the *Plutus* of Aristophanes, and in the *Homeric Hymn to Hermes*, familiar to English readers in Shelley's translation, and one of the longest and most charming of all the *Homeric Hymns*. It tells the tale of the infant god's adventures following his birth in a cave on Mt. Cyllene in Arcadia, the ancient seat of his worship. From there it was carried to other parts of Greece.

Hermes escaped from his cradle, went to Pieria and carried off some of Apollo's oxen, which he drove to Pylos, in the neighbourhood of Olympia. Returning to Cyllene, he found a tortoise at the entrance to his cave, placed strings across its shell and so invented the lyre on which he promptly played. Apollo discovered the theft, went to Cyllene and charged Hermes with the crime. Hermes's mother Maia showed the god the child in his cradle but Apollo took him to Zeus, who obliged him to restore the oxen. By giving him the lyre Hermes won the friendship of Apollo and also various prerogatives, including a share in divination, lordship over herds and animals, and the office of messenger from the gods to Hades.

As herald of the gods, Hermes was god of eloquence. Prudent and cunning, he was master of fraud, perjury, and theft. He was also credited with a variety of inventions apart from the lyre. God of roads, he cared for travelers; and as inventor of sacrifices, he protected sacrificial animals, and was worshipped by shepherds. He was god of commercial transactions and good luck, and patron of gymnastics. The famous sculpture of Hermes by Praxiteles is one of numerous representations of this most versatile of all the Greek gods.

R. F. WILLETTS

FURTHER READING: W. K. C. Guthrie. The Greeks and their Gods. *(Methuen, 1950); C. Seltman.* The Twelve Olympians and their Guests. *(Parrish, 1956).*

Homer

Legendary author of the *Odyssey* and the *Iliad*. Homer's real identity is not known with any certainty, nor if he (or she) was one person or several. Whoever the poet was, he was very likely a bard who sang the epic poems. There is strong evidence to suggest that the *Odyssey* and the *Iliad* are first and foremost oral poems that were later transcribed when writing was reintroduced to the eastern Mediterranean region in the middle 8th century BC. While the ancient Greeks revered Homer as a legendary figure, a real individual, scholars today disagree about the origin of works ascribed to him. Some claim that the *Odyssey* and the *Iliad* are the work of two different poets, or that many different people added and revised the works we now read as a cohesive whole. Others maintain that a single and remarkable genius poet was the source of these texts. They point to the repetition of phrases and the consistency of vocabulary and style. Inconsistencies in the epics are said to be a foible of Homer's fallible memory.

FURTHER READING: Atchity, Kenneth John., Ron Charles Hogart, and Doug Price. Critical Essays on Homer. *(Boston, MA: G. K. Hall, 1987); Martin, Richard P.* The Language of Heroes: Speech and Performance in the Iliad. *(Ithaca: Cornell UP, 1989); Parry, Milman, and Adam Parry.* The Making of Homeric Verse: The Collected Papers of Milman Parry. *(Oxford: Clarendon, 1971).*

Janus

The precise origin and earliest character of Janus eluded even Roman savants. His name denotes any passageway, usually the classical arch, and yields the common Latin word for 'door' (ianua). The god was considered present in every door or gate. Nevertheless he remains best known for his function in certain public arched gateways which did not belong to a fortification system. It is not clear whether ianus primarily meant the passageway itself or its god. Equally unclear was Janus's function within the passageway.

The month of January and invocation of Janus by the Salian Brothers, an ancient priestly group, authenticate Janus's longstanding worship. The Salian Brothers, serving the god Mars, and the month were traditionally instituted by Numa Pompilius, Rome's second king, around 700 BC. Although over five centuries later it became the first month of the civil year, January was reckoned the eleventh month of the liturgical year. The reasons for making January the first month were entirely secular but the Romans interpreted the choice as a sign of Janus's protection of all beginnings, which had developed from his supervision of entrances. On 9 January Janus received his only regular state sacrifice, which took place

Bronze piece with Janus and corresponding symbols

in the Regia, the chief pontiff's house in the Forum, where Rome's priest-king offered a ram. Ceremonies on his behalf must have been observed at the famous arched gateways and his few temples on diverse occasions. Scraps of the very old Salian Hymns contained special prayer-songs to Janus. These were sung in March at planting time when Janus seems to have aided vegetation: rather curiously, since a god particularly concerned with passageways seems to have little relationship with a vegetation deity.

The Good Creator

In the 2nd century BC, Janus appears in connection with two private sacrifices. One was made to Ceres, goddess of the growth of crops, and took place before the harvest. This association recalls the Salians' invocation of Janus as 'the good creator', for Ceres meant no more than 'growth' before her apotheosis. In the harvest ceremony Janus was invoked along with Jupiter and Juno. The second ceremony was an agricultural rite of Mars which required preliminary invocation of Janus and Jupiter. Preliminary invocation of Janus in these and a few other

ceremonies is assumed to derive from his function as protector and promoter of beginnings. However, his name does not stand first in most prayers and rites. In the oldest surviving records the god belongs to a group of vegetation deities and deserves the name of good creator. The passageway does not occur in such invocations.

According to Roman belief Janus was exclusively Roman. Early in the second century Rome's first specialist in the calendar stated that the name January came from Latium, a region surrounding Rome, and had not originated at Rome itself. The Romans also recognized Janus in a cult image taken in 241 BC from Falerii, a town of the middle Tiber valley. The Faliscans were related by language to the Latins and by culture to the Etruscans and Sabines. Rome remained the paramount centre of Janus's cult. Some of her oldest coins carry the usual and famous representation of Janus bifrons, 'two-faced'. Occasionally a four-faced Janus, quadrifrons, is mentioned. The former anthropomorphic Janus belonged to the simple passageway and the latter to the gateways comprising two intersecting paths, where Janus faced in the

direction of each of the four ways.

Some of the god's epithets were thought to indicate his divine functions; Patulcius and Clusivius (or Clusius) pointed to Janus being open or closed (from patere and claudere), while Consivius was related to the root of the word for sowing seed, conserere. These old interpretations are subject to the linguist's doubt. Both Patulcius and Consivius seem to be found in Janus's Salian song. Other epithets are Junonius, Curiatius, and Quirinus. The first recalls Janus's association with Juno in the harvest ceremony. The altar of Janus Curiatius was paired with an altar of Juno Sororia. Curiatius must be referred to the curiae, primitive divisions of Rome. His rites may have comprised purification of adolescents on their coming of age and entrance to their ancestral curia. Quirinus belonged to the same civil system and his name also derived from this word. However, Janus Quirinus was worshipped by all the curiae and was a state god.

The Closed Doors of Peace

Janus Quirinus possessed the most famous 'temple' of Janus, situated off the Forum. The origin of the shrine is clouded in antiquity overlaid by folk-tale. The small rectangular building had double doors at each end, which caused this Janus to be called geminus, 'twin'. The side walls did not reach the roof, but were surmounted by grates. A statue of the two-faced god stood within this bronze enclosure that was presumably a monumental gateway on the street leading from the civic centre. This unusual temple stood as a symbol of war or peace to the Romans. Many Latin writers confirm how the open Janus betokened war and the closed Janus peace, the opposite of what might be expected. In explanation of this anomaly, students in modern times have argued that Janus was imbued with the vigour of war and therefore was closed in peace and open in time of war. Except for the connection with Mars, who was also an ancient god of vegetation and fertility, Janus shows few signs of belligerence. Moreover, when Augustus Caesar

closed Janus Quirinus to herald a new era free from civil war, he mentioned only one closing in 235 BC, some six years after the first war with Carthage.

There is very little truly old evidence for understanding the occasion of opening and closing Janus, when one normally expects a gate or passage to be closed during war. A recent study attempts to solve the problem by arguing that a ianus had originally been a bridge with a simple structure of two uprights and a crossbeam at both ends which was dismantled and thus 'open' during war. This theory depends upon a close topographical connection of ianus to water crossings; since archaic Rome was covered by a network of streams of which very few needed a bridge convertible to defense, this ingenious thesis cannot be proved.

Janus appeared un-warlike to the Romans, and so they stressed his role in peace. Such a divinity of peace does not recall the modern aspiration for peace. Rather the closed Janus put the

mark of success and security upon the Roman empire and its policy of peace through armed intimidation. Putting aside his relation to agriculture, ancient and modern authors have laid particular emphasis on Janus in an original capacity of lord of beginnings. This capacity owes much to the accident of January's position in the civil calendar.

R. E. A. PALMER

Jason & the Argonauts

The story of Jason and his quest for the Golden Fleece is set a generation before the Trojan War, sometime during the Bronze Age, or approximately 1300 BC. There are many versions of the tale that reflect an evolving Greek understanding of geography. There is also evidence that the shifting details of plot in the Jason saga may

Jason and the Argonauts Disembark at Colchis, Charles de La Fosse (1636–1716)

have been due to cultural exchange with cultures east of the Aegean. The Argonauts embark on one of the oldest hero's quests. Jason and his crew sail off to find a legendary golden fleece and have amazing adventures along the way.

The earliest written version of the tale is Eumelos' rendition from the 7th century BC, although the story is certainly much older and would have developed during a period of oral storytelling. Apollonius of Rhodes, librarian at Alexandria, provides perhaps the most well known version in the 3rd century BC.

Jason, Son of Aeson

Jason, son of King Aeson of Iolkos, was raised by the centaur Chiron on Mt. Pelion after Aeson's brother Pelias usurped the throne. When Jason is old enough, he returns to Iolkos to demand his birthright and to be crowned king. On his way to the palace, the goddess Hera, disguised as an old crone, asks for assistance crossing a swift river. Jason politely stops to help her, and in crossing the river with the goddess on his back, loses a sandal in the current. So Jason appears before Pelias with the blessing of Hera as well as with only one shoe. Pelias had been warned in a prophecy to beware of a stranger with one sandal, and so when Jason reveals his intention of reclaiming the throne, Pelias relents immediately, but cunningly imposes just one condition: Jason can have the throne if he delivers to Pelias the legendary golden fleece.

The Quest

Jason accepts the challenge. He commissions a ship from Argus, a master shipbuilder, who names his new vessel, fittingly, Argo. The bow of the ship, donated by Athena, is made from a piece of oak felled from a sacred grove of Dodona; the piece of wood has the power of speech. Jason also recruits a crew that includes Heracles, Orpheus, Argus, Peleus the father of Achilles, Telamon father of Ajax, and others. Heracles and Orpheus would have been later additions to the original story, and the specific heroes on the quest varies. Probably each town or region wanted to include their local hero in the story. Jason's crew become known as the Argonauts (after the ship). They sail east toward Colchis where King Aeëtes has placed the Golden Fleece under the guard of a dragon.

The Isle of Lemnos

Their first stop is Lemnos, an island inhabited soley by women. When the women of the island neglected Aphrodite in their worship, the goddess made them unattractive to their husbands. The men promptly took concubines from another island, and the spurned wives murdered all the men on the island. Princess Hypsipyle, now the Queen of the island, saved her father from the mass homicide by sending him to sea in a wooden cabinet. The Argonauts stay on the island for a year consorting with the women and fathering children, including Jason and Hupsipyle's twins, Thoas and Euneos.

Cyzicus and Cios

Their second stop is Cyzicus, where the Argonauts are received hospitably, but accidentally engage in a nighttime battle with the local Doliones, inadvertently killing King Cyzicus. They discover their mistake in the morning, help bury the king, and depart. They stop next at Cios so that Heracles can replace a broken oar. Hylas, Heracles' protégé and closest friend, is abducted by nymphs on the island who are taken by his beauty, and Heracles abandons the quest to search for him.

King Phineus and the Symplegades

Next, the Argonauts land at Salmydessus, ruled by the blind prophet King Phineus. Phineus is harassed by the monstrous winged Harpies who, whenever there is a meal, would swoop in, steal his food and foul his table so that the king is essentially starving. The Argonauts chase the Harpies away, and in exchange Phineus tells them of the dangers ahead, in particular of the Symplegades, or clashing rocks, which are two cliffs that smash together, crushing any ship that attempts to pass between them. Phineus advises them to release a dove, and if the bird makes it through safely, to row quickly as the rocks recoil. The plan works, and the Argo only sustains minor damage. The Symplegades were fused together thereafter, so travelers could safely pass.

Colchis, the Golden Fleece and Medea

After a voyage through the Euxine Sea, the Argonauts reach Colchis, the place of the Golden Fleece. In typical fairytale mode, Aeëtes is ready to give Jason the fleece if he successfully completes a series of heroic and seemingly impossible labours: to yoke a pair of fire-breathing bulls and sow a field with dragon's teeth, which would sprout warriors that Jason needed to then kill. Medea, Aeëtes' daughter and skilled sorceress, has meanwhile fallen in love with Jason (at Hera's request to Aphrodite), and offers to secretly help him achieve his goals. She provides a potion to protect Jason from the fire of the bulls, and helps him trick the warriors into killing each other. She also gives him a magic potion to put the dragon to sleep so that Jason can steal the fleece.

Return to Iolcus

Jason, Golden Fleece in hand, takes Medea home to Iolcus. Ovid's version has Jason returning triumphant, handing over the fleece and reclaiming the throne with his bride by his side. Other versions include further trouble on Jason's return home. The tragedy that ensues between Medea and Jason is dramatically illustrated in Euripides' play Medea. Jason is said to have died when a piece of the Argo breaks off and crushes him while he is napping. The journey that the Argonauts take is suffused with fairytale elements and does not map onto real places or events as nicely as some of the later heroic sagas. While the story was being formulated, Greek explorers were traveling extensively in search of new trading and colonization opportunities, so the myth likely represents the heroic effort to expand the Greek vision of the world.

FURTHER READING: Apollonius, and R. L. Hunter. Jason and the Golden Fleece: the Argonautica. *(Oxford: Oxford UP, 2009); Euripides, Stephen Joseph. Esposito, Anthony J. Podlecki, and Michael R. Halleran.* Four Plays: Translation with Notes and Introduction. *(Newburyport, MA: Focus Pub./R Pullins, 2004); Apollodorus, and Robin Hard.* The Library of Greek Mythology. *(Oxford: Oxford UP, 2008).*

Juno

In Roman mythology, the wife and sister of Jupiter, identified with the Greek goddess Hera; she was the queen of heaven and protectress of females; she was particularly associated with childbirth and with the month of June, which was considered a favourable month in which to marry: at Roman weddings the bride's girdle was consecrated to Juno.

Jupiter

Rome's most important and powerful god, Jupiter came to Italy with the migrations of Indo-European speaking people. His name's first element, giving us 'Jove', is related to the Greek Zeus and to the Latin and Germanic words for 'day'. Its second element is simply 'father', bestowed on him and a few other Roman gods, just as Zeus was often so addressed. In their own literature the Romans transferred the many tales of Zeus to his Latin counterpart. Jupiter's cult was found in most parts of Italy and his functions readily became fused with those of Etruscan, oriental, and north European gods of like character.

In Italy Jupiter was revered as lord of sky and daylight. Rain and its consequences were owed to him. Thunder and lightning were sent by this god whom the Romans majestically represented with the thunderbolt and eagle which otherwise adorned every military standard. Because the ancient Italians trusted to natural phenomena in ascertaining the divine will, both thunder and lightning, together with the flights of certain birds were scrupulously observed as sent from Jupiter. All important public business could be validly transacted only if and when such heavenly signs were propitious. The Romans developed the interpretation of the signs into a fine art, the 'auspices.' Official consultation of Jupiter probably led the Romans to accord him pride of place among the political gods of the state religion. Since Zeus, too, enjoyed a comparable position in many Greek city states, the Romans and others may have imported into Italy the idea of the god as a defender of the people.

Jupiter's religion exhibits a number of cult practices. On the Aventine Hill, for instance, Jupiter Elicius had an altar, or a mere stone, by which the Romans could summon heaven's gift of rain. Smaller stones might be employed to solemnize oaths, for Jupiter also stood as guarantor of man's good faith. This aspect of his worship strengthened Roman political reliance on Jupiter because he sanctified the many treaties which played a fundamental part in ancient warfare and diplomacy. Besides stones, some trees such as the beech, and certain oaks were sacred to Jupiter; this attachment apparently arose from their relative susceptibility to his lightning. Thanks to his control of the rain, the god was beneficial to Mediterranean farming, and one of Jupiter's many festivals concerned successful grape harvesting.

Not only Rome's chief magistrates but also a priest and his priestess wife, the flamen Dialis and flaminica, ministered to Jupiter. No priesthood supplies a better index to the primitive quality which marks Rome's old religion. The flamen was compelled by law to observe and eschew many practices to which no other priest was bound, with the object of protecting him from pollution. Jupiter's flamen was forbidden to mount a horse, gaze upon the army, swear an oath, touch a corpse, or enter a sepulcher; he must not wear a ring unless perforated and without a stone, lend fire from his hearth unless for prescribed rites, knot his clothing or hair, or walk under grape bowers; he was not permitted to touch or speak of female goats, uncooked meat, ivy or beans; or to eat leavened bread; or to uncover himself out-of-doors where he was seen by his god. On the other hand, he was required to have his hair trimmed only by a free-born barber, and the hair trimmings and nail parings were buried under a fruitful tree; to sleep on a bedstead whose legs were smeared with clay; to sleep no more than three nights away from home; to allow no one to sleep in his bed and to keep sacrificial cakes at its foot; and at all times to wear his special white pointed cap (apex). By an outmoded ceremony he wed only a lady of his patrician caste whom he might not divorce; if she died, he quit the priesthood.

His priestess wife, the flaminica, was bound by her husband's restrictions and by a few of her own. For instance, she wore specially dyed clothing, kept a twig from a fruitful tree in her elabourate headdress, and did not ascend a ladder beyond the third rung. On certain days, she might not comb or arrange her hair although she apparently still wore the headdress. Some of these restrictions obviously belong to the priest of a sky god; others are simple taboos against flatulence or corruption by the dead. It is little wonder that toward 200 BC the flamen botched a sacrifice, thereby forfeiting his office and that there after eligible candidates for the priesthood rarely came forward. Ceremonial limitations left many priestly functions to the chief magistrates, the consuls.

Gorgeous Spectacles

In matters of war and government the Romans ever looked to Jupiter for help and advice. His major shrine on the Capitol gave him the name Capitolinus although the official style was optimus maximus 'best and greatest'. This temple had three chambers, one each for Jupiter, Juno, and Minerva. In the central chamber stood his statue garbed like a triumphant general in resplendent toga. Every fifth year the statue's complexion was reddened with lead paint. The god, as well as his triumphant model, had once been smeared with the blood of a fallen foeman. Founded by Rome's last Etruscan king, its liturgy was partly inspired by the Etruscans although the temple was dedicated by the new republican

Second-century statue of Jupiter of Smyrna, which was discovered in Smyrna (present-day Izmir, Turkey) in 1680 by the French. The statue was presented to King Louis XIV, and Pierre Granier restored the statue, adding the raised arm holding a thunderbolt. Initially displayed at Versailles, the work was seized during the French Revolution. Presently the statue is located in the Louvre Museum in Paris, France.

Iris and Jupiter, **Michel Corneille the Younger (1642–1708); Palace of Versailles, Versailles, Paris, France**

imperial point of view the Roman consul could no more omit this ceremony than he could fail to greet Capitoline Jupiter before and after his military expeditions.

While in late pagan times Jupiter's divinity attracted astrological and philosophical speculation and quickened religious syncretism (or intermingling), his Roman cult retained the savour of its simple beginnings and propagated veneration of the Empire's greatness. From first to last the Romans acknowledged him as their patron and lord.

R. E. A. PALMER

The Kindest Planet

Ever since the development of astrology as a study in itself in the 7th century BC, Jupiter, the largest of the planets, has been supposed by astrologers to be the most kindly-disposed of them, and for that reason is often spoken of in astrological literature as 'the greater benefic', the lesser being Venus, which is smaller. The zodiacal sign ruled by Jupiter, even when he was still the father of the gods and not yet a planet, appears always to have been Sagittarius.

Jupiter as a planet is constantly associated with wealth, high position, getting one's own way, promotion, prosperity, and all forms of status. Anyone who wants to choose a time to begin an undertaking, to make sure that it shall not go wrong, would be advised by an astrologer to pick a time when the Moon is going to be in a strong 'good aspect' of Jupiter. Similarly, if he chooses a time when Jupiter is fortified (that is to say, when he is in a favourable position), there should be no financial difficulties.

Although the chief association of Jupiter is with money matters, he is also concerned with social position, so that any question connected with

government in 509 BC. The god's puissance among the Romans encouraged them frequently to convene voting assemblies in its precinct. On the same height was situated the small temple of Jupiter Feretrius, a god of oaths. On its walls hung three sets of armour taken by Roman chief magistrates from enemy chieftains whom they had slain in battle with their own hands.

Jupiter enjoyed cult through public games that began as religious ceremonies and developed into those gorgeous spectacles for which the Romans were renowned. Feretrius's games included boxing matches and footraces held on oiled animal skins. Others comprised chariot races and, later, stage-plays produced under Etruscan and Greek influence. Like the triumphal games to which they are related, Jupiter's festivals were preceded by a lavishly-mounted parade of statues of almost

every deity installed at Rome, of state priests, and of the magistrates. The statues were borne upon platforms which also held paintings and religious paraphernalia. His games fell in September, October, and November and at one time totalled twenty-nine days. On 13 September, he received a banquet in return for the rain which had made possible the harvest.

Of equal historical importance was the festival of Jupiter Latiaris on the Alban Mount. Since time immemorial the Latins foregathered to offer annual sacrifice under a rotating presidency from the several constituent peoples of Latin stock. In later republican times the sovereign Roman consuls presided over this religious remnant of a Latin league. A truce of the god secured the sharing of the meat of sacrificial victims by the assembled Latins or, later, by their representatives. From an

The planet Jupiter

snobbery can always be answered by examining the aspects of Jupiter. He is also 'the greater benefic' in an entirely general way, and signifies success of any kind, including the recovery of health. Success is always thought to be indicated by the influence of a favourable planet, so even if one were setting out to commit a burglary, say, or any other crime, it would be prudent to try to have Jupiter on one's side. Even if this precaution did not lead to financial gain, it might bring luck to one's illegal enterprise by causing a policeman to look in the other direction at the critical moment.

The signs ruled by Jupiter are Sagittarius, the Archer, which is regarded as positive and masculine, and Pisces, the Fishes, which has been described as negative and feminine, though the sexes symbolically allotted to these two signs should not be taken too seriously. Both signs have a touch of that happy-go-lucky optimism which is one of the most characteristic gifts of Jupiter to his natives.

Typically, a person born under Jupiter will be good-looking, if not handsome; like those born under Leo, although to a lesser extent, he will have the dignity of a natural ruler. He knows what is due to him and expects to receive respect accordingly. He will probably have an impressive manner and in consequence is likely

to be elected to official positions in clubs and other organizations. Such men are often successful businessmen or heads of companies, for they like making money. They usually uphold the established order and their dress is conventionally respectable.

People whose horoscope is dominated by Jupiter in his less favourable position spend their lives betting but are unlikely to meet with much success. Looking on the bright side, however, they may well win a competition, be promoted unexpectedly, or meet with some other kind of unforeseen good fortune.

Keres

In Greek mythology, malignant spirits who brought all kinds of misfortune and trouble including disease, old age, and death; some believed them to be the executors of the will of the Fates and others that they were the souls of the dead.

Labyrinth

Or maze, a complex arrangement of buildings or intricate network of enclosed paths, from whose centre it is difficult to find a way out: to penetrate it and then return symbolized spiritual death and resurrection: to the ancients the labyrinth was linked with the idea of a sacred centre of ritual, reserved only for the initiated; the famous Labyrinth of Cnossos was said to have been built by Daedalus on the orders of King Minos of Crete, to hide the Minotaur.

Lares

As tutelary deities the Lares usually protected a given place which supplied them with their distinguishing epithet.

Far and away the most frequent, if not oldest, manifestation is met within the household (familia), where the single Lar Familiars (Household Lar) received regular monthly offerings of garlands on the hearth as well as daily observance at mealtimes. This Lar protected the household and its wealth, no matter how small, and was invoked on important family occasions: sometimes he also gave oracular signs to the householder. The Lar in fact came to symbolize the home.

In the oldest complete surviving Latin prayer, however, the Lares, together with Mars and certain 'seed gods', are invoked by the Arval Brothers (an ancient Roman college of priests) at the boundaries of the cultivated land (arvum). Where two fields joined, the Lar of each boundary line was honoured by the farmer and his slaves; both the convergence of boundaries and its marker were called compita. The compital shrine was a small tower with niches for every Lar thought to be present; here the Lares Compitales were found. Because the boundaries of property were usually marked by a path or a road, the Lares Compitales are best known from worship at rural crossroads and busy urban

Ancient Roman Lar

intersections. Sometimes they were the only or chief deities at country junctions where a hamlet comprised a few huts. At a normal junction, made by two roads, two Lares would be jointly worshipped; the practice became established, so that no matter how many lines converged, only two Lares were thought to be present. Even the Lar Familiars was depicted in duplicate, although each household had only one Lar. The Lares Semitales were venerated for their protection of paths (Semite) and the Vials their protection of highways (viae).

The great annual festival of the Lares was the movable feast of Compitalia, which fell soon after the winter solstice. Like other winter festivals, Compitalia called for artificial light, and the liturgical use of candles first appears here. Indeed, several aspects of Compitalia became an integral part of the Western Christmas festival. The Lares' victim was the pig, which was traditional Christmas fare until challenged by fowls.

Very early the Lares enjoyed the veneration of the humble and they became the most important gods of society's lowest stratum: slaves and freedmen. Such people were often foreign by birth, and the Lares exercised a strong force in their assimilation into Roman society. Slaves and freedmen especially observed Compitalia, for it was one of the few state cults to which everyone was admitted, regardless of condition. Much merrymaking used to accompany performances of crude, extemporized farces. As early as the 5th century BC, the Roman government expressed concern over the presence of foreign rites at the urban compita. It is very likely that drama was first performed in Rome by foreign slaves and freedmen for these winter festivals.

Imperial Takeover

Rome and her colonies were officially divided into neighbourhoods (vici), and the countryside into villages (also vici), to which belonged a public cult of Lares Vicinales or Compitales. Because the greater part of the population often consisted of slaves and freedmen, the freedmen mayors and slave attendants of each neighbourhood and village supervised regular worship.

Shortly after 12 BC, the Emperor Augustus converted this cult into the worship of the Lares Augusti, Lares of 'increase' associated with the worship of his genius, his personal 'procreative force.' Every householder's genius had been propitiated beside his Lar Familiars; in this way Augustus successfully adapted a long established cult to the new Imperial cult without imposing his direct worship in Italy (although outside Italy he was worshipped as an actual god). On compital altars portraits and symbols honoured the emperor and his family; sometimes Augustus donated statues of neighbourhood gods, who then acquired the epithet Augustus. In the months of May and August (the latter renamed after the Emperor) the altars were strewn with flowers on his behalf.

At many Roman intersections the Lares' marble altars stood before a small temple housing statues of two Lares and a genius. At most compita in Italy there would be a simple altar of stuccoed brick, built against a wall on which were painted the three figures. Lares were represented as Greeks wearing tunics and holding a wine bucket and Greek goblet; usually they appeared to dance while their faces suggested drunkenness. In contrast, a dignified Roman toga clothed the genius, who held a sacrificial saucer and cornucopia.

Grunting Gods

Lares rarely enjoyed grand worship in state temples. Among the exceptions were the Lares Praestites, 'protectors' of the Roman people. The 'grunting' Lares Grundules, called after the sacrificed pig, numbered thirty and protected the thirty civil divisions of Rome. The title 'Lar' could also be applied to other gods, such as Silvanus, lord of the forest. Aeneas, the legendary Trojan ancestor of the Roman people, is addressed as a Lar on a dedication of around 300 BC. This designation probably reflects the custom of adding the title Lar to foreign deities or heroes after their cult had been appropriated by slaves and freedmen: Orpheus, for instance, was venerated as a Lar.

The Lares' cult effected a remarkable social change by admitting the slave or ex-slave, now a citizen, to the native religion and giving him a public task. In 214 BC Philip V, Macedon's last great king and an enemy of Rome, acknowledged the value of the Roman practice of bestowing minor public office on freedmen. The Italians of southern Italy even imported the Roman cult of the Lares on to the island of Delos, their mercantile centre in the Aegean, in the 2nd century BC.

An invaluable contribution to Roman culture was made through the development of theatre from its origins in the festival of Compitalia, while universal participation in compital worship helped to assimilate foreigners into the mainstream of Roman life. The Lares Augusti marked the first stage of the Imperial cult, which later became overwhelming, and continued to thrive until the time of the Christian emperors. But such was the tenacity of this pagan domestic cult that vestiges still linger with us on 25 December and New Year's Day.

Manes

In Roman religion, the spirits of the dead; the name may be euphemistically derived from the Latin for 'good'; it came to be used for the spirit of an individual dead person but had earlier meant the dead as a collective group of divine beings, Di Manes; the dead had a festival in February, when they returned from the underworld to haunt the world of the living.

Mars

Among the ancient Italians there was no greater god than Mars, after Jupiter.

He was known by an unusual variety of cult names: Mars, Mavors, Maurs, Mamers, Marmar, Marmor, Mamurius, and the honourific compound Marspiter. Many Latin and neighbouring communities named a month after him, and our month of March preserves the memory of his veneration. The Roman month Martius embraced the spring equinox and by its season reinforced the god's oldest functions in agriculture. March marked the first month of the oldest known liturgical year at Rome. Certain state priests promoted the growth of crops at the onset of the year, prepared for the new year by cleansings and otherwise marked what we today keep as the New Year. For a time 15 March opened the official year but later yielded to 1 January, which acquired from 1 March such customs as decoration with evergreens. However, March retained many ceremonies of the new year as well as the constant cult of Mars which was mainly entrusted to the Salians, priests whose title seems to be derived from salire 'to dance, leap'.

On fixed days in March the Salians proceeded along an established route where they would stop at certain points and perform rites that included the chanting of some of the oldest hymns in the Latin language, beating time on the ground according to the ritual three-step, and carrying outmoded spears in which Mars lurked, and shields, one of which was sent from heaven. Their dancing and beating of spear on shield was probably thought to advance the growth of the crops. However, the priests' military accoutrements and the regular resumption of warfare in March always underlined the god's martial aspects. The surviving scraps of the Salian Hymns mention many Roman gods, and Mars himself in the form Mamurius Veturius, evidently the Mars of the old year. The hymns certify the Salians' concern for agricultural growth and the welfare of the infantry (armed with spears of a kind different from those which the priests themselves carried). Much of the Salians' intervention with their god was directed toward cleansing the community and its utensils.

Peculiar to Mars in Roman religion

Roman god Mars Cast of the 'Sarcofago matti' (dating from around 220 AD)

is the use of the horse. On 14 March a racing festival, Equirria, was kept for Mars on the Campus Martius, 'Field of Mars'. On the same ground every 15 October another race was run, after which a horse of the winning chariot team was sacrificed to Mars. The blood of its tail was dripped onto the hearth in the king's former residence, the Regia. The ashes were later compounded with the cremated remains of unborn calves sacrificed on 15 April and applied in the cleansing held on 21 April, Rome's birthday. The horse's blood may have been intended to ward off barrenness, while the cremated calves were sacrificed to invite fertility into the community.

A third race came in late February and presumably marked the end of the old year. The last month of the liturgical year was crammed with cleansing rites. The Quirinalia in February honoured Quirinus, an epithet sometimes applied to Mars. Both Mars and Quirinus had Salian priesthoods as well as their own flamen, a Roman priest peculiarly bound by religious restrictions. Quirinus as a distinct god was an offshoot of Mars who acquired considerable prestige of his own. As a promoter of peace, Quirinus represents the willingness of Mars to cease warring and to accept terms from the enemy.

Leaping the Boundary

At the end of May another priesthood, the Arval Brothers, annually kept their agricultural cult by invoking the name of Mars thrice in three different forms, by thrice repeating the petitions and by dancing the ritual three-step (tripudium). No older prayer than the Arval Hymn fully survives to us. After asking help of the Lares and before and after inviting the seed gods, the Brothers begged Mars to prevent the invasion of blight and the collapse of growing grain, to leap the boundary and to remain on the land. This prayer was sung five miles from Rome, apparently at the border. The god's arrival by avoiding contact with the boundary itself demonstrates an irrational fear which still survives: brides are carried over the threshold lest their stumbling bring barrenness. Mars was expected to remain on the land, but not to import barrenness. His protection of Roman ploughland (aruum) is paralleled by old evidence from one Umbrian town where, like the Campus Martius, two fields belonged to the Martial woodpecker, where Martial Growth (Cerfus Martius) was hailed for cleansing the community and for damning foreigners, and where this Martial Growth controlled two divine powers, Protection and Fright.

The Umbrian ceremonies are attested earlier than an elabourate ritual for cleansing Roman farmland by circling it with a suckling pig, a lamb, and a calf (suovetaurilia), with prayers and sacrifices to Father Mars who would defend and increase the land, its human and animal occupants, and all

Portrait of Hadrian as the god Mars, detail from a statuary group; Marble, Roman artwork (c. 120–140 AD)

the vegetation. In another Roman ritual of the same era, Mars Silvanus, Mars of the Woodland, received sacrifice within the woods for the good health of the cattle. From its oldest survivals the cult of Mars shows a primary concern for the health and welfare of all living animals and crops.

The Avenger

Just as old but less clear at the outset is the Mars who was the god of war. The Salian priests certainly observed in part a cult of war. After it became a formal republican assembly of all citizens, the Roman infantry always met on the Campus Martius and never within the city's sacred boundary (pomerium). The Field of Mars held the oldest known altar to Roman Mars. At the only archaic temple to Mars, which stood more than one mile from the city on the Appian Way, the cavalry formed for its annual parade into the town, and the infantry rallied at the outset of a campaign. Consequently it is often asserted that Mars was purposely kept from the city because he was bellicose. Indeed he was worshipped outside where the Romans expected him to promote growth. However, the Salians worshipped him only in the city and there, too, kept their shields and spears, which they addressed 'Mars, awake!' The early lack of urban temples does not prove that Mars was solely a war god in origin.

Some of the Martial temples may be of relatively late construction on sites where he did the greatest good, on the land. The Emperor Augustus greatly enhanced the god's material condition at the end of the last century before Christ. In 53 BC, the political and financial magnate Licinius Crassus had gone to Parthia (modern Iran) to seek military glory. Instead, Crassus was slain, his army routed and massacred, and his standards captured. Julius Caesar and Mark Antony vainly hoped to recover the first standards lost to an

enemy within memory, but the former succumbed to death and the latter to Cleopatra. It was left to Augustus to recover the standards by diplomacy. Not only did he represent his success as a military victory by depicting a kneeling Parthia and a triumphal arch on his coins, but he also lodged the standards in one of the two urban temples he built for Mars Ultor, 'the Avenger'. Thus Augustus made Mars responsible for a real military victory over Caesar's murderers at Philippi, as well as for a revenge upon the invincible Parthians. The Avenger's temple in Augustus's forum attained such importance that the grand plaza gradually exchanged the Emperor's name for the god's. Until some seventy years ago the street of Christian Rome which ran above the Forum Augustum was still called Via Marforio.

The early equation of Italic Mars with the Greek Ares lent great emphasis to the literary role of Mars as war god. Ares appears in Greek poetry mainly as a divine personification of war and violence. Some argue that Ares means 'destroyer', which if true would explain his relative lack of cult. Ares enjoyed prestigious family connections in mythology, where he is represented as a most unpleasant god. In terms of divinity Ares cannot compare with Mars, but most of the mythology of Mars was borrowed from Greek poets. Two peculiarly Roman tales show the difference.

One explains why the month of Mars comes at the year's beginning. The god sought Minerva in marriage. The withered hag of a matchmaker, Anna Perenna, pretended to have gained Minerva's consent, but herself wed Mars. The festival of Anna Perenna (which means little more than the 'everlasting year') fell on 15 March when a riotous and promiscuous mob kept her holiday. The marriage of Mars marks the cycle of the year at the return of spring.

Veiled Emigrants

Mars and Jupiter are the best known of the few oracular deities of the Italians. Through his special bird, the woodpecker (picus Martius), Mars could indicate future events. To be born in the month of Mars clearly distinguished a child and thus promoted the names Marcus and Mamercus. The Marsi of central Italy and the Mamertini of southern Italy are two peoples named after the god. The origin of the latter illustrates the double function of Mars. In prehistoric times a community troubled by want of food or by the scourge of a human enemy would vow all that was produced in a given spring to Mars and Jupiter. Jupiter received the animals born in that season. Upon reaching adulthood men born at that time were sent veiled (perhaps so that they could see no ill omen) from the boundaries of the dedicating community to found a new community. Such consecrated men were dedicated to Mars. Thus, we are told, the Mamertini earned their name.

An animal often led the consecrated emigrants. The Italic Hirpini were named after the wolf in these circumstances. The Picentes may have taken their name from the woodpecker. Although without any linguistic merit, the most famous of such names is Italus and its derivatives from vitulus, 'calf'. This belief originated among Greeks who remembered one band consecrated to Mars that was led by a calf. Accordingly, when her Italian allies broke with Rome in the late '90s BC, the Marsi had coins for paying troops of the Italian confederacy marked with the Italian calf trampling the Roman wolf, the Martial beast which had given fresh life to the infant Romulus and Remus.

Mars in Astrology

The 'Rogue Male' of the planets, Mars is considered rather dangerous, and likely to be involved in any act of violence. The colour attributed to him is red, the colour of anger, appropriately enough, for the closer he comes to the earth, the more obvious is the planet's reddish colour. Although Mars is said to be baleful and can be harmful to either sex, to women he is the natural significator of men in general, and husbands in particular; he also signifies the active callings of soldiers, policemen, athletes, sportsmen, and metal-workers. Even a scholar, if young or a husband, can be signified by Mars.

His character is impatient, tireless, excitable, easily moved to wrath but also readily appeased. He is neither subtle nor profound; if one assumes that a Martian is bluffing, one soon finds out one's mistake. In manner, the Martian is generally held to be rough and crude, lacking in refinement and uninterested in the arts. Learned men, however, need to have a good deal of Mars in their composition to persist in their often unrewarding and even tedious studies. Religious persons are frequently strongly influenced by Mars, for the religious need courage and tenacity.

The Gift of Energy

The greatest advantage of Mars is that he is never easily fatigued. He represents energy, and in consequence is never too tired to go on, and never too lazy to bother. He always insists on doing his work thoroughly. The man who does enough but no more is not a Martian, for a Martian enjoys labour and regards it with understanding, rather than as an imposition for which one is justified in exploiting one's employer. His pugnacious temperament will enable the Martian to fight his way through life, especially in the years of adulthood.

If Mars is the only dominant planet, there is a tendency for the rough and brusque manner identified with Martians to emerge; but there are four quarters of the horoscope in which

planets can dominate, so there must be many Martian people in whom the wish to use their energy is not their sole and prevailing drive.

One very common personality defect of Martians is that, although they have plenty of energy, they may be content to use it in whatever way is familiar to them, and lack the imagination and vision to launch out in a different direction. Another defect of which Martians should beware is that often they cannot accept things as they are and feel they must change them at all costs. A Martian schoolmaster would be likely to administer punishment to give vent to his own feelings, rather than because he considered it for the good of the offender. But Mars is as courageous as he is hasty; although he does not deliberately take chances, he is never afraid to run risks and seems to be utterly fearless.

FURTHER READING: For the god Mars, see R. E. A. Palmer, The Archaic Community of the Romans *(Cambridge Univ. Press, 1970). R. E. A. Palmer.*

Mercury

The name of the Roman god of trade derives from the Latin words for 'goods' and 'payment'. His worship thrived at the meanest level among tradesmen and shopkeepers. Unlike many Roman deities, he enjoyed no great state cult and priesthood. From first to last Mercury quickened business and fostered general prosperity. The Roman god of commerce was likened to the Greek god Hermes, who made him a literary gift of many attributes unknown to the Mercury of the true cult.

Rome's only temple for Mercury was dedicated in 495 BC on the Aventine Hill; its foundation accords with the major religious event at the

beginning of the Roman republic. The Aventine region and its cults were especially important to plebeian politics. A famine in 496 was followed by the dedication of a temple on the Aventine to Ceres Liber and Libera in 493. Although the trinity bear Latin names, they are in fact the Greek Demeter, Dionysus and Kore, honoured with a temple built by Greeks and paid for with Roman money at the instance of the Sibylline Books of Destiny, which contained the ecstatic utterances of the Sibyl, and which were a constant source and inspiration of Greek and Etruscan religion to the Romans.

Sometimes it is assumed, perhaps correctly, that Mercury's temple belongs to the influx of Greek religion and that it rose before the others in hopes that trade rather than growth itself, Ceres, might have alleviated the dearth of grain. Whereas the temple to the trinity was destined to become an important religious and political centre for plebeian political aspirations in the face of patrician exclusion, Mercury's solitary temple never acquired great glamour despite its obvious popularity.

Every May, on the anniversary of its founding, the temple became a meeting place for Roman merchants. Like many another club, this guild met the businessmen's need for a religious association and for an expression of their solidarity. (Craftsmen met under the protection of Minerva and had their own guilds.) The month of the dedication and the annual meeting seem purposely chosen to honour the Greek Hermes' mother, Maia. Since the Roman Mercury had no such mother, the Roman state and its merchants were apparently influenced in worship by Greeks, even down to mythological details.

The temple and its cult were entrusted to a board of Mercuriales who were drawn from the second rank of society, in contrast with the social eminence of other Roman priests. In two cases membership on this board was combined with membership on the board of Capitolini, who were in charge of the Capitoline Games held in honour of Jupiter. One man boasted that he was the elected leader of the Capitolini, Mercuriales, and the residents of the Aventine district; this priest had made his career first in the Roman army and later in the lower rungs of the civil administration under Augustus.

Clubs of Mercury sprang up wherever Latin-speakers went. These businessmen's associations sometimes styled Mercury Felix and thus retained the older sense of the word, 'productive, prosperous'. Despite the paucity of temples, Mercury was frequently honoured in Rome and other business centres with altars, statues, murals, and even small roofed shrines set especially at urban intersections.

The neighbourhoods worshipped him beside their ubiquitous Lares, guardian spirits. Augustus took a keen interest in fostering his lowly cult; accordingly, Mercury assumed the epithet Augustus, which recalled not merely the Emperor's devotion and benefaction but equally that title's derivation from the verb augere, 'to increase'. Before the time of Augustus neighbourhood Mercuries had acquired such peculiar titles as Malevolus, 'Ill-willing', in the case of one who faced no shop, and Sobrius where he was honoured by a milk libation in a district without a tavern. In contrast to the latter is a guild of wine merchants who were incorporated as the Club of Father Liber and Mercury. Liber was the Roman god of vine and wine.

In poetry Mercury always reflects the Greek Hermes. In one Roman poem he is made to sire the Roman Lares, who earned this prestigious parent through the humble association of neighbourhood religion.

Mercury, ancient Roman bronze figurine

Mercury in Astrology

The planet Mercury is not often seen with the naked eye, for it is never more than 28 degrees from the sun, and therefore seldom emerges from the golden glow of dusk or dawn. Because it is the smallest of the planets, and closely dependent on its parent, it is inevitably associated with children. Childish vices—lying, fraud and thieving, for instance—as well as childlike virtues such as ingenuous charm, are also attributed to Mercury. It is possible that masochists (using the word in a general sense to describe people who enjoy being treated severely as if by a stern parent) may be under the planet's influence.

Despite its childish qualities, simplicity was never a characteristic of this planet, for it was thought to influence the entire field of education, including all types of learning. Intellectual brilliance, quick-wittedness, and scholastic ability are therefore considered to be typical qualities of people born strongly under Mercury.

Mercury rules trade and commerce and those born under this planet are always intrigued by technical skills, and are often knowledgeable about trades such as carpentry and engineering. A Mercurian will always have an answer for any question; and although it may not always be correct, it will at least be glib and convincing. Although not all Mercurians are plausible rogues, the plausible rogue will almost always be a Mercurian.

The shy, timid, and tongue-tied people of this world need the Mercurians to speak up for them, and a discussion about whether or not the time is ripe for wages to be raised often turns out to be an argument between two Mercurians. It is likely that neither of them will become heated, for Mercury often appears to be rather cold and aloof, even in sexual affairs: unlike many other people, Mercurians think of these as just a part of the glo-rious game of life. When they marry, many of them do not really take their partners 'for better for worse, for richer for poorer . . . till death do us part'—as they think that, if the desire seizes them, the game can as easily be played with a different partner.

Among typically Mercurian professions is that of the journalist, for instead of being directly involved in life he is mainly concerned with viewing it objectively. A person born under Mercury may succeed in any learned profession, or as a schoolmaster who

Statue of Mercury, clock tower, Cardiff Castle, Wales

may have a wide general knowledge without being an authority on any one subject, or as a doctor. When a Mercurian is connected with the arts, it is often possible to discern a lack of the heavy, thoroughgoing seriousness which some artists seem to feel is the least that life deserves.

Mercury the Metal

Since the Renaissance there has been one fundamental principle in all alchemical thought: that matter is composed of the three 'philosophical elements' of mercury, sulphur, and salt. This theory had a very considerable influence.

The idea of what constitutes an 'element' has undergone considerable changes since the days of early science. The universe was at one time conceived of as a composite of tiny particles which had specific qualities. According to the teachings of Greek philosophers including Aristotle (384-322 BC), and also the early alchemical writings, the primary qualities are those of fire, water, earth, and air. These four 'essences' found their completion in the 'quintessence', the spiritual.

Many systems of correspondences were constructed on this basis. For instance, certain elements had an affinity for certain colours, planets, tastes and 'humors' (the four liquids present in the body, differing combinations of which determined both one's temperament and one's physique). This kind of systematizing was very important at a time when empirical science was considered to be less important than the cultivation and refinement of the old tradition; but in this form it dealt only with what we would call physical states of matter. It soon became clear that there were differences in nature which could not be totally explained simply by taking into account the differing combinations of physical particles; that there were also chemical differences in the modern sense.

Mercury, patron of the merchants

Following the philosophical dogma that the multitude of phenomena must be reduced to fundamental and simple elements, the earlier alchemists taught that all matter consisted of two different kinds of components: 'mercury' and 'sulphur'.

The alchemists began by dealing with the theory of metallic transformation. They thought that metals such as lead could be reduced to 'mercuric' and 'sulphuric' components when treated in the right way. The differences in weight, appearance, and so on were explained by a different composition of these two elements. The principal theory of alchemy was that the natural maturation of metals, from 'immature' or base substances to 'noble' and precious metals like silver and gold, could be artificially set in motion. The alchemists therefore experimented with methods that seemed likely to change the proportion of the combined elements. However, with the rapid growth of scientific knowledge in the Middle Ages it soon became apparent that this simple theory did not really work.

Salt, the Third Element

Paracelsus, the great Swiss scholar, enriched the theory by introducing a third 'philosophical element'—that of salt. The wealth of natural phenomena could now be explained more satisfactorily. According to this theory, salt is the element of palpability, tactility, tangibility; it represents noninflammability and fixity. It is because it contains salt that matter has weight.

Mercury, or quicksilver, stands for the fugitive qualities of matter, for its spiritual element, for mobility, and for the property of some material things to become liquid, so enabling the elements to influence each other. So without the spirit of mercury nature would remain motionless and unchangeable.

We can easily understand the great importance the concept of mercury had in the teachings of alchemy, whose basis is the artificial induction of evolution from the 'impure' to the 'noble'. It was said that the nearer a metal came to the ideal of 'golden nobility', the more mercury it contained. In many alchemical treatises, therefore, 'mercury' also stands for the materia prima, the First Matter of the Philosophers' Stone, and sometimes also for the Stone itself. Care must therefore be taken when reading alchemical texts not to confuse these various meanings of 'mercury'.

Sulphur is the element which gives natural things the quality of combustibility. No matter, according to the alchemists, could ever burn without containing a certain percentage of sulphur. One example, often cited in the writings of the Paracelsists, is a good illustration of what is meant by this theory of three elements; if wood is burned, the flames are nourished by its content of sulphur. That which flies up into the air as smoke and smell is the fugitive mercury. Salt is what remains in the ashes.

Such an all-embracing concept could also be extended to the philosophical sphere, giving alchemy its two aspects, the 'chemical' and the 'spiritual'. Man, being a microcosm himself, a miniature reflection of external nature, was also composed of three elements: body, soul, and spirit, corresponding to the three elements in the rest of nature.

SAL	salt
CORPUS	body
SULPHUR	sulphur
ANIMA	soul
MERCURIUS	mercury
SPIRITUS	spirit

When the alchemists wrote of transforming material things by rearranging their proportions of salt, sulphur, and mercury, a real chemical change could be meant, but the text could also have a hidden meaning; it could really deal with human transformation, thus misleading those who were greedy only for material wealth.

Of the three Paracelsian elements mercury is the one which is mentioned most often; it corresponded to everything that was regarded as belonging to the sphere of spirit. But again, 'mercury' could designate different things. Mercurium nostrum, 'Our Mercury' is often described as being different from ordinary mercury or quicksilver, which has the property, unique among metals, of remaining in a liquid state at normal temperatures. If this metal is dropped it forms into tiny elusive silver balls. The ancient scientists did not know whether quicksilver should be regarded as a metal or as a liquid. The German encyclopedist Johann Heinrich Zedler (1732–1754) describes it as:

A mineralic or metallic sap or humor (liquor), which is very heavy, liquid, and volatile and looks like a silvery fusion. It is a liquid which does not moisten, forming compounds with all metals, especially accepting gold eagerly, mixing and amalgamating with it; and it can be separated from it by a hot fire, but at moderate heat forms a compound again that never can be separated. Mercury is so piercing that—as Sir Kenelm Digby (1603–1665) says—'if you put it on the great toe of your foot and take a ducat in the mouth, it will get a whitish surface' . . . It is regarded as the mother of all other metals which, depending on their different mixture with metallic salt and with sulphur,*

> *In Greek mythology, a magic herb given by Hermes to Odysseus to protect him against the enchantments of Circe is described as having a black root . . .*

and depending also on the different influences of the celestial forces, are said to grow in their different ways.

In the early part of the eighteenth century the doctrine of Paracelsus was evidently still very much alive.

'Our mercury' is what is otherwise referred to as the First Matter (that is, the original matter) of the substance which is to become the Philosophers' Stone. George Starkey, an English alchemist writing at the turn of the sixteenth century, in his book *The Stone of the Philosophers: Embracing the First Matter and the Dual Process for the Vegetable and Metallic Tinctures* says:

All true philosophers agree that the first matter of all metals is a moist vapor, raised by the action of the central fires in the bowels of the earth, which—circulating through its pores—meets with the crude air and is coagulated by it into an unctuous water, adhering to the earth, which serves it for a receptacle . . . If it is sublimed leisurely through places which are hot and pure, where the fatness of sulphur adheres to it, this vapor (which the Philosophers call 'their Mercury') is joined to that fatness and becomes an unctuous matter, which . . . where the earth is subtle, pure and moist, fills the pores of it—and so gold is made.*

A Complexity of In Meanings

The term mercury may stand for the First Matter, but in the paradoxical language of the alchemical treatises it may also designate the matter undergoing transmutation, and finally the product itself, the mysterious Philosophers' Stone. C. G. Jung, the great Swiss psychologist, showed that it may also designate water, fire, the spirit of the air, spirit in general, or the soul.

Because of the medieval doctrine that postulated the existence of two elements, mercury and sulphur (before Paracelsus added salt), only two components of matter are mentioned as being of importance for 'the great work' in most of the old texts: something red and something white, or—in the language of poetical allusions—a red and a white rose, which are to be combined in the 'alchemical marriage' to form the supreme unity of the Philosophers' Stone. Alternatively, alchemists may speak of a male element, the red lion, and of a female element, the white eagle or the lily, which find their bridal bed in the retort in order to bring forth something new and potent out of the fire.

Modern chemists have often tried to follow the alchemical prescriptions literally and have, for instance, said that the red lion must be antimony trisulphide, the lily silver chloride, and so on—but it is hard to believe that the mysterious Stone would not be something more important and powerful. So we have to be content with thinking of 'sulphur' and 'mercury', or of soul and spirit, in whatever sense, as being combined mysteriously in order to bring forth the final stage which makes it possible to transform impure metals to gold, and to heal all diseases by making the elixir of life.

The Alchemical Marriage

The assumption of an original dualism of the two elements leads us back to the days of Alexandrian alchemy in Hellenistic times, when the gnostic systems exerted a powerful influence. Secret doctrines of all kinds and ages often speak of the two opposing principles which must be united in order to form again the divine integral unity as it must have existed before the Creation tore it asunder.

Dualism means tension, opposition, multitude—and so a dynamic universe is created; but the two halves, despite their different qualities, tend to be re-united in varying proportions of the components. In the language of alchemy, the element of sulphur and the element of mercury are found in different proportions in all natural things and in order to stimulate their evolution it is necessary to separate them, to lead them back to their original simplicity, and then to unite them in the perfect way. This union of the two pure elements is the 'alchemical marriage' of 'spiritual sulphur' with 'spiritual mercury'.

The idea of this marriage was conveyed in a variety of allegorical forms in alchemical manuscripts; such allegories expressed the necessity of combining the opposites, normally referred to as sulphur and mercury, in order to take part in the creative plan. The important thing was to know the right degree and proportion.

In a psychological sense we could assume this to mean leading the spirit (mercury) along the right path so that it is able to accept the soul (sulphur), and also the 'burning' sphere of instincts and desires, in a creative embrace which would bring forth a unified whole, a mature personality.

But this view would be too incomplete and theoretical if we were to forget the third principle, the bodily element of 'salt', which makes it possible to shape a system able to reflect the wholeness of human nature, into which the material process is involuntarily projected. Only by this means could the 'great work' of the alchemist become the perfect mirror of what the 'philosophers' wanted to see when beholding their furnaces and alembics.

HANS BIEDERMANN

Minerva

Roman goddess, identified with the Greek Athene; patron of arts and crafts, and the inspirer of wit and resource, she was a protector of cities among the Etruscans.

Moirae

The three Fates of Greek mythology, Clotho, Lachesis, and Atropos, first named in Hesiod's *Theogony*; moira originally meant a person's 'lot' or 'rightful portion' in life: the Fates were sometimes said to be present at birth because that is when an individual's lot is decided; in modern Greek folklore they appear on the third night of a child's life and fix the course of his life.

Moly

In Greek mythology, a magic herb given by Hermes to Odysseus to protect him against the enchantments of Circe (*Odyssey*, book 10); it is described as having a black root, a flower like milk, and being hard to uproot; it has not been convincingly identified with any real herb, though mandrake, garlic, and rue have been suggested.

Muses

In the earliest Greek traditions the Muses were goddesses who inspired poetry and song; gradually they came to be thought of as presiding not only over different kinds of poetry but also over the arts and sciences in general. As a result, Greek education in historical times was thought of as a combination of 'music' (roughly, any art over which the Muses presided) and gymnastic (or physical education). A museum (*mouseion*) was first a shrine, seat or haunt of the Muses, a home of music or poetry, and later a philosophical school and library, such as that of Plato in Athens, or the Museum ('temple of the Muses') at Alexandria.

The latter is described by Strabo, the geographer, who paid a visit to Alexandria in 24 BC, as being in the royal quarter of the city. It included a covered walk, an arcade with recesses and seats, and a large building with a common hall where the scholar members of the Museum went for meals. This scholarly association had a common fund. Its president, who was a royal nominee, was known as 'the priest of the Muses' shrine'. It is probable that members of the Museum were given an annual salary, but it is not known what detailed branches of scholarship were pursued. Certainly schools of medicine and mathematics were formed, lectures were delivered, and there was organized scientific research. There were two libraries, the chief librarian's post going to a man of letters who was also tutor to the royal household.

Mosaic of the bath of Achilles—King Peleus, Achilles' father, and the three Moirae Klotho, Lachesis, and Atropos

In Homer's *Iliad*, after the Olympian deities have feasted, Apollo plays his lyre as the wine goes round and the Muses sing, 'answering one another'. In one of the Homeric Hymns the Muses sing, again antiphonally, of the immortal gifts of gods and the trials of mankind, while the Horai (Hours) and Charites (Graces) dance hand-in-hand to Apollo's music, and the god himself actually takes part in the dancing.

The old bards derived their inspiration and usually their real knowledge of things from the Muses who were, for the epic poet Hesiod, 'the daughters of Memory'. The epics begin with invocations to the Muses. Odysseus, for instance, in Homer's *Odyssey*, compliments a minstrel by saying he must be inspired by Apollo or the Muses.

The Role of Apollo

Although Apollo's association with these goddesses is clearly attested in the early epics, and can reasonably be assumed to have derived from prehistoric times, the Greek traditions also suggest that the Muse goddesses and the god Apollo were brought by different routes to form their association on the Greek mainland, perhaps in Boeotia in central Greece.

For the Muses were originally mountain goddesses from the north, from Pieria and Olympus, whose later cult extended southward to Helicon and Parnassus. In historical times in antiquity their main centre was at Thespiae, an ancient town in Boeotia, where they were worshipped by a society named after Hesiod.

The origin of Apollo is more controversial, some scholars favouring a northern, and some an eastern origin, while others suggest a compromise twofold origin from north and east.

Opposite page:
The Muse Terpsichore,
Cosimo Tura (1430–1495)

A Company of Nine

Apparently the Muses were once three in number, but were later thought of as a company of nine. They were: Calliope or Calliopeia, 'the beautiful voiced', the epic Muse, who was represented with a tablet and stylus and sometimes with a roll of paper or a book; Clio, the Muse of history, who was depicted either sitting or standing, with an open roll of paper or chest of books; Erato, 'the lovely', Muse of erotic poetry and of mime, who was sometimes shown with the lyre; Euterpe, 'the well-pleasing', Muse of lyric poetry, was represented with a flute; Melpomene, 'the singer', was portrayed with a tragic mask, the club of Hercules, or a sword; Polyhymnia or Polymnia, 'Muse of the many hymns', was depicted in attitudes of meditation, normally without any characteristic symbol or object; Terpsichore, 'delighting in dance', was shown with lyre and plectrum, an instrument used for plucking stringed instruments, as Muse of choral dance and song; Thalia, or Thaleia, 'the festive one', Muse of comedy, of playful and idyllic poetry, was portrayed with a comic mask, shepherd's staff or ivy wreath; Urania, the heavenly Muse of astronomy, was represented with a staff pointing at a globe. These neat distinctions were developed in later antiquity, however, and names and functions differ according to the sources.

The traditional association of Apollo and the Muses is as familiar in Greek mythology as is their joint patronage of poetry, dancing and music. This association appears to derive from prehistoric times and is comparable with actual choral performances by a female chorus under a male leader. The poet Pindar (5th century BC), in one of his odes, describes how the Muses danced in a chorus led by Apollo with his seven-stringed lyre at the marriage of Peleus and Thetis, the parents of Achilles.

However that may be, those who argue for the more primitive and separate role of the Muses, before their association with Apollo, emphasize that the god was absent at the funeral of Achilles, as Homer describes it. For the poet says that the Nereids stood around the body, weeping bitterly as they wrapped it in the winding-sheet, while the nine Muses, answering one another, sang the dirge. A male would have had no part in an old traditional dirge such as this, performed exclusively by women.

The Muses have exercised great influence on the European cultural tradition. This is natural, as they were deeply embedded, from the earliest times, in the most basic cultural impulses of social life.

R. F. WILLETTS

Narcissus

A young man renowned for his perfect beauty but who spurns those who love him, he falls in love with his own reflection in a pool of water and dies. Ovid tells of Narcissus and Echo, a nymph who falls in love with him. Echo tries to show her love, but Narcissus rejects her; Echo spends the rest of her days in caves and caverns pining for her unrequited love, until her only remnant is her voice. Ovid has Nemesis punish Narcissus for his treatment of Echo by making him fall in love with his reflection. Another version has a different spurned lover Ameinias calling on the gods to avenge Narcissus' harsh treatment. Artemis arranges for Narcissus to fixate on his reflection, and this version has him committing suicide in despair that he cannot possess the object of his love (himself). The blood from his suicide produces the narcissus flower. Sigmund Freud and later psychoanalysts defined narcissism, or self-love, as a type of psychological disorder, and the myth has also been used as a metaphor

Thalia, muse of comedy, holding a comic mask; Detail from the Muses Sarcophagus representing the nine Muses and their attributes

for social commentary by authors like Oscar Wilde and Andre Gide.

FURTHER READING: Ovid, A. D. Melville, and E. J. Kenney. Metamorphoses. *(Oxford: Oxford UP, 2008); Graves, Robert.* The Greek Myths. *(Baltimore: Penguin, 1955); Storr, Anthony.* Freud: A Very Short Introduction. *(Oxford: Oxford UP, 2001); Wilde, Oscar.* The Picture of Dorian Gray. *(London: Oxford UP, 1974).*

Nemi

Site of a sacred grove of Diana in the Alban Hills, south of Rome, whose priest was Rex Nemorensis, 'the King of the Wood'; no one could hold the priesthood except a runaway slave who, having broken off a bough from the sacred tree, would engage the reigning priest in mortal combat, kill him and succeed to his office; the custom was the starting point of Frazer's *Golden Bough*.

Neptune

At first Neptune had no connection with the sea. His origins remain in doubt because the equivocal evidence points to both an Indo-European derivation like Jupiter's and to a purely Italian derivation like Mars's. Some would relate his name to that of an ancient Vedic water god and a shared linguistic root for 'moisture', while others draw attention to the Italian commonness of such compound names innus and to a possible equation with nethuns-sl, an incomprehensible word found in a single Etruscan liturgical text.

In Rome's oldest civil calendar the feast of Neptune was observed on 23 July in the interval between two distinct festivals of sacred groves. The Neptunalia may be linked to the grove observances because the single known detail of the ceremony is the construction of shacks from tree boughs that were ritually called 'shades'. Often, Neptune's summer veneration is explained by a desire to increase the water supply. Indeed, his only really old shrine was situated by the Tiber River. When his altar sweated water in 206 BC, the occurrence was duly recorded in the priestly chronicles. Such sweating, by no means unusual in the annals of Roman religion, conforms to the god's power. The Romans had regularly prayed to Neptune for his salacia, which later they believed to be the name of his wife. The word refers to the water's power to leap (salire) from a fresh source. Thus it seems that Neptune caused fresh water to flow.

In 399 BC the Romans first introduced the Greek ceremony of a banquet (lectister-nium) for the Twelve Gods of Olympus. Then Neptune was paired with Mercury, whereas in 217 BC Minerva was his partner at the feast. Presumably the first occasion saw Neptune as master of maritime trade and the second in relation to the importation of foreign crafts. However the banquets may be interpreted, Neptune never fully became a sea god. At Rome his cult partners were sometimes the freshwater sprites called Nymphs. At Comum on Lake Como where a local Neptunalia was celebrated, Neptune was joined by the anonymous Gods of the Water (Di Aquatiles) who must have belonged to the great lake. Elsewhere in Italy a ferryman would make an offering to Neptune. On the Danube he was coupled with the deity of that great river.

The Riches of the Sea with Neptune, Tritons, and Two Nereids, Luca Giordano Giuseppe Recco (1634–1695)

The triumph of Neptune, Roman mosaic from La Chebba, Tunisia, late 2nd century BC. Women representing the four seasons occupy each corner, along with agricultural scenes and flora. Bardo National Museum, Tunis, Tunisia

There were also maritime shrines to the god. For instance, a few miles north of Rome at Anzio a row of matched altars was dedicated to the Winds, Calm, and Neptune. A final example may illustrate the adaptation of the Latin Neptune to a great variety of circumstances. In 209 BC Cornelius Scipio successfully assaulted New Carthage by taking advantage of his knowledge of tidal ponds and marching from the coast. This prompted one historian to make Scipio invoke Neptune 'leader of the march'.

The decline of Neptune's actual Roman cult cannot be easily explained, because fresh water was always needed in ancient Rome and was venerated in the popular form of many nameless deities called Fontes 'springs'. The state cult may have shrunk into insignificance with the vast water supply made available by the aqueducts.

In historical times Neptune possessed almost no personality of his own because the Romans had long since made him over in the image of the Greek Poseidon, chiefly a maritime god.

Neptune in Astrology

Discovered in 1846, the planet Neptune was named after the Roman god. Astrologers once supposed that events strongly influenced by Neptune would have something to do with the sea, but this is now thought to be untrue.

Although the influence of Saturn is supposed to be the most unpleasant of any of the planets, that of Neptune can be equally bad or even worse, in an entirely different way. Saturn's unfortunate influence only demands infinite patience until it passes away; on the other hand, Neptune's influence causes violent emotional storms and disturbances, perhaps harder to bear. In marriage, if Neptune is strongly influenced by one of the malefic planets—Mars or Saturn —the couple will be unable to continue living together.

Yet the general influence of Neptune is not necessarily bad, provided one enjoys uncertainty: for instance, Neptune combined with Venus would provoke perpetual excitement about love affairs, with constant vulnerability to the attractions of novelty. Neptune with Jupiter would provoke worries about financial or other success.

If Neptune is in conjunction with the Sun, there is a danger of excessive self-interest or narcissism; the same may be true if Neptune is in close aspect to the ascendant or midheaven. If Neptune, in close aspect to Jupiter, is conspicuous in the horoscope, imprudent or exaggerated optimism may result; but with Saturn the opposite —exaggerated pessimism— may occur. When Neptune dominates the horoscope, everything, whether good or bad, becomes exaggerated; in fact Neptune may be called the 'planet of exaggeration'.

Neptune in conjunction with Mercury would make a good but sensational journalist, quick to see opportunities for exaggeration. Neptune with the Moon, however, is easily alarmed by 'scare' stories. The most famous Neptunian was Horatio Bottomley the financier, who rarely drank anything humbler than champagne, and who ruined thousands of small investors after the First World War by wasting their savings on a fraudulent get-rich-quick scheme.

Odysseus

Or Ulysses (from the Latin form of his name), King of Ithaca who was one of the Greek leaders at the siege of Troy; prominent in the *Iliad* and the central character of the *Odyssey*, which describes his adventures on his ten years' journey home after Troy had fallen; later writers depict him as a crafty rogue; he may have been a real chieftain around whom legends gathered.

Oedipus

In Greek mythology, a king of Thebes who was fated to kill his father and commit incest with his mother; to prevent this, as a baby he was abandoned in the hills with a spike driven through his feet, hence his name, 'swell-foot'; he grew up unaware of his true parentage, killed his father, Laius, solved the riddle of the Sphinx, and married his mother, Jocasta; when the truth was discovered, he blinded himself, and went into exile; Freud named the 'Oedipus complex' after him.

Olympus

Mountain on the borders of Thessaly and Macedonia, close to 10,000 feet in height, the highest peak in the Greek peninsula and the home of the Greek gods; also the name of several other mountains in Greece and Asia Minor.

Orpheus & Orphism

There is really no such thing as Orphism. There is Orpheus, the legendary singer, about whom various stories are told; and there is Orphic literature, that is, a mass of poems, mainly now lost, composed in different places at different periods for different purposes, and for the most part having nothing in common except that Orpheus was claimed as their author. Until not very long ago, it was taken for granted that these poems collectively represented the teaching of a body of people called The Orphics, and a great religious movement called Orphism was constructed and extensively written about.

The truth is that no prophet or sect had a monopoly of Orpheus' name. The 'Orphic' poems fit into no overall

Oedipus and the sphinx

scheme. The most that can be said is that under the Roman Empire one poem of a somewhat encyclopedic nature achieved a sort of canonical authority: new Orphic poems took account of it, and academic theologians accepted it as the authentic revelation of Orpheus. Its vogue is one thing that might be called Orphism.

Orpheus, like several other legendary singers, was held to come from Thrace, the semibarbarous, semimythical country to the north of Greece; or from Mt. Olympus, where the Muses themselves were born. And according to an alternative account of his parentage, Orpheus was born from the Muse Calliope and the most musical of gods, Apollo. But he was a mortal, with mortal descendants. Genealogies were constructed which made him the ancestor of other famous minstrels, including Homer. The number of generations inserted in these genealogies

implies a belief that Orpheus belonged to a period well before the Trojan War (13th century BC, on our reckoning). That is a period well covered by a network of Greek legends and genealogies which may preserve some genuine memories of the Mycenean age. But Orpheus, as a Thracian, stands outside the Mycenean world, and is only very loosely connected with the main body of heroic mythology.

Legends of Orpheus

Probably the best known of the stories about him is that he sang so beautifully with his lyre that not only the creatures of the wild came and stood entranced around him, but even the rivers stayed in their courses, and the rocks and trees came sidling down from the mountain. This eccentric miracle has no context, it is not associated with any particular occasion. It is true that a similar effect is

produced when Orpheus sings for the Argonauts, but that was at sea, and the typical trees and rocks are absent. The story was that Orpheus took part in Jason's famous expedition to get the Golden Fleece. Though not a stalwart fellow, he came in very useful, for among the dangers that had to be overcome on the voyage were the Sirens, who lured sailors to their shore with their beautiful singing, to sit and listen till they wasted away. Orpheus saved the Argonauts by striking up in competition. The tale belongs to the type common in folk literature, in which a group of companions undertake a difficult task and are able to survive a series of dangers because each of them has some special skill. It is older than the *Odyssey*, in which the Sirens are one of several motifs transferred from the Argonauts to Odysseus. But the identity of the Argonautic minstrel is not fixed in the tradition, and Orpheus himself need not be so ancient. We cannot trace him definitely earlier than the 6th century BC.

His other famous exploit was his descent to Hades to recover his wife—usually called Eurydice—after she had been fatally bitten by a snake. Again it was his singing that was important, enabling him to prevail upon Pluto and Persephone to make an exception and release their visitor. But (the story usually proceeds) he failed to bring her safely back: he looked back at her before they reached home, and the poor dear was at once compelled to return. This was a piece of magic, like others in myth and ritual, that could only be accomplished with averted eyes. But Orpheus remained one of the few, like Theseus, Hercules, and Odysseus, who penetrated to the land of the dead and returned to tell the tale.

As for his eventual death, one story was that Zeus struck him with lightning: an ambiguous fate, often the wages of sin, but sometimes the means of translation to a higher existence in

Orpheus, Roelant Savery (1576–1639)

Elysium or even heaven. The more widespread version, however, was that for one reason or another he was set upon by the Thracian Bacchants and torn limb from limb. Again, this is a typical theme. Orpheus is only one of a number of people (normally either young children, or men who interfere with the service of Dionysus) who are torn apart by Bacchants. But in his case there was a surprising sequel. His head, thrown into the River Hebrus, continued to sing. It was carried out to sea and across to Lesbos, where it was found on the shore still caroling away. It was installed in a chasm on the island, where it issued oracles to inquirers. Once more, a folktale element is involved, for there are several stories about murder victims whose severed heads retain the power of speech. We may say generally that the myths about Orpheus are of this sort, folktales that have attached themselves to a convenient hero. There seems to

be no residue of historical memory, and in answer to the questions who Orpheus really was and when he lived, if he lived at all, we must confess that we have no notion.

Orphic Poems

The practice of foisting theological poems on Orpheus begins, so far as we can see, with Pythagoras and his early followers, about 500 BC. Pythagoras was an intellectual priest-prophet who claimed to be an incarnation of Apollo. His teaching combined a superstitious insistence on old religious precepts and taboos with the novel doctrine of transmigration of souls through different animal bodies and different regions of the universe; probably also a mystical reverence for numbers. Writers in the fifth century speak of his 'making a selection' of certain writings, or specifically of his publishing under the name of Orpheus. We hear of rites which are 'called Orphic and Bacchic but are

really Egyptian and Pythagorean'. We know the titles of several poems of metaphysical content, nominally by Orpheus but remembered as the work of early Pythagoreans called Brontinus, Zopyrus and Cercops, and we can see reflections of Pythagorean thought in their subject matter. The 'Robe' may have developed a myth of Pherecydes (540 BC), for whom the earth's surface was a robe worn by the earth goddess after her marriage to Zeus the sky god. For Brontinus the weaving of the robe may have been more than a metaphor—an insight into the physical process by which vegetation spreads across the earth in spring.

The 'Net' must have been a rather similar poem. The knitting of the net illustrated the formation of a living creature, with its tissue built up loop by loop, its soul being the air captured in the interstices. Then there was the 'Mixing Bowl'; the mixing process played an important part in cosmological theory of the time and the cosmic mixing bowl reappears in Plato. Apart from these metaphysical expositions, there was a descent to Hades, probably a straightforward apocalypse in which Orpheus gave an account of his quest for Eurydice, and revealed to mankind the fate of souls in the other world.

In the second half of the fifth century we find Orpheus mentioned as an inventor of spells and incantations. But his principal gifts to mankind, according to Aristophanes, are 'sacraments, and abstention from bloodshed'. This implies a religious vegetarianism, a typically but by no means exclusively Pythagorean discipline. The sacraments referred to may include those of the Eleusinian Mysteries, for it is not much later that we find Orpheus named as their founder. The hero of Euripides' Hippolytus (428 BC) has been to the Eleusinian Mysteries, he follows a vegetarian diet in his desire for purity and holiness, and he 'has Orpheus for his master, paying service to the vapourings of many writings'. A little later, Plato tells of people who persuade both private individuals and the greatest cities (surely a reference to Eleusis) to take sacraments that bring purification and release from sin, personal or inherited; they offer 'a throng of books, of Orpheus and Musaeus' (another mythical singer). The purified, it is said, feast with the gods forever, while the rest lie in mud. In the next generation, Theophrastus notes it as a mark of the superstitious man that he takes his family every month to the 'Orpheus-ministers', who no doubt charged him a suitable fee for his salvation.

It was such a man, perhaps, who took with him to the funeral pyre an allegorical commentary on an Orphic theogony, not far from Salonica: the scroll was only charred, and a few years ago it came to light, the oldest surviving Greek papyrus and the only one found in Greece itself. Full publication of the text is impatiently awaited. To the same period, the late fourth century, belongs the oldest of the famous gold tablets, which turn up in tombs in widely separate places (Thessaly, Crete, Italy) down to the 2nd century AD. Although they say nothing of Orpheus, they throw light on that desire for personal salvation which often did take Orpheus for its evangelist. They are reminders to the soul of what to do and say in the other world; they are mainly in verse. The longest reads: 'Now you will find to the left of the halls of Hades a spring, and beside it a white cypress standing. Do not approach this spring. You will find on the other side cool water flowing from the Lake of Recollection; but there are guards before it. Say "I am a child of Earth and Sky, of heavenly race, you know it well: but I am parched with thirst, I perish. Give me, quickly, the cool water from the Lake of Recollection." And they shall give you to drink from the holy spring, and after that you shall enter the kingdom of the Heroes.' There are similarities to the Book of the Dead here, and many scholars admit an Egyptian influence.

But we must return to Plato, for only one side of his Orpheus has been described. He mentions Orpheus more often than any earlier writer, and this may not be unconnected with the fact that he was much influenced by Pythagoreanism. A Pythagorean origin should perhaps be posited for the Orphic theogony that he and presently Aristotle mention. (It is not yet clear whether it was the same as the theogony of the Salonica papyrus.) Like the old theogony of Hesiod, it gave a gene-

Orpheus surroundend by animals; ancient Roman floor mosaic, from Palermo, now in the Museo archeologico regionale di Palermo, Picture by Giovanni Dall'Orto

alogy of the gods, interspersed with narrative episodes. Its content seems not to have been startlingly different from Hesiod. But we cannot tell how it ended; and the ending will have been the important part, containing a religious message to which the genealogy merely served as a background. If it was Pythagorean, it may have set out the doctrine of transmigration, which Plato knows as an 'ancient account' told by 'godly' poets. He also mentions 'ancient sacred accounts' which tell of penalties imposed on souls by judges; and the imprisonment of the soul in a body as a punishment is linked with the name of Orpheus.

The Apparition

The theogony had a long and varied career. First, it was chosen as the opening poem of the Epic Cycle, an artificial chain of epic poems spanning the whole of legendary history, and this involved certain alterations and omissions. Secondly, at least one rival Orphic theogony appeared, totally different in content. It features Unaging Time, portrayed as a winged serpent, with extra heads of a bull, lion and god, coiled with a female counterpart, Destiny. Time produces Light, Darkness, and Chaos, and in the middle a shining egg. From it a splendid creature hatches, with golden wings, four eyes and horns, various animal heads, and the organs of both sexes. He has many names: Zeus, Pan, Dionysus, Eros, Firstborn, Phanes ('Apparition'), and more obscurely Erikepaios. The world is filled with radiance at his appearance, but he himself is invisible except to Night. He mates with her as well as with his own female parts, producing heaven and earth, and other gods, and so our world takes shape. This extraordinary poem is thoroughly oriental in inspiration, having its closest parallels in Iranian theology, and was proba-

bly composed in the East in the 3rd century BC.

There were now two or three theogonies by Orpheus in circulation, telling very different stories. The conflict was resolved soon after 100 BC, when a redactor forcibly conflated them, together with whatever other 'Orphic' material came to hand. There was a tale that Homer's poems had had to be reconstructed after his death from 'rhapsodies' (the Greek word means recitations) which he had left behind in different towns. So it was pretended that the new epic had been constituted from Rhapsodies of Orpheus, 24 of them as in the *Iliad* and *Odyssey*.

> *The Titans, diverting him with a curious assortment of ritual objects, cut him into seven pieces, which they boiled and tasted.*

Instead of being the permanent ruler of the world, Phanes was now the first of six divine kings. He was no longer Zeus and Dionysus: they were the fifth and sixth kings, born long after him. Yet Zeus remained the creator of the world, for he swallowed Phanes and the universe with him, and then produced it all over again. The climax of the complicated narrative came when Dionysus was set on the throne at the age of six. The Titans, diverting him with a curious assortment of ritual objects, cut him into seven pieces, which they boiled and tasted. But Apollo, by burying the pieces, was able to restore the child to health; the Titans were blasted with thunderbolts, and from the dirty smoke that this produced, man was created. His soul is immortal: after death it is judged, spends 300 years in pleasant or nasty surroundings, and is then reborn in a new body. But men aim to achieve

release from this round of ills, and Dionysus and Persephone are appointed to help them, if they perform the correct sacrifices and purification rites.

The dissection and cooking of Dionysus must be compared with the myths of Bacchants tearing people apart, and seems to be a mythical reflection of a procedure of animal sacrifice. We first hear of the death of the god as a local legend from Delphi in the early 3rd century BC. It is presupposed in a broken papyrus of about 220 BC which contains notes for a sacrificial ritual and prayers for personal salvation addressed to Demeter, Persephone, and Erikepaios (here probably a name of Dionysus). This reveals a cult in Greek Egypt very like what we would have to postulate, besides the rival theogonies described, to account for the contents of the Rhapsodies. It is noteworthy that Ptolemy IV, who ruled Egypt from 222 to 205, was a great devotee of Dionysus and claimed descent from him. He issued an edict that all who held Dionysiac sacraments must register in Alexandria, state who they had learnt their ceremonies from, and deliver a signed copy of their holy story. Various 'Orphic' poems must have been collected as a result.

'Orphic' Cults

The Pythagoreans still had shares in the name of Orpheus. As their interests spread, in the last centuries before Christ, to subjects like medicine, astrology and divination, their Orpheus modified his poetic output accordingly. Varro (116–27 BC) knew a poem called the Lyre, said to be about summoning up souls, and perhaps based on an analogy between the seven strings of Orpheus' lyre and the seven planetary spheres through which, in post-Platonic speculation, the soul ascended to heaven. The Elder Pliny

(23–79 AD) more than once cites Orpheus as an authority on herbs, a topic which Pythagorean writers were investigating by 50 BC at the latest.

The fact that Orpheus was adopted as the founder of the Eleusinian Mysteries should mean that he composed the sacred poetry, and a chronicle of 264 BC probably named him as the author of a cult poem on the rape of Persephone. In fact we possess such a poem, among the hymns ascribed to Homer, and parts of it are quoted as 'Orpheus' in a papyrus of the 1st century BC. The practice of attributing to Orpheus poems composed for local cults became increasingly prevalent in the Hellenistic period and under the Roman Empire. As early as 320 BC he is the founder of Dionysus-mysteries. Later we find him linked with cults in Aegina, Sparta, and Phrygia. We hear of a Corybanticum and of Enthronements for the Divine Mother, both belonging to rites in which initiates in the service of the Great Mother were set on a throne and danced round by the others. We hear of a Girding Song (in some cults, the initiate put on a special girdle); Verses for sacred investiture; Verses for founding a shrine; Verses for naming; Cosmic invocations for Salvation; Oaths. There must have been much more. One specimen of 'Orphic' cult poetry has come down to us intact: a collection of 87 hymns, very homogeneous in style and probably the work of a single author in the 2nd or 3rd century AD. He refers to himself as Orpheus, and alludes to the Rhapsodies. The hymns were apparently used by members of a private religious society who met at night in a house somewhere in west Asia Minor and prayed to all the gods they could think of, to the light of torches and the fragrance of eight varieties of incense. Occasionally their ceremonial extended to a libation of milk. Dionysus is prominent, being the recipient, under different titles, of eight hymns. We

get a picture of cheerful and inexpensive dabbling in religion by a literary-minded circle.

The tradition of sub-scientific Orphica continued concurrently. There is record of a *Book of Eighty Gems* (on the magic properties of stones), various astrological poems, and directions for divination from birds, dreams, eggs, entrails, and earthquakes. Two compositions that stand apart from the rest are the Testament, possibly a Jewish effort, in which Orpheus repudiated his earlier teachings and acknowledged a single God, and the Argonautica, a short and derivative epic in which Orpheus described his participation in Jason's expedition. The poem is hardly earlier and perhaps later than the 4th century AD. It was consciously designed as an addition to an already bulky corpus of Orphic literature, for Orpheus begins by reviewing his previous compositions. He summarizes part of the Rhapsodies, and mentions among other things Corybantic rites, Demeter's search for Persephone, cults of Lemnos, Samothrace, Cyprus, and of Osiris in Egypt; poems on astrology, divination, purification, propitiation of gods and departed spirits, and an eyewitness account of the underworld.

Such was Orphic literature at the time: a vast hotchpotch. But pride of place is given to the Rhapsodies;

and Dionysus is the god with whom Orpheus is most firmly associated in cult. The reason is perhaps simply that the Dionysiac mysteries were more popular than any other. If it had fallen to a Greek god to conquer Europe, it would have been Dionysus; and the Orphic Rhapsodies would have been our Bible. Among our Apocrypha might have been the Bacchica, a late poem which reidentified Dionysus with Zeus and Phanes, holding all these names to be titles of the divine Sun. But for the Neoplatonist philosophers of the fifth and sixth centuries, 'Orpheus' meant primarily the Rhapsodies. They discussed the poem in seminars and written commentaries, quoted it constantly, and misunderstood it completely, finding in it an allegorical exposition of their own vapid metaphysics. In antiquity as in modern times, Orpheus was all things to all men.

M. L. WEST

FURTHER READING: I .M. Linforth. The Arts of Orpheus. *(Arno reprint);* W. K. C. Guthrie, Orpheus and Greek Religion. *(Methuen, 2nd edn., 1952);* W. Strauss. *Descent and Return: the Orphic Theme in Modern Literature.*

Orpheus and Orphic and Dionysiac mystical rites

(Harvard Univ. Press, 1971); J. Warden, ed. Orpheus: the Metamorphosis of a Myth. *(Univ. of Toronto Press, 1982).*

Ovid

Roman poet, 43 BC to 18 AD, Ovid specialized in the 'elegiac couplet' (hexameter line followed by pentameter line). He was very prolific, and many of his works survive, including a series of erotic poetry, poems dedicated to the monthly festivals (*Fasti*), several works reflecting his time in exile, and *Metamorphoses* (Transformations), which are important sources of classical mythology. He was renowned in his time as a great poet, and his influence continued throughout the Western literary tradition, inspiring works by Shakespeare, Cervantes, Dante, singers and performers of medieval literature, and even James Joyce, whose Daedalus character is informed by Book VIII of *Metamorphoses*.

FURTHER READING: *Ovid, A. D. Melville, and E. J. Kenney.* Metamorphoses. *(Oxford: Oxford UP, 2008); Fantham, Elaine.* Roman Literary Culture: From Cicero to Apuleius. *(Baltimore: Johns Hopkins UP, 1999); Galinsky, Karl.* Augustan Culture: An Interpretive Introduction. *(Princeton, NJ: Princeton UP, 1998).*

Pan

Perhaps the most appealing introduction to the worship of Pan, the strange deity of the Greek countryside, is the Homeric Hymn to the god. It is imbued with an idyllic charm, a salute to the god of flocks and herds, whose old home was in remote Peloponnesian Arcadia, surrounded by mountains.

The poet begins by appealing to the Muse to tell him about Pan, son

Pan with panflute

of Hermes, with his goat's feet and his two horns, a lover of noise. This strikes a traditional note at once for, although genealogies vary, Hermes and Pan were both shepherd gods of Arcadia. The god, continues the poem, wanders through the woodland glades with dancing nymphs who tread the sheer hill crests, invoking Pan, the long-haired and shaggy deity whose haunts are the snowy ridges, mountain peaks and rocky ways. He goes through dense thickets, now drawn to gentle streams, now climbing up to the topmost peak from which the flocks can be watched. Often too he darts across the mountain slopes as a keen-eyed hunter.

The Arcadians themselves were famous as hunters and it was natural for their goat-footed god to represent an occupation that was so familiar to his worshippers. It was also natural for them to describe the herdsman god as playing his pipes in the evening when the sport was over, vying with bird songs. At times the clear-toned mountain nymphs are with the god, moving nimbly, and singing their songs, that echo around the mountain top, by a spring of dark water, while Pan joins in the dancing. He wears a lynx-pelt on his back as he delights in the songs in a soft meadow, where the crocus and the fragrant hyacinth are mingled with the grass.

This passage is reminiscent of a choral ode from the *Helen* of Euripides (translated by Richmond Lattimore):

I was down by the shining blue
water, and on the curl of the grass
there in the golden glare of the sun
laid out the coloured wash
in the bed of the young rushes
to dry. There I heard my lady
and the pitiful sound as she cried out,
the voice of sorrow, lament without lyres,
a sharp voice of pain, of mourning
as cries aloud for grief some nymph,
a naiad, caught
in the hills for all her flight, gives voice
to pain, as under the rock hollows
she cries out
on Pan and his captured marriage.

Nymphs Bathing, Antonio Muñoz Degrain (1840–1924)

Hermes took his son in his arms and there was boundless joy in his heart. Carrying him closely wrapped up in the skins of mountain hares, he went swiftly to the abodes of the immortal gods. (The hare, by the way, is a symbol of Pan on some ancient coins.) He set the child down beside Zeus and showed him to the other gods. They were delighted, Dionysus especially; and because the child gave them all such pleasure, they called him Pan which, according to the Homeric Hymn, is derived from the Greek word for 'all', pas. This derivation is also given by Plato; and it has further been suggested that the Orphic identification of Pan with the cosmos, 'the all', must have been caused by this particular piece of etymology.

'Panic' Terror

Pan had no part in the old traditional Olympian pantheon, and in the 5th century BC Herodotus spoke of him as one of the more recent Hellenic deities. No doubt he had been revered in the fastnesses of his native Arcadia long before his name and cult spread to other parts of Greece.

Pan was certainly a late arrival in Athens, where he was worshipped in a cave under the Acropolis, perhaps because he was supposed to have helped the Athenians at Marathon by casting 'panic' terror into the Persian ranks. Certainly Pan could cause sudden panic among herds, when the animals, seized inexplicably by fright, would rush away; and panic among armies was also thought to be clearly the work of Pan, as the name bears witness.

Herodotus tells how the fast runner, Pheidippides, was sent off to Sparta before the battle of Marathon. On the way he was accosted by Pan, who addressed him by name and bade him ask the Athenians why they neglected him when he was so kindly disposed toward them, had often helped them in the past and would do so again in

the future. As soon as they could turn their minds to such matters the Athenians therefore set up a shrine to Pan under the Acropolis and established in his honour yearly sacrifices and a torch race.

Pandora

In Greek mythology, the first woman, created by Zeus to punish men after Prometheus had brought them the gift of fire; she opened the great jar or box in which all evils had been confined, so letting them loose to plague the world; her name, which means 'All-giving', suggests that she was originally an earth goddess.

Persephone

In the literature of Greek mythology Persephone appears most often as the young daughter of Zeus and Demeter, who was carried off by Hades (or Pluto) to be his bride. Her name has taken various forms—Persephoneia, Phersephone, Persephassa, Phersephatta, Periphone—according to literary or spoken dialect. No etymology has been found for it in Greek in any of the various forms. It is therefore likely that it was pre-Greek and was difficult for Greeks to pronounce. The classical Latin Proserpina seems to be a simple mispronunciation.

Homer calls her 'dread Persephone' and makes her the wife of the lord of the underworld, terrible herself and sender of terrifying ghosts and apparitions, like Hecate—with whom she was sometimes identified. She controls the appearance of specters, including that of Tiresias in the *Odyssey* (book 11) when Odysseus consults the oracle of the dead.

In this book, indeed, she seems more truly ruler of the underworld than

The Abduction of Proserpina, Rembrandt (1606–1669)

Persephone and Hades

Hades himself. As such she perhaps descends from a pre-Greek goddess who would have been, like the Sumerian Ereshkigal, mistress of the underworld. Hesiod in the *Theogony* is the first to call her daughter of Demeter and alludes to her rape. But the superb myth of her abduction and of Demeter's angry grief appears for the first time in the *Homeric Hymn to Demeter*.

Persephone was playing as a maiden away from her mother on the Nysian plain in a meadow with the daughters of Ocean. As they were gathering flowers, she came upon the narcissus, a marvelous radiant flower, and reached for it with both hands. At this, the earth suddenly opened and Aidoneus (Hades) sprang out with his golden chariot and immortal horses. He caught her up and carried her away across the world and down to the infernal regions while she lamented and cried shrilly upon her father Zeus. But no one heard her except Hecate in her cave and the sun god Helios, until Demeter too heard when it was too late. Demeter was led by Hecate to Helios, who alone had seen how her daughter had disappeared, and the sun god tried to comfort Demeter by saying that Aidoneus, brother of Zeus, was no unworthy husband.

Pomegranate Seeds

Demeter in her wanderings arrived at Eleusis, disguised as an old woman. There she nursed the king's child, warming him in the ashes of the fire to make him immortal, until she was discovered doing so by the queen. She then revealed herself as a goddess and a temple was built for her at Eleusis, where the goddess of crops sat mourning, making a dreadful year for mortals during which nothing grew. Finally Zeus sent Hermes to order Aidoneus to restore Persephone, so that the human race should not perish. Aidoneus obeyed, but Persephone had eaten six pomegranate seeds, and Hermes brought her back to Demeter in the chariot of Aidoneus. Demeter, as she held Persephone in her arms, felt a misgiving and asked her whether she had tasted any food down below. If she had done so, she must spend a third of every year among the dead. Zeus confirmed that she should spend this period of time in the underworld and the rest among the gods.

The Nysian plain has a name that is otherwise associated with Dionysus, whose sacred mountain was Nysa. For this reason some scholars have argued that Aidoneus in the Hymn is another name for Dionysus, who had connections with the underworld.

The place where Aidoneus's chariot descended is variously given according to local cults of Persephone. In Attic cult it was Erineos, the place of the wild fig tree by the river Cephisus near Eleusis. This tree had a connection with the subterranean Dionysus. Though the Hymn has a special link with the cult of Demeter at Eleusis, Enna in the heart of Sicily became in later literature a favourite scene for the rape, for it had a native Sicilian cult of the infernal powers.

Variations on the Myth

Less well-known is the myth of Theseus and Pirithous, who made an expedition to the underworld in the hope that Persephone could replace Pirithous's lost wife.

Nonnus, an epic poet of the 5th century AD, retails, perhaps with some additions, an Orphic myth outside traditional lore. Persephone, kept at home by her mother but desired by all the gods, was conveyed to Sicily and there guarded by dragons, until Zeus himself, taking the form of a dragon, seduced her. She became the mother of Zagreus, the earlier form of Dionysus, whom the Titans tore to pieces.

Commentators have pointed out that the myth of Persephone is the sacred story that accompanies the ritual of sowing corn. Demeter is the corn mother, representing the seed corn that is stored underground during the deadening heat of summer, until it is brought out again in the autumn, is sown, and sprouts. The sprouting is the return of Persephone the Maiden. Demeter and Persephone are in a sense one, as the growing corn that vanishes and reappears.

E. D. PHILLIPS

FURTHER READING: C. Kerenyi. Eleusis: Archetypal Image of Mother and Daughter. *(Princeton Univ. Press, 1967); T. W. Allen, W. R. Halliday, and E. E. Sikes.* The Homeric Hymns. *(AMS Press reprint).*

Plato's Myths

All Plato's dialogues are themselves stories. They are imaginary conversations, often with vividly drawn characters and settings so well presented that readers find them easy to imagine and remember. And they are full of stories of all sorts, and word-pictures which could sometimes be developed into stories, which are designed to bring home to the reader the various points which Plato wants to make.

Plato knew that if you want people, not just to accept the conclusion of an argument as correct, but to believe something effectively and act on it, you must engage and convince every part and level of their psyche, including what we should call their imagination and feelings as well as their reason (and, for Plato, reason in its highest operation has in it a large element of what we should call imagination). It is not a matter of just assenting to the conclusion of an argument, but of directly seeing or experiencing something, a flash of imaginative intuition in which an eternal truth makes itself immediately present to the mind. These intuitions are rare and Plato seems to have thought that stories would help in the early stages of preparing the mind for them.

The stories he tells in the dialogues, which are usually referred to as Plato's 'myths', are of many different kinds and degrees of elabouration. Some of them are straight allegories, like the story of the birth of the love god, Eros, in the Symposium. At Aphrodite's birthday party in the heavenly palace of Zeus, the Spirit of Business Success, having drunk too much, had a rest in the garden, and the Spirit of Poverty slipped in and induced him to make love to her, and so Eros was begotten; a strange intermediate being sharing the characteristics of both his ill-assorted parents.

A strange story which Plato uses in a subtle way is the myth told by Aristophanes, again in the Symposium. This tells how once upon a time human beings were spherical, with two faces (one on each side of the head) four arms and four legs. There were three sexes, male, female, and hermaphrodite. They were strong and could move very fast by turning cartwheels, and they threatened to storm heaven in the arrogance of their strength. Zeus thereupon split each of them in two, and Apollo shaped and rearranged the halves into the sort of human beings we are today. Since then we have all been half-humans who go about looking for our other halves, and falling in love with them when we find them. Love (homosexual or heterosexual, according to the sex of the complete human one is really half of) is just the desire of wholeness, the desire to become a complete human being by reuniting the two halves.

In the *Statesman* there is a very odd cosmic parable, designed to show that there are two forces at work in the world, the divine reason and a sort of basic irrationality. It tells how in one cosmic period God spins the universe one way, and in the next it spins itself the other way and everything goes into reverse until God takes control again. Of course, none of it is intended to be taken literally, and the details cannot be interpreted one by one allegorically—they are just part of the imaginary picture. This is also true of the greatest of Plato's myths, which are stories about the destiny of man and the origin of the world. There are four great stories, in the *Gorgias*, *Phaedo*, *Republic*, and *Phaedrus*, which present imaginative pictures of man's life in the other world to which he rightfully belongs and where he returns when he is not incarnated in an earthly body. The story in the *Phaedrus* gives an imaginative explanation of why true philosophical lovers fall in love, and of how they should live and love in order to escape as quickly as possible from the wheel of reincarnation, and return finally to the divine world from which they came. In explaining this, Plato uses an image of immense power and great influence, that of the soul as a chariot (the reason) driving two horses, a vicious one (the bodily passions) and a spirited but tractable one (the higher emotions).

The Divine Craftsman

The other three stories are all about the life of the individual soul between incarnations, when it is judged for its behaviour in this life, brought to a place of punishment or reward, where it remains for a very long time, and eventually is either reincarnated in another earthly body (human or animal) or escapes finally from reincarnation.

In these stories Plato is concerned to get across, imaginatively, doctrines in which he certainly believed—that the soul is immortal (before birth as well as after death); that it rightfully belongs to a higher world, the world of pure intelligence and its eternal objects; and that we are morally responsible, and our fate after death will be determined by the way we choose to live here. But he does not commit himself to the details of his stories—they are just part of the imaginative picture. The basic ideas with which he operates, and many details of the geography of the other world, are taken from a sectarian religious tradition, probably not very ancient, the tradition of the groups called 'Orphic' and the Pythagorean philosophers.

Plato's myth about the origin of the world occupies nearly the whole of quite a long dialogue, the *Timaeus*. This is exceptional. Most of the myths are quite short, and the dialogues in which they occur are predominantly philosophical discussions. Plato seems to have put his account of how divine intelligence made the world (and he certainly believed that it did) into story form for two reasons. Firstly, one cannot give an absolutely certain and completely rational account of something like the physical universe, which is always changing. One can only tell a likely story about it. Purely rational discourse can only be about the unchanging realities known by

Plato's Academy mosaic

pure intelligence. The other reason may be that divine intelligence is for Plato something mysterious. It is very difficult indeed for human beings to know what it really is; they can only make more or less inadequate comparisons to suggest what it is like. So in the *Timaeus* divine intelligence is compared to a perfectly good Craftsman who wants to share his goodness generously by making the best possible world according to the best model, the Real Living Thing, an organic unity or universe of immaterial eternal realities. The story tells how he set about making the physical world on this model, and how he coped as best he could with the built-in irrationality in all that is material.

The *Timaeus* was intended to be followed by another long story-dialogue, the *Critias*, of which we have only the beginning. This was to tell in full one of Plato's most famous stories, the story of Atlantis, which is summarized in the introduction to the *Timaeus*. The story relates how the great, rich, arrogant imperialist power of Atlantis invaded the civilized world from its island base in the Atlantic Ocean, and how it was defeated by prehistoric Athens, which Plato intended to represent as his ideal state of the Republic in action; the best possible human city, trained and led by philosopher kings, going out to defeat the forces of tyranny and set the whole world free. The story was to end with Atlantis sinking beneath the sea. Whether Plato knew (as his speaker in the story says) some ancient tradition of a great disaster can never be certain—some dim memory of the volcanic eruption which destroyed Thera (Santorin) might have survived, and he may have known of it; but he was quite capable of making the whole thing up himself. What is certain is that it would not have been a story mainly about Atlantis but about an idealized ancient Athens which was also Plato's Republic, and that Atlan-

Pluto abducting Persephone, colonnade in the park at Versailles, Paris, France

tis itself would not have been any sort of ideal state, but an evil and aggressive power.

A. H. ARMSTRONG

Pluto

The god commonly known as Pluto in Roman times and later, was also and more often in earlier times called Hades (Aides), though that name has come to be used in modern languages for the underworld where he lived as lord of the dead. In Greek there is also the form Aidoneus, used by Homer in the *Iliad* and in the Homeric Hymn to Demeter; in Latin he is called Dis, a translation of the Greek Plouton

which means 'wealthy', and Orcus, commonly derived from the Greek horkos, 'oath', because his name was used in oaths. He is also called the subterranean Zeus (Zeus kat-achthonios) as in the *Iliad* (book 9). Among the gods he is the most hated by men, who rarely honour him with cult, and the most separate from other gods. He remains nearly always in his own realm, the House of Hades. The name Hades is generally agreed to mean 'the unseen one'. Hades is the son of Cronus along with Poseidon and Zeus, but he is seldom active in Greek myth.

According to Homer, when Zeus and the other Olympians had overthrown Cronus and his Titans, Zeus divided the world between himself,

Poseidon and Hades: Zeus had the sky, Poseidon the sea, and Hades the misty darkness, while the earth and Olympus were common to all (*Iliad*, book 15). In the *Odyssey* Hades as a person is mentioned in Book 11 but always along with Persephone. In the *Theogony* of Hesiod the underworld, including Tartarus, is described as a vast abyss and the prison of the overthrown Titans. Its entrance in the far west is reached by Day and Night in turn as they travel across the sky to 'the awful home of murky Night', which never holds both at once. Somewhere near the entrance, 'there in front', stand the echoing halls of Hades, god of the lower world, where he dwells with Persephone. A fearful hound guards the house, evidently Cerberus.

The Cap of Invisibility

There is only one famous action of Hades or Aidoneus in Greek myth: his breaking through the earth with chariot and horses to carry off Persephone. The narcissus, which Persephone tried to pluck, had special links with the underworld. Horses, too, had a connection with it in its most alarming aspects and Hades is often called klytopolos, 'owner of renowned horses'. Hades is active once more in a curious myth told in the *Iliad* (book 5). Hercules wounded him with an arrow 'at Pylos among the dead' and caused him so much pain that he went up to Olympus to have the arrow drawn out of his shoulder by the healer god Paieon. The commentator Eustathius explains that Pylos here is not the town mentioned in Homer but the gate of the underworld. This passage again suggests that Hades was believed to have his dwelling near the entrance of the underworld as a war-

den of the dead, which would suit one of his titles, pylartes, 'fastener of the gates'. But this pitiless guardian of the dead was simply strict and rigorous, he was not any kind of devil, and his realm, except for some places where notorious offenders were punished, was not a hell, but the common destination of mankind.

A mythical object which by its name was connected with Hades was the helm or cap of Hades, Aidos kynee. The name has the general sense of 'cap of darkness' or 'cap of invisibility'. It is worn by Athene in battle with Ares in the *Iliad* (book 5), by Hermes in battle against the giants and by Perseus in his attack on the Gorgons. It is not worn by Hades, nor in Greek art is it shown on his head, nor is it certain that he really owned or lent it.

As one of the chthonic or underground powers, Hades or Pluto has

Pluto, detail of a sculpture by François Girardon (1677–1699)

not simply the gloomy aspect which he wears in the epic tradition, nor is he only the lord of the underworld. This is obvious from the name Pluto, connected with ploutos, 'wealth', a word which originally meant the wealth of crops which grow out of the ground and of precious minerals which lie beneath it. In this aspect he is thought worthy of cult by Hesiod: 'pray to Zeus beneath the ground'. It was in this aspect again that Hades was associated in cult with Demeter and Persephone at Eleusis. He is called 'another Zeus' by Aeschylus in his Suppliants and as Zeus katachthonios he is mentioned in Homer with Persephone as enforcer of a father's curse. He is in this sense a power supporting life and the family.

The entrance to the realm of Hades was seen in many caves and clefts to be found about Greece and also in parts of Italy settled by Greeks. The most famous in Greece were the cave of Taenarum in southern Laconia and a whole region of Thesprotia in the northwest. Thesprotia had rivers called Acheron and Cocytus and a lake called Acherusian, all of them names belonging to the mythical Hades, and also an oracle of the dead which, in some traditions, Ulysses visited. Pausanias remarks that Theseus and Pirithous invaded Thesprotia to carry off the king's wife. This looks like a version of their descent into Hades to carry off Persephone. Plutarch says that the heroes went to Epirus to steal the daughter of Aidoneus, king of the Molossians, who had a wife called Phersephone and a dog called Cerberus.

The Greek colonists carried these stories with them when they reached the volcanic region of Campania. They discovered another mouth of the underworld in Lake Avernus, and applied the names of the infernal rivers to various streams. Aeneas, in the sixth book of the *Aeneid*, is shown entering the underworld under the guidance of the Sibyl. Pluto, however, does not appear himself in the *Aeneid*, nor indeed in the story of Orpheus in the *Fourth Geòrgic*, though he is mentioned as terrifying and unyielding in taking back Eurydice, once Orpheus had looked back at her as he led her out of the underworld.

E. D. PHILLIPS

Pneuma

Greek word for air, breath and spirit, the subject of elabourate physiological and philosophical speculation in the ancient world: the identity of, or close connection between, air and breath, without which men cannot live, and the soul or spirit or vital spark which animates the body, is a very widespread idea.

Poseidon

The second greatest of the Greek gods was Poseidon. No other male deity ranks as the brother of Zeus, except Hades. In the *Iliad*, he is the god whom Zeus has the greatest difficulty in bending to his will. Threatened, he protests that his status is equivalent to Zeus's; the universe has been shared out equally among the three sons of Cronus, and Poseidon has the sea, Hades the underworld, and Zeus the sky.

For Homer, Poseidon is the god of the sea. He has a golden palace in the depths of the waters, the sea creatures dance at his passing by, and when he leads the Greeks to battle the waves surge up to their encampment. He causes storms at sea and sailors pray to him for a safe voyage. But he is also the god of the earthquake, and this appears to have been his primary role at the time when the formulaic epic language was taking shape, for his standard epithets all refer to it: enosichthon or ennosigaios, 'earth-shaker'; gaie(w)ochos, 'earth-carrier'; eriktypos, 'loud-booming'.

To delve further into his past, we assess his importance in the cults and legends of Greece, and discover a significant fact. The Hellenes entered Greece in two main waves. The first came about 2000 BC, and during the following centuries was much affected by cultural influences from the subject people and the civilization of Minoan Crete. The second wave came about 1200 BC, flooding large areas with a dourer folk known to us as the Dorians. In these areas, Poseidon has his cults, but is noticeably less prominent in myths. In Sparta the dialect form in which his name appears shows that he was taken over from the pre-Dorian population. We infer, firstly, that his worship spread itself in Greece before the Dorian invasion and was diminished by it; secondly, that it was not shared by the invaders. In other words, it was not brought by the Hellenes from an earlier home but was native to Greece. Greece was always a land shaken by earthquakes, and if the pre-Hellenic population feared any god, they must have feared the earth-shaker. His name does not lend itself to explanation from Greek, and is probably indigenous.

In Homer his only peer is Zeus, who certainly came with the Hellenes, and afterward we see Zeus steadily growing in power and universality, while Poseidon declines. Perhaps Poseidon had once been the greatest god in Greece. It is natural enough that the god who makes the earth heave and toss should be identified as the one who makes the sea heave and toss. It is also possible that the belief that the earth rested on the sea—the starting point of scientific speculation in the 6th century BC—goes back to much earlier times: the god of the sea might then indeed be called the 'earth-carrier'. It is no less natural that he should

Poseidon fighting Polybotes

sometimes be associated with springs and rivers, which are frequently seen to change their courses in earthquakes. And when he appears in genealogies as the first ancestor of a royal line, or in cult as 'Father', 'God of the clan', and so on, he is clearly exceeding the prerogatives of a seismic force. At Athens 'Poseidon!' was a colloquial expostulation, like 'for heaven's sake!' These do look like survivals from a time when he was really great.

But he has passed his prime by the time literature comes into view. If he is primarily the god of the sea in Homer's eyes, he is no longer mighty in the land. He maintains his place in the ceremonial calendar, and one of the great national sports meetings, held every two years at the Isthmus of Corinth, was consecrated to him. But he is honoured like a great man in retirement. He is made to fit in with other arrangements. Other gods develop and take on new aspects in response to changing needs, but Poseidon remains static, more and more confined to the sea. His title Asphalios, 'god of security', originally of geophysical significance, came to be understood as 'saviour of ships'.

By the 6th century BC, earthquakes were being explained from natural causes by the sophisticated. In 373 BC an earthquake and tidal wave destroyed the town of Helice (along the coast from Patras), together with a notable shrine of Poseidon. Such an occurrence was not calculated to increase respect for the ancient gods, any more than when Zeus struck his own temples with lightning.

M. L. WEST

Prometheus

The oldest and fullest account of Prometheus comes from the poems of Hesiod (700 BC). Prometheus was a son of the Titan Iapetus. His brothers Atlas and Menoetius were both punished by Zeus for unruliness, and he too crossed the tyrannical ruler of heaven.

Gods and men were settling their affairs at Sicyon (not far from Corinth) prior to living apart. A bull was sacrificed, and Prometheus carved it up for eating. He served Zeus with a good meaty portion, but covered it in skin and paunch to make it look unattractive; while for mankind he set bones dressed up in juicy fat. Zeus complained at the unfair division, whereupon Prometheus, with a cunning smile, invited him to choose his own portion. Zeus promptly seized the better-looking one (the pious poet assures us that he was not really taken in), and ever since then men sacrificing animals have given the bones and other inedible parts to the gods, and divided the meat among themselves.

The Theft of Fire

As Karl Meuli has explained, the procedures of blood sacrifice go back to the hunting societies of Paleolithic times. The basic reason for killing the animal was to eat it. The remains were treated with care and arranged in a particular way, perhaps in the hope of restoring the animal alive to the herds. The Greeks, however, had come to think of it as a feast which men shared with the gods, and they consequently felt the need to justify the inequality of the division. The Prometheus story does so: it is an example of pure myth, a story designed to account for a feature of the world we live in, its details governed by present facts. The wrapping of the bones in fat corresponds to actual Greek sacrificial practice; the wrapping of the meat in the paunch may reflect a method of roasting.

Angered at the deception, Hesiod continues, Zeus withheld fire from men (perhaps with the idea of preventing them from cooking their meat); he 'would not give it to the ash-trees', the

Prometheus Bound, Jacob Jordaens (1593–1678)

source from which men derive it. But Prometheus stole it in a fennel-stalk and delivered it to us.

The story belongs to a widespread type. Fire is a magical element that does not seem to belong on earth, and the myths commonly tell how it was stolen from heaven—often by a bird —and hidden in the trees. In Greece there was more than one local story. At Argos the bringer of fire was the hero Phoroneus, son of a tree nymph. Prometheus appears at Athens as one of the gods specially worshipped by potters and smiths. There was an annual torch-race from the altar he shared with Hephaestus, perhaps originally

a ceremony for renewing the purity of another altar's fire. Prometheus's fennel-stalk was not a torch, it was an established means of transporting fire, which will live safely and inconspicuously on the white inner pith. But the external similarity of the torch-race in Prometheus's honour might have been responsible for his being identified as the thief who loped off with the stalk of fennel.

Zeus's next move was to send mankind a pernicious commodity to counterbalance the desirable one that they had got. On his instructions the divine craftsman Hephaestus made a beautiful girl, various goddesses

adorned her, and Hermes gave her a deceitful disposition. She was named Pandora, and sent to Prometheus's foolish brother Epimetheus. Although Prometheus had warned him not to accept a present from Zeus, he married her, and all mortal women are her descendants. It was she who took the lid off the great jar in which all evils had been confined, letting them loose among us: only Hope remains in storage.

Many cultures have myths of the origin of women, as a separate event secondary to the creation of man. Eve was made from Adam's rib. Epimetheus was probably invented by someone who wanted to link the origin of women with the Prometheus story, but considered Prometheus himself to be too clever to be taken in by Zeus's trick. Prometheus's name suggested something like 'Forethought', so he was given a brother 'Afterthought' (as a prologue has for its opposite an epilogue); a pair of brothers, one clever and one stupid, or one good and one bad, is a common theme in folktales. Genealogists later brought Prometheus, Epimetheus, and Pandora into connection with Deucalion and Pyrrha. These were the ancestors of mankind in the mythical tradition of north and central Greece. After a flood of which they were the sole survivors, they had to throw stones behind them, and those thrown by Deucalion turned into men, those thrown by Pyrrha into women. This legend was reconciled with the story that women were descended from Pandora by making Pyrrha the daughter of Epimetheus and Pandora.

The jar of ills was an independent motif. Homer speaks of two such jars, in Zeus's keeping, one of ills and one of good things. Zeus dips in and dispenses to men as he thinks fit. Hesiod rather confusingly uses a single jar, primarily as a container of ills, but then also as a retainer of Hope. In daily life jars are used to store good things, but in myth they are useful for keeping evil spirits in bondage. It was much later, under the influence of the allegory of Cupid and Psyche, that Pandora's jar became a box.

Prometheus Bound

To prevent any further roguery, Zeus bound Prometheus in invincible bonds, and secured them by driving them through the thickness of a column. He then sent an eagle to feast on Prometheus's liver. Each night it grew again, and each day the eagle returned to its work, for constant repetition is proper to the torments of sinners. Later, however, Zeus's wrath abated, and he allowed his son Hercules to win glory by shooting the dutiful bird; yet Prometheus remains in bondage, for there is no thwarting the will of Zeus.

Hesiod probably thought of Prometheus as being bound somewhere at the world's end, where his brother Atlas stands supporting the sky's weight. The column to which he is fastened may have a connection with the idea of pillars of heaven. This conception alternates in Eurasian folklore with that of a world tree or a world mountain which reaches up to the sky. In later versions of the Prometheus myth, the miscreant is shackled to a mountain—Caucasus, from the Greek viewpoint a remote eastern outpost of the earth. The story that the Argonauts saw Prometheus on their legendary Black Sea voyage might go back to a source of Hesiod's time.

There is some evidence that the Caucasus is in fact the original home of the myth. Throughout that region it is related that earthquakes are caused by the struggles of a fierce giant who tried to steal the water of life from the mountain heights, or was otherwise impious, and as a punishment was bound by God to a pillar or in a cavern in the mountain. In many versions a vulture pecks at his heart. He

The Defiance of Prometheus

Monarch of Gods and Daemons,
  and all Spirits

But One, who throng those bright
  and rolling worlds

Which Thou and I alone of living
  things

Behold with sleepless eyes! regard
  this Earth

Made multitudinous with thy slaves,
  whom thou

Requitest for knee-worship, prayer,
  and praise,

And toil, and hecatombs of
  broken hearts,

With fear and self-contempt and
  barren hope.

Whilst me, who am thy foe, eyeless
  in hate,

Hast thou made reign and triumph,
  to thy scorn,

O'er mine own misery and thy
  vain revenge.

Three thousand years of sleep-
  unsheltered hours,

And moments aye divided by
  keen pangs

Till they seemed years, torture
  and solitude,

Scorn and despair, – these are
  mine empire:—

More glorious far than that which
  thou surveyest

From thine unenvied throne,
  0 Mighty God!

Almighty, had I deigned to share
  the shame

Of thine ill tyranny, and hung
  not here

Nailed to this wall of eagle-baffling
  mountain,

Black, wintry, dead, unmeasured;
  without herb,

Insect, or beast, or shape or sound
  of life.

Ah me! alas, pain, pain ever, for ever!

The crawling glaciers pierce me with
  the spears

Of their moon-freezing crystals, the
  bright chains

Eat with their burning cold into
  my bones.

Heaven's winged hound, polluting
  from thy lips

His beak in poison not his own,
  tears up

My heart; and shapeless sights come
  wandering by,

The ghastly people of the realm
  of dream,

Mocking me: and the Earthquake-
  fiends are charged

To wrench the rivets from my
  quivering wounds

When the rocks split and close
  again behind:

While from their loud abysses
  howling throng

The genii of the storm, urging
  the rage

Of whirlwind, and afflict me with
  keen hail.

And yet to me welcome is day
  and night,

Whether one breaks the hoar frost
  of the morn,

Or starry, dim, and slow, the
  other climbs

The leaden-coloured east; for
  then they lead

The wingless, crawling hours,
  one among whom

—As some dark Priest hales the
  reluctant victim—

Shall drag thee, cruel King, to kiss
  the blood

From these pale feet, which then
  might trample thee

If they disdained not such a
  prostrate slave.

Shelley, *Prometheus Unbound*

will have to stay there till the end of the world, but when he does break free his rage will destroy everything. Some accounts add that he once found a helper who nearly freed him; we think of Hercules.

Local variants are more reminiscent of the punishments of other Greek sinners. The water of life flows just out of the prisoner's reach: in the same way Tantalus was tormented ('tantalized', as we still say) by food and drink that kept eluding his grasp. Or beside the giant a great wheel turns, day and night; he never takes his eyes off it, for when it stops, he will become free.

Ixion was bound on a revolving wheel. Tityus, like Prometheus, was fed on by birds of prey—two vultures.

In the Caucasus, then, we have a straight Nature myth with logical connections (the pecking bird accounts for the prisoner's intermittent wrath); in Greece, a loose group of curious stories. The myth can be traced back to about 400 AD in the Caucasus (a similar one was current in the Hindu Kush when Alexander the Great got there, 700 years earlier), and there is no reason why it should not be thousands of years older. It would not be the only myth to reach Greece from the heart of Asia.

Prometheus Unbound

Prometheus's punishment forms the subject of Aeschylus's play *Prometheus Bound* (second quarter of the 5th century BC). He is now represented as having given men a great deal more than fire; he is a dignified culture hero instead of a trickster. Formerly men lived in caves, ignorant of everything. Prometheus taught them to measure seasons by the stars, to reckon and write, to harness animals to their service, to sail the sea, to make medicines, to interpret dreams and omens, to mine metals. By Aeschylus's time the Greeks were speculating about the origins of civilization, and while some saw it as a self-activated evolutionary process, others thought in terms of a divine or human instructor: Prometheus, or Palamedes, or the centaur Chiron, or Hephaestus and Athene, each nomination being based on some hint in traditional legend.

Aeschylus shows Prometheus as defiantly proud of his achievements in spite of the punishment they have brought him. Man's advancement is for the good, and Zeus must come to terms with it. In mythical language, he must come to terms with Prometheus, for if the craftsmen of Athens flourish, their god must flourish too: they will not have him a helpless prisoner at the world's edge. The story that Hercules relieved him of the eagle is accordingly developed into a full release. *Prometheus Bound* was followed in stage performance by *Prometheus Unbound*. The play is lost, but we know that after the lapse of 30,000 years Hercules freed Prometheus. Zeus only relented under pressure, however. It had been prophesied that a certain goddess would bear a son mightier than his father. As an insatiable wooer of goddesses, Zeus badly needed to know

Prometheus Bound, Nicolas-Sébastien Adam (1705–1778)

MAN, MYTH, AND MAGIC

Pythagoras

Prometheus creates man, Italian Renaissance plaquette

The discoveries attributed to Pythagoras, the Greek mystic, mathematician, and philosopher, in the fields of geometry, music, and astronomy have had a major influence in Western history, yet he left nothing of his own in writing. He was born c. 580 BC and died c. 500 BC. The details of his life and of his doctrine are known only through the writings of followers, commentators, and detractors.

A native of Samos in Greece, son of Mnesarchus, an engraver or merchant, Pythagoras studied with various Greek masters. He won the heavyweight boxing championship in the forty-eighth Olympiad, and then set out upon long journeys, some of which are almost certainly fabrications of his followers. Although the Pythagorean doctrine of the transmigration of souls and reincarnation bears much resemblance to Indian doctrines, the accounts of Pythagoras having spent years studying with the Brahmins in India are probably false. It is also extremely unlikely that he travelled to Britain and studied with the Druids. But it is highly probable that much of his time was spent traveling throughout the Near East, learning from the priests of the temples of Egypt and Babylon.

The extent of the knowledge he brought back from these travels has always been a controversial subject. It is usual to discount those ancient sources which claim that Pythagoras was principally a transmitter of ideas rather than their discoverer, not because there are facts to support this view but largely because Western scholars prefer to believe that all pre-Greek civilization was primitive—even though technically and artistically accomplished—and devoid of mathematical, scientific, philosophical, or astronomical knowledge.

Recent work, however, has shown

who it was, and only Prometheus could tell him. (It was Thetis. She was accordingly married off to a mortal, and bore Achilles.)

In the 5th century BC Greece's true classicism was already in decline. Certain analogies might be drawn with the Romanticism of the nineteenth century, and Aeschylus's treatment of Prometheus could be taken as an expression of one trend of thought which exalted man's indomitable nature and capacity for self-improvement. But events discredited this kind of enthusiasm, and dialectic discredited myths about the gods. The dramatists dropped Prometheus. A historian of the end of the century rationalized him: he was a Scythian king whose subjects incarcerated him because he could not stop the incursions of the Eagle river, until Hercules diverted it. Sophists and philosophers composed variations on the myth to suit their purposes, in particular developing the idea of Prometheus as a craftsman who fashioned mankind from clay, which presently became a cliché. From at least the late fourth century, allegorical interpretations were put forward. The fire that Prometheus brought represented philosophy, and he was accordingly the first philosopher. For the Stoics he was that divine Forethought which shaped man in the beginning, and then, lodging in him, apprehended the utility of fire. His punishment is heart-eating worry.

M. L. WEST

FURTHER READING: C. Kerenyi. Archetypal Images in Greek Religion, 5 vols., vol. 1, Prometheus. *(Princeton Univ. Press, 1963); H. J. Rose.* A Handbook of Greek Mythology. *(Dutton, rev. edn., 1959); J. G. Frazer.* Apollodorus. *(Loeb Library, Harvard Univ. Press, 1921, vol. 2 appendix), and his* Myths of the Origin of Fire *(Hacker reprint); world trees and mountains may be pursued in M. Eliade,* Patterns in Comparative Religion *(New Am. Lib.).*

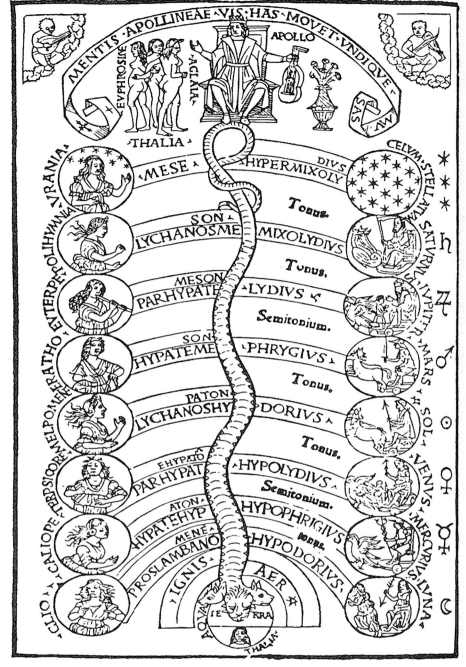

The Music of the Spheres; Pythagoras, the Greek mathematician and philosopher, is credited with saying, 'There is geometry in the humming of the strings. There is music in the spacing of the spheres.'

mous initial success, Pythagoras made the fatal error of attempting to carry his ideals into the practical world of politics. He succeeded in establishing a philosophical and ethical aristocracy in a number of Greek city states, but the hold was tenuous and foredoomed: the desire for external liberty and the incapacity to submit to the discipline essential to internal liberty that so commends the Greeks to the modern West asserted itself.

Cyron, rejected by the brotherhood because of his violent nature, became its implacable enemy and succeeded in fomenting rebellion. In successive coups, the brotherhood lost all temporal power and ultimately, in a massacre, most of its advanced members.

Thereafter, though never a secular or organized force, the Pythagorean doctrine was carried forward into Western culture by his followers. It is expounded almost unadulterated in Plato's *Timaeus*, seems to vanish for several centuries, reappears in the 1st century AD in the Neo-Pythagorean writings of Apollonius of Tyana, and again vanishes. It reappears with Plotinus, Proclus, and the Alexandrine Neoplatonists, and is injected into Christendom by Boethius in the 6th century AD, an influence that was most strongly felt in the Middle Ages.

But whereas in philosophy and literature the Pythagoreans are known, in art and architecture they are somewhat shadowy presences; their influence and knowledge is obvious but the names of those responsible for keeping the tradition alive and pure are unknown. Meanwhile, as is invariably the case, innumerable followers distorted and misused his teaching in numerology, black magic, astrology, and so on.

'Number is All'

The Pythagorean doctrine resembles other mystical and religious teachings in that it held that the universe is a divine creation and that in the divine

that certain discoveries invariably attributed to Pythagoras—such as the 3, 4, 5 triangle—were known in Egypt and Babylon, raising again the question of sources. It is no longer improbable that, as the philosophers Porphyry (c. 233–308 AD) and Iamblichus (c. 250–325 AD) maintained, Pythagoras learned his geometry and astronomy in Egypt, and his astrology and science of numbers in Babylon and Phoenicia.

Returning from his travels, Pythagoras set up a school or 'brotherhood' in the Italian city of Croton, dedicated to musical experimentation (he taught that all phenomena were fundamentally harmonic by nature, a view largely corroborated by twentieth-century physicists), and to the study of geometry, mathematics, and astronomy combined with a religio-ascetic discipline.

His teaching having met with enor-

plan man was placed to fulfill a unique purpose: carrying a spark or germ of divinity within him, his role was to conquer and destroy his animal nature (the biblical Old Adam) and nurture and encourage the divine. The doctrine differed from other systems in the emphasis it placed upon number, and upon the essentially numerical disciplines of geometry, arithmetic and music. A much-quoted Pythagorean principle was 'Number is all'.

Until very recently, this aspect of the teaching was treated with little respect in the modern West. While Pythagoras was given full marks for his geometry, music, and theory of the solar system, his so-called 'number mysticism' was believed to be an inherited residue of the superstitious past. It has been said that 'Numbers . . . were conceived at that early stage of thought, not as relations or qualities predicable of things but as themselves constituting the substance or essence of the phenomena'. However, since it is now clear that the qualitative distinctions we make between phenomena are fundamentally numerical, the Pythagorean doctrine reappears in modern dress. Our senses operate through the reception of vibrations of differing frequencies. Red is red because of its frequency or 'number', and so it is with every sense impression that we receive, without exception.

Creation was explained by the Pythagoreans as the division of the primordial unity into multiplicity and diversity. Other traditions expressed the same idea in terms of myth or legend, with deities representing the various universal principles of birth, love, strife, fertility, growth, maturity, death, renewal, and so on, a mode of expression inescapably inviting embellishment and misrepresentation. Conceivably it was to avoid this danger that Pythagoras taught his disciples the numerical, geometric, and

harmonic bases underlying the myths. But if this was his objective, it failed; once the vows of secrecy were broken, all were free to make what they would of 'All is number'.

Numbers, to the Pythagoreans, were not abstractions as they are to us. They were symbols representing cosmic principles. Each number had a form or forms, made up of unity points, and from a study of these forms and the manner in which they generated sequences of numbers, an understanding of the underlying principles could be achieved. Thus numbers were held to be triangular, square, linear, or rectangular by nature.

Though ultimately requiring complex considerations upon many levels, the whole of the philosophy of numbers flowed from distinctions originally created by the primordial division of the One into multiplicity. According to the Pythagoreans this act of genesis necessitated ten opposing categories: odd and even, limited and unlimited, one and many, right and left, male and female, rest and motion, straight and curved, light and darkness, good and evil, square, and oblong.

Though at first glance a curious mixture of geometry, biology, and

ethics, and disparaged by scholars as based upon 'fanciful analogies', a brief geometrical demonstration can show how the Pythagoreans derived at least a few of their categories simultaneously.

The number 2, the prototype 'oblong' number, was written • •.

The next oblong number was 4:

which generated the next, 6:

Thus it may be seen at a glance that all oblong numbers necessarily generate rectangles which change shape with each step (tending constantly closer and closer toward the square but never finally reaching it). Oblong numbers may therefore be said to be in 'motion', 'unlimited', 'many' and by extension and application, and by analogies perhaps not altogether fanciful, 2 acquired its other properties as well.

Contrast it to 3, the first 'square' number. (Strictly speaking, 1 was not a number, but a symbol for the Absolute containing the possibilities for all numbers within it). The number 3 generates 5, which generates 7: successive squares which, because constant in shape, may be said to be at

Pythagoras, as a symbol for Arithmetic, Palazzo Ducale in Venice

'rest', hence 'limited', hence partaking of the nature of 'one' as opposed to 'many'.

Upon such considerations, the Pythagoreans arrived at specific numbers and specific figures which, embodying certain principles held to be particularly important, were regarded as sacred. The figure known as the Tetractys, for example, representing 10, was holy because it summed up in triangular form the principle of 1, 2, 3, and 4; its internal relationships determined the musical octave, the trinity at its core was enshrined in the seven notes of the octave, the harmonic laws upon which all things come into being.

As Theon of Smyrna (c. 130 AD) wrote: 'if the single string in the monochord is divided into four equal parts, the sound produced by the whole length of the string forms with the sound produced by three-quarters of the string (the ratio being 4:3) the consonance of a fourth'. In the same way, the ratio 2:1 corresponds to the octave, and the ratio 3:2 to the fifth.

It was in their desire to impose such simple numerical relationships upon everything in the cosmos that the Pythagoreans came up with the doctrine of the harmony of the spheres. They assumed the earth to have a perfect spherical shape and therefore, by extension, they thought that the surrounding universe should also have this form.

According to Aristotle (who never referred to Pythagoras himself by name, and possibly did not believe he had existed) the Pythagoreans maintained that at the centre of this spherical universe was an invisible fire, round which ten spherical shells revolved concentrically. The inmost but one of these spheres carried the earth through one rotation per day; and the inmost sphere bore an invisible 'Anti-Earth'. On spheres progressively further from the centre

the planets moved: in order, moon, sun, Venus, Mercury, Mars, Jupiter, and Saturn; and the tenth sphere bore the fixed stars.

The most remarkable feature of this theory was the harmony of the spheres. It was natural for the Pythagoreans to suggest that the radii of the spheres were related in simple ratios, and from this they deduced that the movement of the spheres would result in a diapason of tones whose pitch depended upon the radius, and hence the relative velocity, of each sphere. It is not that we are unable to hear this heavenly music: accustomed to it from the moment of our birth, we do not notice it.

It was according to such harmonic principles that the Pythagoreans conceived their cosmos. Study of the Tetractys revealed to them an unfolding and rich world of meaning and significance and, bizarre as some of their philosophy may appear to us, it remains a fact that, following recent discoveries in quantum physics, wave mechanics, and relativity theory; a number of eminent physicists and mathematicians have taken up a position which they call 'Neo-Pythagorean'.

J. A. WEST

Rome

Roman religion has no equal in the ancient Mediterranean although its type of polytheism is shared throughout pre-classical and classical Europe, North Africa and the Near East. Polytheism was never a mode of theology as we understand it today. A formal body of dogma and an organized congregation or network of congregations have no place in a

Night view of the Rome's historical forum; in the foreground, the temple of Saturn

Roman mosaic with Neptune and Amphitrite in the *Casa di Nettuno e Anfitrite* in Herculaneum

study of Roman paganism. Even the notion of religion remained outside the ancient cognizance.

The Latin word religio, whose original definition is obscure, meant 'awe', 'scruple', and also 'superstition', although the Romans sometimes acknowledged the last as a distinct and extreme attitude. One's devotion and sense of obligation to the divine could be expressed by the idea of pietas, which was by no means due merely to the gods. It was a bond of obligation which could be felt in accordance with bloodties, ethnic solidarity, or contractual agreement. Whereas pietas and similar notions reflect a personal recognition of a deity's existence, the worship (cultus) of a deity manifested itself in sacrifices, gifts and utensils (sacra), which shared with other sacrifices, gifts and utensils the common denomination of the ritus that was normally designated by its ethnic origin. Hence, such modern expressions as 'Greek rite' have a very long history.

The Roman Rite

Some Roman gods were worshipped in a non-Roman rite. For instance, a sacrifice to Saturn took place in the 'Greek rite'. In this case the Roman officiant did not cover his head with his toga but poured the wine while bareheaded. Normal Roman ceremonial practice dictated a covered head—evidently to avoid ominous sights. Constant flute music was also required—evidently to avoid ominous sounds. The 'Roman rite' of Italy implied a covered head, flute music, and other practices which distinguish it from the rites of diverse communities and peoples. Theoretically rites were as numerous as there were clear ethnic divisions. The various rites are an integral part of Roman imperial religion.

Occidental religion tends to concentrate man's attentions upon one deity and to prescribe norms of behaviour that constitute morality, but little in the way of moral precept emerges from pagan religion. Further,

a modern focus upon the single deity tends to narrow our attention on the breadth of Roman religion. While the importance, not to say power, of the Roman gods cannot be denied, the role of these gods can never approximate the omnipotence and unity of Western man's one God. Some Roman gods did not even begin as gods but as forces, activities and spheres of influence beyond man's ken and control. The one God acknowledged today has received superhuman attributes; that is attributes which are human though somehow better than human. Creating, knowing, loving, and the like can be understood only in human terms. For the Romans a god enjoyed human shape, but religion involved much besides manlike gods. The history of Roman religion exhibits traces of nongods becoming gods, so that we must admit the possible growth of a notion of deity. However, this growth derived its material from religious forces, powers and entities otherwise outside the nature of the world, if not outside knowledge or fear.

The majority of Roman gods rarely received cult as the simple god. Rather, the gods usually bore an epithet or surname which distinguished them from others whose realm of efficacy differed. Consequently the universality of one pagan god was never possible. From place to place his epithets evinced his peculiarity. The gods of the Romans may conveniently be divided into groups of natural forces and their phenomena, physical activity, single abstract conceptions, deities of a given place and, finally, divinities of unknown origins. Among the gods of nature stand Jupiter, Mars, and Ceres. Jupiter was once the sky and the day. So he might be worshipped as a god of the sky and be called Thunderer or the like after some heavenly appearance. Mars belongs to the forces of springtime, and so his cult was concentrated in March.

Ceres ruled the growth of crops and vegetation in general. Her origin leads naturally to the next group, the type of physical activity. At an earlier stage Ceres was no goddess. Ceres or cerus was a verbal noun from the root 'to make grow' (creare) or 'to grow' (crescere). It was Growth itself. By the classical period Ceres had acquired all the attributes of a fertile lady and had narrowed her attentions upon agriculture, with the notable exception of her invocation at a wedding. She was identified with the Greek grain goddess, Demeter, as early as the fifth century. Indeed her oldest Roman temple may have been totally the result of Greek influence. Be that as it may, Ceres in cult and in story rarely exhibits a purely Roman background.

Venus represents the same type of deity. She began as the physical activity of coaxing and luring, but was early assigned a role in keeping watch over vegetable gardens. In some parts of central Italy the same priestess served both Ceres and Venus. A third such deity was Juno, whose name must be related to the word 'youth', a period of animal life which she as a goddess preserved and prolonged. In many instances the Romans forgot the origin of such gods.

These divine types differ in origin very little from the manifest abstraction which never, or only occasionally, assumed a human form that could overwhelm the deity's beginnings to such a degree that a Roman could not understand its principal function. In this category are Tellus, Dis, Fides, and Salus. Tellus signifies the earth, which is anything but an abstraction. However, tellus was most certainly the state or essence of earth, 'earthness', rather than a natural power such as growth or physical activity such as coaxing. The sole major festival of Tellus was

named for the slaughter of pregnant cows, which were cremated so that the bountiful ash might be employed in fertilization. Tellus was enriched and was not in itself a force or deity. However, under Greek influence the 'earth' became a mother goddess.

Dis shows affinities with Tellus and also influence from a Greek quarter. Dis belonged to the underworld. His name means 'rich', which was thought a suitable translation of the Greek Pluto. Whereas Tellus received annual sacrifices, the underworld's Dis received sacrifice every century (saeculum) at the splendid and gorgeous Secular Games. Tellus had one Roman temple which had been vowed in wartime on account of an earthquake. Her old cult was performed in the open away from temples. Dis had

Many gods and goddesses enjoyed temples, precincts, chapels, or altars in Rome.

the one altar, buried except for a few hours every century. Evidently neither deity was represented by a man-like statue, although the Romans considered one a goddess and the other a god. Tellus remained quite Roman in cult in spite of learned attempts to equate her with the Earth of Greek mythology. Dis, on the other hand, was an integrated foreigner.

The many deities invoked at the Secular Games exhibit a miscellany of Roman, Italic, and Greek gods, worshipped by prayers and with utensils emanating from equally diverse quarters. The core of the ritual went back to the middle of the 4th century BC. The Games were controlled by the Fifteen Men (formerly Ten Men) For Sacrificing, a powerful priesthood in

charge of imported state cults. The cult of Tellus, however, was carried on by the chief pontiff and the Vestal Virgins, the oldest civil priests of Rome. Yet Tellus, 'Earth', and Dis, 'Rich', share similar beginnings and interest in the soil's goodness.

Of the same type are Fides Publica and Salus. The former, 'the People's Trust', had a very old cult and precinct. The latter, 'Welfare' or 'Safety', received a temple very late although the notion of the people's well-being dominated many areas of the civil religion. Both were acknowledged as gods to the extent that they were given temples, but neither had a human representation and, so far as we know, they were female only because of their grammatical gender. Ceres, Venus, and probably Tellus, originally, had a neuter grammatical gender and became 'feminine' in the process of becoming deities with functions seemingly appropriate to women.

Ops offers herself as an example. The grammatically feminine word means 'abundance', 'resource', and 'provender'. On 25 August she received worship from the Vestal Virgins at the King's House. On 19 December fell her oldest civil festival, which the Romans recognized as a ceremony for a deity generous in the bestowal of natural resources. Hence, she was honoured after the harvest and in the dead of winter. Yet this 'goddess' could not withstand the tendency to anthropomorphism and became in the popular mind the wife of Saturn, for no better reason than the occurrence of his great festival on 17 December, two days before hers. The one temple Ops certainly had was probably not very old. Sacrifice at the King's House suggests that originally the cult was domestic and later raised to a public status.

Many gods and goddesses enjoyed temples, precincts, chapels, or altars in Rome. However, such honours did not necessarily imply a conception of a man like deity. Even statues sometimes did not blur the Romans' understanding of the god's primitive existence as a force or activity. It is frequently urged that Etruscans and Greeks lent the Romans their anthropomorphic conception of the divine. Considerable as this outside influence was, man's instinct to fancying man-like gods still prevails. Very early Romans applied 'Father' and 'Mother' as cult titles. What was akin to the Roman imagination was the myth-creating belief in marriages among gods and their offspring. Most divine marital and filial ties the Romans transferred from Greek to Latin poetry. So far as we can ascertain, the Roman gods passed celibate lives before Greek ideas were introduced.

A very different force is met in the divinity which the Roman community wished to ward off. On 25 April every year a civil priest offered sacrifice to the force of the rust blight, Robigus, which might strike the crops. The rites were held at places five miles from the city, apparently in order to keep the rust from crossing some archaic boundary. More unusual, indeed unique, was the altar dedicated on the edge of the city to Verminus, god of cattle worms. The rearing of this altar by a prominent patrician was prompted by a great plague in 175 BC, which wrought death among the cattle and the men such that corpses were heaped untended in the streets. The Romans explicitly speak of Robigus and the like as 'gods'. However, they clearly never saw them as beneficent deities. They sought their benevolence, and in this context there is much truth to the view of Roman religion as perpetual appeasement of natural forces.

Because the primitive religion, which the Romans conservatively kept, closely adhered to the agricultural economy of its decidedly unintellectual practitioners, most festivals, ceremonies and deities betray and reflect the lives of tillers and herders, within the cycle of the year. If the well-being of a people is not reckoned only in its battles, it is reckoned by its material resources. In this context Romans sought a right relation with their gods or, more specifically, with natural forces and activities, in terms of their society. Hence the state religion took little account of deities of trade and manufacture, who did indeed exist and in some later cases thrived apart from the major civil cults.

A history of Roman religion would need to trace the development of an agrarian religion into an imperial religion that borrowed and modified gods and cults from many peoples within its vast empire and upon its fringes. Sometimes old deities changed and added to their own attributes those of other gods with whom they were identified. Sometimes the alien god was introduced with or without a slight Roman veneer. Later stages in Roman religion may reflect merely the Latin outcropping of some Etruscan, Greek, or near Eastern religion. Although inherently interesting and equally Roman phenomena, the borrowings remained just borrowings, unless we are to except Christianity.

Calendar and Cult

The civil calendar retains the oldest stratum of Roman religion. This calendar was an official almanac of religion which the state priests were bound to observe, even though the first serious Roman student of his religion (Varro, in the 1st century BC) tells us how knowledge of some cults had deteriorated till only the name was known. The basic features of the calendar's liturgy roughly parallel the farming year in central Italy. The planting, promotion of growth, harvesting, storing of crops fall at their appropriate moment. February is given over to cleansing and March to decorating as the year ends and begins. December and January betray some signs of festivals of lights, but generally the Romans seldom took their eyes off the ground to gaze at the heavens. They left that task to others when they wanted it done.

Roman cult was rarely ever personal or congregational. Almost all civil sacrifice fell to the priests named for life or to annually elected officials. The priestly class at the top was identical with the ruling class. A priest came from the social elite and rarely felt his religious duties to be in conflict with his political ambitions. An official clergy as we understand it did not develop. This lack does not indicate the absence of priestly expertise. On the contrary, the normal expectation of priesthoods by members of the same clan presupposes traditional religion preserved by these clans.

Empty of moral content and gradually losing all semblance of relevance to the priests' prevailing social condition as an imperial elite, ancestral Roman religion lapsed into a formalism unusual in its consequences. Native scruple and aristocratic ambition made religious acts the object of bitter political quarrels so long as the aristocracy ruled. Temples, statues, altars, and gifts came to the gods because of aristocratic munificence. Religious formalism promoted a religious legalism that ultimately converted the Roman mind into one of the keenest instruments of legislation and jurisprudence.

Principal Priesthoods

The most important priesthoods were the panels of pontiffs, augurs, and Ten Men For Sacrificing. The pontiffs oversaw many aspects of sacral law and jurisprudence. The chief pontiff served the state in the capacity of religious spokesman in the formal conduct of religion and frequently presided over meetings of the pontifical college which included the one priest-king, the flamens, and the Vestal Virgins.

The pontiffs, and more particularly the chief pontiff, regularly decided matters of law and sacrilege put to them. The augurs were charged with constant surveillance of the well-being of the land and people from a religiously technical point of view. Their technical expertise also had political ramifications, for they could disrupt public assemblies and void elections by proclamation of some religious miscarriage or detection of an ill omen. Foreign cults and rites were entrusted to the Ten Men For Sacrificing.

Some deities, but by no means all, enjoyed the services of their own priest, called a flamen, and the flamens exhibit an early stage of Roman religion.

Another kind of priesthood was the sodality, the Luperci and the Salii being representative examples. The Luperci, divided into two bands, performed a purification of the Palatine Hill on 15 February. Garbed only in loincloths, they struck unclean objects with a strip of goatskin called 'Juno's cloak'. The Salii, also divided into two bands, performed throughout March on behalf of Mars, whose divinity was associated with the new year of growth and war.

Ordinary religious ceremonies included the dinner or the sacrifice. A sacral supper might be offered only to the god or gods, and every September Jupiter alone received a dinner of the harvest fruits. Extraordinary situations could demand a banquet for a group of deities. Equally efficacious were regular suppers of which men and a god partook. While in later times invitations

to a sacral dinner might be limited to priests and magistrates, early universal custom respected inclusion of all worshippers. This kind of ceremony differs from the sacrifice, which was usually a total offering of one food to a god.

The Romans gave their gods what they themselves ate. Animal victims were the pig, sheep, or cow, rarely the goat and only in one known case the horse. The animal had to be ritually pure; otherwise, some attention might be paid to its selection according to sex and colour. Besides animals the Romans offered foodstuffs of grain and fruit or wine and milk. Incense was introduced very early and was presumably acquired locally long before the oriental frankincense was imported. Burned sacrifice was made on an altar, which might be a stone hearth or turf specially cut and piled for the ceremony.

Sarcophagus with putti (chubby, naked infants with and without wings) depicting a sacrifice of goat

Cleansing ceremonies were many. A common type was the procession of a pig, sheep, and bullock (suovetaurilia) around the area to be purified and their slaughter for the good of the soil. Like other ancient peoples, the Romans firmly believed in the divinity of a given place or some social unit. Sometimes the local god was called simply Genius of This Place or God Who Watches Over This Place. Otherwise the deity had the name of the place itself. Any sojourn in a place prompted sacrifice if not a more permanent gift. Also the full range of governmental offices and communities, as well as the multitude of military units, worshipped their several Genii or the like.

The Romans were keenly aware of the strength that the land imparted to its inhabitants. When they conquered and wholly absorbed another people, they ritually summoned the chief local god (or gods) from the conquered land to Rome where the alien god was properly domiciled. The vanquished town and its farmland might be placed under a perpetual curse by uprooting its boundary-markers, sowing salt in its furrows, and consigning the town and land to gods of the underworld with prayer to Jupiter and Tellus, Heaven and Earth. This ceremony was called devotio, as was that personal act of self-dedication whereby a general would literally sacrifice himself to the enemy to gain a victory for his people.

Devotio was but a particular kind of vow or promise which Romans were wont to make in a moment of stress or need. Many religious donations from high and low stemmed from the vow (ex voto). The customary form for keeping one's promise was to pay or loosen the vow (votum solvere). Romans seldom offered what was not due.

Augury not only acknowledged the necessity of keeping the land productive and clean; it also embraced the act of bird-watching, called the auspices, which figured prominently in Roman public and private life. Distinct from augury was the skill of haruspicy, which the Romans borrowed from the Etruscans, in whose families the semiofficial skill was practiced. Haruspicy was that form of divination whereby the gods' will was made known through scrutiny of an animal's entrails.

The Gods at Home

Most Romans left the celebration of the civil gods to the state priests. At home and within the tradition-bound clans, private worship continued unabated for centuries. Indeed the extent, variety, and tenacity of private cult demonstrates how gods were so deeply rooted in pagan hearts. The primitive centre of the household cult was the hearth. The name of the goddess Vesta means no more than the hearth fire. Vesta's public cult of the City's fire, kept by her virgins, grew as her domestic cult declined.

Other domestic deities were the Penates, Lares, and Genius. The Penates were gods of the food cupboard (penus). The Lares occupied the hearth but also functioned elsewhere. The Genius typifies the house cult and the Roman mentality. The word sig-

Sacrificial attendant (*victimarius* or *popa*) with axe for killing the animal

nifies the procreative force of the male householder. It was honoured at least on every birthday by libations of wine. The Genius joined the Lares in a small shrine with an artificial hearth set in every dining room and was often portrayed between the two Lares. He was a model householder, wearing a toga, holding in one hand a horn of plenty and in the other a wine saucer.

Although some ancient authors give the impression that the domestic gods received little more than perfunctory attention, the physical remains, especially those of Pompeii, eloquently counter such an impression. Every household had its altar. Besides the painted or sculptured Lares and Genius are found a wide variety of statuettes of other gods, coins left in safekeeping and ceremonial utensils, not the least important of which was the candelabrum or oil-lamp that reminds us of the candle—which the electric bulb has replaced—before the madonnas in Italian kitchens and on Italian street corners.

The humble cults flourished on the streets and in the countryside. When the Emperor Augustus encouraged some form of worship of the ruler, he allowed the imperial Genius to join the neighbourhood Lares so that his family's pre-eminence came daily to the attention of the Roman lower classes. Another typical and wide-spread deity of the lower class was Spes, 'Hope'. Innumerable tablets, statues, reliefs, paintings, altars, shrines, and chapels which have come to light in Italy and throughout the Roman Empire attest the religious depth and sincerity of untold thousands. Although the popular enthusiasm for the great state cults declined, no one can assert that religious apathy prevailed among the Romans. Indeed, Christianity's 'victory' was truly a victory, the often bloody finale to a

long battle. The imperial cult, worship of the dead emperors as gods and the live one as a divine Genius or Divine Will (numen), was by no means so superficial as might be believed. The early Christian emperors permitted it to continue in certain areas, although they forbade actual sacrifice.

Although Roman religion welcomed cults and gods from many foreign and conquered areas, it did not freely digest all ancient manifestations known elsewhere. For instance, magic and astrology never figure in Roman religion. Prophets and oracles might be heeded but they remained peculiar or alien. Visions were not uncommon, but divine epiphanies (appearances

> *The religious beliefs of the Roman people remained without the slightest moral tone: they wanted to be in good standing with the forces of Nature.*

of the gods) were rare. The Romans sought knowledge of the future from either haruspicy or the lots. The latter were usually wooden tokens or strips inscribed with some ambiguous phrase which the divinity of a place issued. Although men hawking lots or fortunes could be found in Rome, the great centres of prediction by lots were at a little distance from Rome. The most famous of all such shrines was the magnificent temple complex set atop the citadel hill of Praeneste, modern Palestrina. The deity of this place, called Fortuna Primigenia, issued lots to the high and the low for centuries.

Romans and Italians reported to the pontiffs unnatural occurrences which, if they happened in grave times, might cause mass hysteria and required expiation—androgynous babies, animals with too many limbs or heads, rains of bloody meat, mice gnawing gold, bulls mounting brazen cows, and like

phenomena. On rare occasions such prodigies could even prompt human sacrifice. Thus what was contrary to nature could cause acts contrary to the norms of Roman religion.

The religious beliefs of the Roman people remained without the slightest moral tone: they wanted to be in good standing with the forces of Nature. The Roman's attitude toward his gods somewhat resembles the situation in early Israel. Romans expected the deity to act generously on their behalf or not to act at all. If the deity acted in the manner expected, he was rewarded with a gift of an offering or a sacrifice. If he failed too often or acted too badly, he was abandoned for another.

The Romans believed that certain deities watched over them and supposed that others took care of their neighbours. To this end, they felt it necessary to deprive their enemies of their gods, their sacred utensils and all means of worship. The modern mind may find this mode of religion criminally selfish but the Romans seldom questioned the efficacy of a religion which had grown outward from a bend on an Italian river to embrace the greater part of Europe, North Africa, and the near East. They sought only to improve it by admitting new gods to their worship. They found it quite difficult to hold with a belief in one god when many gods had served them so long and so well.

R. E. A. PALMER

FURTHER READING: C. Bailey. Phases in the Religion of Ancient Rome. *(Greenwood Press, 1972); R. M. Ogilvie.* The Romans and their Gods. *(Norton, 1970).*

Saturn

In literary presentations of classical mythology from Roman times onward, the figure named Saturn has been filled with the content of the Greek Cronus, one of the Titans who were sons of Mother Earth and who ruled before the Olympians and were overthrown by them. Scholars have therefore tried to discover what kind of deity the Roman Saturnus was in origin, and why and when he was selected to be a Roman Cronus. It is a matter of some importance that in classical times the Greek Cronus seems to have been confined to myth, and hardly to have received any cult. This would be natural for a figure driven from

power by his son and therefore no longer important for human destinies. The name of Saturnus was connected by such ancient writers as Festus and Varro with the sowing of crops (Satus) but this derivation is doubtful. It may be Etruscan, as F. Altheim has argued: he regards it as connected with the place-name Satrium and the Etruscan clan called Satre. This would mean that Saturnus was the god of this clan, but that fact alone would not show what kind of god he was. Festus mentions that Saturnus's name occurs in the very ancient song of the Salii, an archaic priesthood of Rome. His festival the Saturnalia is recorded in the earliest form of the Roman calendar of festivals. He is connected with another deity—the goddess Lua, to whom

captured weapons were dedicated.

On an Etruscan bronze from Piacenza, which is in the form of a liver used in divination, the name occurs on the left or ill-omened side. But even this Etruscan origin does not exclude a close and very early connection with the Greek Cronus. Greek influence in south Italian and Etruscan religion goes back nearly to the days of the earliest Greek settlements of the 8th century BC. Why an Etruscan clan should adopt Cronus from the Greeks and rename him after itself is a question hard to answer, given his faded and mostly sinister character in Greek myth. But Greek religion of earlier stages than the Olympian mythology of Homer continued to survive in many parts of the Greek world. Its

The temple of Saturn at Villa Torlonia, Rome, Italy

Fresco showing Saturn, flanked by Aquarius and Capricorn; Angera Castle, Hall of Justice, Varese, Lombardy, Italy

divine figures are little known, but Cronus may have been important among them.

The temple of Saturn was on the slope of the Capitoline Hill in Rome. There is little evidence from inscriptions outside the city for his cult in Italy. The festival of the Saturnalia was famous for the temporary suspension of the authority of the higher classes over the lower and of masters over slaves. Saturn, who as an exile saw the world upside-down, was the natural patron of slaves on such an occasion.

Saturn was also, rather oddly, connected with weights and measures, and the minting of coins: he was even guardian of the treasury. The Saturnian meter of older Roman poetry was a rhythm originally Greek but apparently adapted to a language of stress rather than quantity, as Latin was in earlier times. The adjective Saturnius had sometimes a special quality.

Saturnia Juno means simply Juno as daughter of Saturn, as Hera was daughter of Cronus in Greek myth. Saturnia tellus in Virgil means Italy as a rich land reserved for the finest breed of men. But in Saturnia regna, 'Saturn's reign', there is much more of the Greek content of 'life under Cronus' when human life had been easier and gentler, before Zeus made it hard.

God of Chill and Gloom

This is the usual character of Saturn in classical Latin literature. But his sinister aspect never disappeared, and in later astrological belief it became predominant. This is the origin of the word 'saturnine'.

The cruelty and crimes of the reigning Cronus, his exile at the hands of Zeus, and the gloom and despair in which he spent the rest of his days were well-known features of Greek myth, which reappeared in stories

told of Saturn under classical Greek influence. To Greek myth, by the date when classical Latin literature arose, there had been added another element, the Babylonian lore connecting various gods with various planets. The influence of these planets on human destiny was the influence of these gods transmitted by a particular channel, and portioned out according to their predictable movements in the heavens. The planet that the Romans came to call Saturnus had in Babylonian or Assyrian belief been linked to the god Ninurta, whose province was war and hunting as practiced by the Assyrian kings. The cruelty of this background became attached to the planet and this character was attributed to the planet Saturn all through medieval times.

Saturn with his earlier savagery and later banishment, as taken over from Cronus, became a god of chill, gloom, and cruelty. This character was liable to appear in children born when his planet was in the ascendant. A further addition to this lore was made from the theory of temperament developed in Greek medicine. In a combination of astrology with the medical theory of humors in one of its cruder forms, Saturn came to represent melaina chole, black bile, or melancholia; a frame of mind, ferocious like the purely bilious temperament, but also gloomy to the point of madness. Those whose temperament was entirely Saturnine tended to be full of hidden malice, to be grumpy celibates and cruel to children, and to have a permanent feeling of bondage and captivity and a love of concealment. When they were mad or in their mad fits, such people would be like Shakespeare's King Lear after his deposition.

E. D. PHILLIPS

Planet of Limitation

Until recently the most distant of the known planets, Saturn was looked upon for centuries as being cold and slow. Astrologers have described him as the most evil and dangerous of all the heavenly bodies.

'Limitation' and 'control' are the keywords applied to Saturn; his influence brings caution. A person ruled by him is likely to succeed in life through a combination of hard work and forethought. He will make his plans for the future, and then keep rigorously to his timetable, looking cautiously ahead for unexpected events.

A person's power of self-control will depend to a large extent on Saturn's influence over him, but this control can be misused, and he may become emotionally cold. In fact, Saturnians have been described as people who are 'cold in charity'. The sense of limitation imposed by Saturn may cause someone ruled by him to be over-conscious of the narrowness of his existence, and to feel a sense of inadequacy.

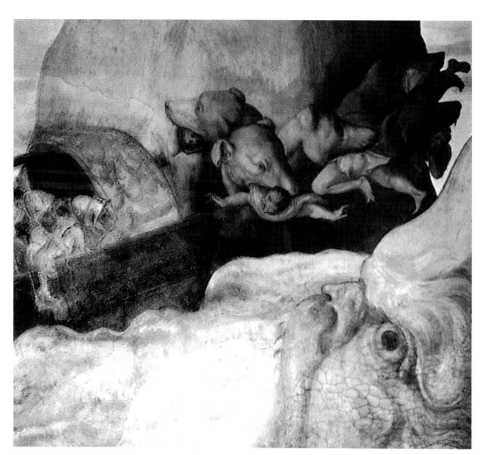

The painting is an Italian fresco of Odysseus's boat passing between the six-headed monster Scylia and the whirlpool Charybdis. Scylla has plucked five of Odysseus's men from the boat.

On the other hand, the influence of this planet enables a person to endure with patience the difficulties he may encounter, even though he feels them keenly, and it also instils in him the urge to overcome these difficulties and the ability to bear any responsibilities that result from them.

Someone who is ruled by Saturn will be cautious in love, as in everything else, and will think long and hard before deciding to marry. Once married, however, a male Saturnian will be a good provider, while a woman influenced by this planet will prove to be capable and economical.

Saturn traditionally rules the later years of a person's life, the time when he accepts his responsibilities and settles down; people born under this planet are often late in developing their innate skills and talents.

Black is the favourite colour of people ruled by Saturn, and in appearance, too, they are often dark with serious and grave features. A 'saturnine' temperament is gloomy, but it has its positive side: the saturnine humor has been described as the one that most influences intellectuals.

A Saturnian will be happiest doing routine work, or in an organization where he can look ahead and plan for the future, knowing that his advancement is likely to be steady and that there is a pension waiting for him at the end of his working life. For this reason he is best suited to a career in business, government or politics, or in the Church or the army.

FURTHER READING: L. Greene. Saturn: a New Look at an Old Devil. (Weiser, 1976); D. Talbott. The Saturn Myth. (Doubleday, 1980).

Scylla & Charybdis

In classical mythology, Scylla was a monster with six heads, eighteen rows of teeth, twelve feet, and a voice like the yelping of dogs, who lived in a cave and snatched seamen from passing ships; nearby lurked Charybdis, a whirlpool; Odysseus sailed between the two, which were later located in the Straits of Messina between Italy and Sicily.

Selene

Greek moon goddess, of little importance in myth or cult; said to have been the sister or daughter of the sun; she fell in love with Endymion, who fathered her fifty children, the fifty months between each celebration of the Olympic Games; other, more important, goddesses connected with the moon were Hera, Artemis, and Hecate.

Silenus

In classical mythology, one of the Sileni, woodland spirits who became associated with Dionysus and the satyrs; represented as an elderly, fat, hairy but bald-headed man with the ears of a horse, riding an ass or carrying a wineskin; he is profoundly wise and constantly drunk; sometimes said to have been the teacher of the young Dionysus or the father of the satyrs; Socrates was compared with him for wisdom and ugliness.

Sisyphus

King of Corinth, a cunning trickster and by all accounts a scoundrel, Sisyphus is the subject of many minor adventures in Greek literature, but is most famous for the final punishment Zeus metes out on him. He fathers Odysseus by seducing the daughter of Autolycus, his neighbour and rival. When Aegina, daughter of the River God Asopus, is abducted, Sisyphus sees the culprit: Zeus. Sisyphus passes on this vital information to Asopus, thus incurring Zeus's wrath. Sisyphus evades punishment first by tricking Hades into his own handcuffs, then by deceiving Persephone to let him out of Tartarus for a few days. Finally Hermes escorts him back to the Underworld, where he is forced to roll a huge boulder up a hill, which he can never fully accomplish. Each time he gets near the top of the hill, the boulder slips and rolls back down. Sisyphus is married to Merope, one of the Pleiades (Seven Sisters). Sisyphus' punishment is used as a metaphor for daily life by the French-Algerian author Albert Camus in his essay *The Myth of Sisyphus*.

FURTHER READING: Camus, Albert, and Justin O'Brien. The Myth of Sisyphus, and Other Essays. *(New York: Vintage, 1991); Graves, Robert.* The Greek Myths. *(Baltimore: Penguin, 1955); Hamilton, Edith, and Steele Savage.* Mythology. *(New York: Penguin, 1969).*

Skepticism

A Greek philosophical attitude or school that holds that all knowledge is suspect and that we should suspend all judgments. The goal of this philosophy was to obtain a tranquil mind, and thus a happy life. There were two major groups of Skeptics between 270 BC and 200 AD: the Academics and the Pyrrhonians.

Questioning Knowledge

Skeptics were generally opposed to the kinds of certainties proposed and maintained by the Stoics, who held that knowledge could be obtained from the senses if the experience was clear and forceful. Skeptics argued that any information gathered through the senses should be cast into doubt,

Bust of Selene in a clypeus (a large shield), detail from a strigillated lenos sarcophagus

Mark Henderson talking about his book *The Geek Manifesto* to the Mersyside Skeptics society

since two people could have different experiences of the same event, and a person might have faulty senses to begin with. All judgment, therefore, should be suspended.

The Academic Skeptics were those philosophers who were members of Plato's Academy who adopted the skeptical approach. These thinkers were inspired by Socrates, whose method was to cast doubt on judgments that his interlocutors held with steadfast or reasonable certainty. In 272 BC, Arcesilaus became the head of the Academy and introduced many of the Skeptical philosophical frameworks that dominated that institution for the next two centuries until the end of Philo's leadership in 79 BC. Over that time, leaders of the Academy were more or less strict in their interpretation of skepticism. For one thing, extreme skepticism, which was allegedly maintained by Pyrrhon of Elis in the 4th century BC, leads to absurd forms of life. For example, Pyrrhon's friends were forced to help steer him away from cliffs and other

dangers in his path, since he would not accept the truth of any sense perceptions. Since the goal of Skepticism, as with all Hellenic philosophy, was to find the path to a happy, virtuous life, some Academic skeptics tempered the extreme nonjudgment of their methods by allowing for everyday judgments to be made, only denying the possibility of large philosophical conclusions concerning ethics, physics, and logic. Academic Skepticism ended when Antichos took charge of the Academy in 79 BC, re-establishing a Platonic dogmatism devoted to metaphysical knowledge.

Pyrrhonian skepticism takes its name from Pyrrhon of Elis, but was a later skeptical movement led by Aenesidemus in the 1st century BC. This form of skepticism, influenced by the asceticism of Pyrrhon and its goal of a tranquil life, is less well documented than the Academic version, but tends to emphasize the relative nature of perception and the importance of accepting the limitations of our epistemological powers. By accepting

our limitations, humans can live a more tranquil life, instead of fretting endlessly over metaphysical, religious, or ethical dogmas.

FURTHER READING: Long, A. A. Hellenistic Philosophy: Stoics, Epicureans and Sceptics. (Berkeley: University of California Press, 1974); Long and Sedley, eds. The Hellenistic Philosophers. *(Cambridge: Cambridge University Press, 1987); Annas and Barnes, eds. T*he Modes Of Scepticism. *(Cambridge: Cambridge University Press, 1985); Annas, J. 'Scepticism, Old and New,' in M. Frede and G. Striker, eds.,* Rationality in Greek Thought. *(Oxford: Clarendon, 1996); Bett, R.* Pyrrho, His Antecedents, and His Legacy. *(Oxford: Oxford University Press, 2000); Colish, M. (1985).* The Stoic Tradition From Antiquity to the Early Middle Ages, vol. 1. *(Leiden: Brill, 1985); Sihvola, J., ed.* Ancient Scepticism and the Sceptical Tradition. *(Helsinki : Philosophical Society of Finland, 2000).*

Spinning

Activity symbolically connected with fate; in classical mythology the three Fates spin the thread of each man's life, weave it, and sever it; the fact that spiders spin webs to catch flies has contributed to their folklore and symbolism.

Stoicism

This ancient Greek and Roman philosophy emphasizes virtuous living in accordance with nature as well as acceptance of one's role in a totally determined universe. Stoicism began with Zeno of Citium, a thinker and teacher operating in Athens beginning in 300 BC, and ending with Roman Emperor Marcus Aurelius in the 2nd century AD. Stoicism draws some of its central ethical tenets from the Cynics, who taught ascetic living and indifference to pain and social convention.

Like the Academics, those thinkers from the tradition of Plato's Academy, the Stoics formed their philosophical framework on three main foundations: logic, physics, and ethics. In line with Plato, the Stoics understood that right and virtuous living should be based on rationality and truth. They differed significantly from the Academics in most specifics, however. For example, Stoics claimed that the universe was entirely material. This strict monism had various consequences for their philosophy, namely the absence of true freedom. If the entire universe is made of matter, and that matter is governed by physical laws, then all events are determined in advance. This means both that humans are not truly free and that prediction or divination of the future is possible. So, logic governs physics, which leads to a strict ethical position: all actions that are in accordance with nature and its rational laws are good and virtuous. Because

the universe, and humans within the universe, necessarily operate according to their nature, it would be technically impossible to bypass being virtuous. But the Stoics insist that even if this is the case, we should thoughtfully accept the rational life, consciously acting in our nature. To attain the goal of rational action, we should abandon emotional responses entirely. Emotions are antithetical to reason and can only cloud the truth.

This indifference to the world as well as utter lack of emotion is at the heart of modern uses of the word 'stoic'. A stoic person, in the modern sense, endures all difficulties and trials without complaint or despair. In fact, indifference for the ancient Stoics signaled a fundamental acceptance of one's place in a fully determined universe. Death, illness, loss of wealth or material possessions, or any other

external evil should be treated as a necessary part of the determined universe. Emotional reactions to these sorts of events, as well as their opposites, is both unnecessary and undesirable since it encourages a loss of logical attitudes to the world.

After the founder Zeno of Citium (not to be confused with Zeno of Elea who is remembered for 'Zeno's Paradox'), the most famous and influential Stoics are, from Greece, Chrysippus and Epictetus, and from Rome, Cicero, Seneca, and Emperor Marcus Aurelius. Chrysippus was a genius of logic studies, introducing a number of advanced propositional logic techniques that were only rediscovered in the second half of the twentieth century. The later Stoics are the best documented; their writings are largely those that have survived. Cicero, apart from contributing to the Stoic philo-

Chrysippos of Soli, second founder of Stoicism

sophical bibliography, wrote prolifically in the fields of politics and rhetoric. Cicero was known for his political career and his sophisticated writing style. Seneca was likewise celebrated for his learning, wisdom, political intelligence and literary talent. He taught and advised Empereor Nero, and composed a number of tragic plays that may have strongly influenced generations of writers, including Shakespeare and his contemporaries. Marcus Aurelius, Emperor of Rome from 161 to 180 AD, was a politician, general, and prolific author. Aside from his campaign against the northern Germanic tribes during the Marcomannic Wars, Aurelius is known for his Meditations, a lucid and powerful essay on Stoic duty and virtue.

FURTHER READING: Irvine, William Braxton. A Guide to the Good Life: The Ancient Art of Stoic Joy. *(Oxford: Oxford UP, 2009); Epictetus, and Robert F. Dobbin.* Discourses and Selected Writings. *(London: Penguin, 2008); Seneca, Lucius Annaeus, and Robin Campbell.* Letters from a Stoic. Epistulae Morales Ad Lucilium. *(Harmondsworth: Penguin, 1969); Inwood, Brad.* The Cambridge Companion to the Stoics. *(Cambridge: Cambridge UP, 2003); Marcus, Aurelius.* Meditations. *(Hollywood, FL: Simon & Brown, 2012); Wolfe, Tom.* A Man in Full: A Novel. *(New York: Bantam, 2001).*

Theseus

For the Athenians, as for us, Theseus was one of the more important heroes of Greek legend. But his full renown is of relatively late growth and peculiar to Attica. In fact Theseus has two aspects, which may be called the heroic and the political. In his heroic aspect he is an adventurer, subduer of monsters and chaser of women, after the fashion of Hercules, on whom he came to be modelled. In his political aspect he is a symbol of Athens and of Attic unity and power, indeed almost the only hero to become such an established symbol. He is treated for all purposes as a historical figure, even by sober writers of prose such as Aristotle. For this reason Plutarch brackets him with another legendary figure in his *Parallel Lives of Greeks and Romans,* the founder of Rome, Romulus.

Though for ordinary Greeks legend was not separate from the history of earlier periods, in the case of Theseus this distinction must be made in some form. But it is not enough to argue simply that the heroic Theseus in his marvellous adventures is purely legendary, while the political Theseus is historical in the sense of being a man who really lived. For the political Theseus is a figure answering to other needs of the Attic imagination, but hardly less fictitious.

As a pan-Hellenic hero, Theseus is a relatively minor figure of the generation before the Trojan War, by no means of such stature as his contemporary Hercules or some other figures. He is connected in legend with Troezen in the eastern Peloponnese but otherwise only with Attica, apart from the regions visited in his adventures and wanderings. For the Athenians of classical times he was not only the slayer of the Minotaur but also the author of a great political change, the synoikismos, that is to say the incorporation of all Attic communities into a single state ruled from Athens. In Attic legend he is also the pattern of

Theseus Fighting the Minotaur, Étienne-Jules Ramey (1796–1852)

Opposite page:
The Minotaur, George Frederic Watts (1817–1904)

the humane ruler who receives refugees and unfortunates, since Attica is never in his time ravaged by war.

From Plutarch's Life of Theseus and from two other compilers, Diodorus and Apollodorus, the outline of Theseus's life can be told. This is fortunate because there is no continuous and complete narrative in extant poetry, and even vanished epic poems of Attica such as the Theseis and the Minyas, which are later than the *Iliad* and the *Odyssey*, do not seem from remaining fragments or from references in other writers to have told the whole story.

Sword beneath the Rock

Theseus was born in Troezen to Aethra, daughter of King Pittheus. In Athenian legend his father was King Aegeus of Athens, who returned to Athens before he was born, leaving under a hollow rock a sword and a pair of sandals, to be claimed by his son when he was big enough to raise the rock. In the Troezenian legend his father was the god Poseidon, who has an important part even in the Athenian legend. Having lifted the rock, Theseus then made his way to Athens.

However, he did not take the easy way by sea. He went by land, overcoming and killing dangerous robbers. Such were Periphetes, who attacked travelers with his club; Sinis who bent down pine trees, tied his victims to the tops and then let the trees spring up and apart to tear them limb from limb; Cercyon who forced men to wrestle with him until he killed them; Sciron who made travelers wash his feet on the top of a precipice so that he could kick them over; and Procrustes who forced them to fit one of his two beds, stretching out the shorter travelers to fit the longer bed and lopping the taller to fit the shorter. He

also killed the ravaging sow of Crommyon. On being welcomed by Aegeus at Athens, he was very nearly poisoned by a drink offered by the witch Medea, then married to Aegeus; but Aegeus recognized him and cried out in time.

Aegeus then told Theseus of the affliction that the Athenians suffered at the hands of Minos of Crete. In vengeance for the killing of his son Androgeus in Attica, Minos every year carried off a band of Athenian youths and maidens to be given as victims to the Minotaur. This was a monster with a human body and a bull's head, usually said to have been kept in the labyrinth of Cnossus, a building designed in the form of an intricate maze, from which no one who entered could find his way out.

> . . . *The Minotaur. This was a monster with a human body and a bull's head, unusually said to have been kept in the labyrinth of Cnossus . . .*

Food for the Minotaur

Theseus went voluntarily as one of the victims. When he arrived on Crete, he won the help of Ariadne, daughter of Minos. She gave him a ball of thread to unwind as he made his way into the labyrinth and follow so that he could find his way out again. He killed the Minotaur with his sword and then set off homeward in triumph with the captives, who were no longer needed as food for the Minotaur. He took Ariadne with him, but left her behind on the island of Dia off the coast near Cnossus or, as was more commonly said, on the island of Naxos, where the god Dionysus found her and took her as his wife.

As Theseus approached Athens, he forgot to change the black sail of the ship, a sign of mourning for the young

Athenians, for a white one which would be a sign of deliverance. This he had promised to do if he came home safe. Aegeus, who was looking out for him, concluded that he had perished and hurled himself from a cliff.

Theseus thus became king of Athens. He had to fight rivals, the sons of Pallas, brother of Aegeus, but prevailed over them. He subdued the wild bull of Marathon, being sheltered on his way by an old peasant woman, Hecale. On an expedition with Hercules and others to Themiscyra, where the Amazons lived on the south coast of the Black Sea, he carried off an Amazon, Antiope or, according to others, Hippolyta, and made her his wife; he later repudiated her and married Phaedra, daughter of Minos. The Amazons made war on him, invaded Attica and were with a great effort defeated. By his Amazon wife he had a son, Hippolytus. He also carried off Helen as a girl from Laconia, but she was brought home by force while he was away by her brothers Castor and Polydeuces.

Theseus was in Hades at the time with his friend Pirithous the Lapith, who was attempting to carry off Persephone, queen of the underworld. Pluto, however, cunningly persuaded Theseus and Pirithous to sit on seats, to which their flesh grew. Theseus was rescued by Hercules, who could not free Pirithous.

When Theseus eventually returned to Athens he found that the people were disaffected. He left for the island of Scyros, where the king Lycomedes, fearing that he meant to annex the island, treacherously thrust him over a cliff. A skeleton of great size, said to be his, was found on Scyros centuries later and carried to Athens by Cimon.

The adventures given in this framework appear here and there in surviving poetry, including some celebrated

Third century Roman relief of Achilles at the court of King Lycomedes, the ruler that killed Theseus by pushing him off a cliff.

plays, which introduce something of his other aspect of statesman. Within extant poetry the earliest mention of Theseus is in a speech by Nestor in the *Iliad* (book 1). Nestor compares the warriors at Troy to their disadvantage with the earlier generation which included Pirithous and Theseus, son of Aegeus. 'They were like the immortals, the mightiest of men, who fought the mightiest of enemies, the beast-men of the hills.' The reference is to the centaurs whom Pirithous and his Lapithae subdued with the help of Theseus. In the *Odyssey* (book 11) there is mention of the ghost of Ariadne in Hades 'whom Theseus wished to bring from Crete to Athens but who was slain by Artemis on Dia by the witness of Dionysus': a puzzling passage. The *Odyssey* also relates that Odysseus, after seeing the phantom of Hercules, also hoped to see the ghosts of Theseus and Pirithous. The expedition of the

two heroes to Hades must have been known to Homer.

According to Hesiod as reported in Athenaeus and Plutarch, Theseus abandoned Ariadne because he took a fancy to the maidens Hippe and Aegle. A damaged papyrus contains a fragment of a Hesiodic poem *The Descent of Pirithous*, in which the ghost of Theseus in Hades tells the ghost of Meleager how he and Pirithous came down to carry off Persephone. Meleager apparently hears the story with disgust.

In the remains of the *Epic Cycle*, poems of the same type as the *Iliad* and *Odyssey* but later and inferior, there is an occasional allusion to Theseus. In the *Nostoi* (Homeward Journeys of the Heroes from Troy) it is said that the love of Antiope for Theseus led her to betray Themiscyra to him and Hercules. In the Cypria Theseus is said to have carried off Helen and to

have kept her until she was rescued by her brothers, the Dioscuri.

Among the lyric poets Alcman, as reported by Pausanias, tells how the Dioscuri, retrieving Helen, took Athens while Theseus was away and captured his mother Aethra. Stesichorus says that Helen was pregnant at the time of her rescue, and gave birth at Argos to an infant which she handed over to her sister Clytemnestra, before she herself married Menelaus. Pindar tells much the same story, explaining that Theseus kept Helen because he wished to become brother-in-law of the Dioscuri.

Palace under the Sea

But the most celebrated treatment of Theseus in lyric is found in two poems of Bacchylides. In *Dithyramb 18*, Aegeus is presented in conversation with a chorus about the approach of a remarkable stranger coming from

Troezen. Aegeus has heard that he has killed Sinis and the other robbers and the sow of Crommyon. Two men are accompanying him; he wears a sword, a Laconian helmet, a red tunic and a woollen Thessalian cloak. His hair is flame-coloured and he darts from his eyes a red flame like the earth-fire of Lemons. He is in the flower of his youth, his thoughts are of weapons and he is making for Athens. In Dithyramb 17, Theseus is shown sailing to Crete in the charge of Minos with the captive youths and maidens. He disputes with Minos, who is laying his hands on one of the maidens, claiming that if Minos is son of Zeus he himself is son of Poseidon. Zeus gives a clap of thunder as a sign for Minos, who throws his ring into the sea, challenging Theseus to dive for it. Theseus plunges in and reaches Poseidon's palace under the sea, where he is greeted by Amphitrite and presented with a bright garment. He comes up to the surface still dry,

and the Nereids sing around him as he returns on board.

In Attic drama Theseus is prominent in Sophocles' *Oedipus at Colonus* and in Euripides' *Mad Hercules*, *Hippolytus*, and *Suppliants*. In the Oedipus at Colonus the aged and blind Oedipus, exiled from Thebes, is received in Attica at Colonus as a refugee with his two daughters. Theseus gives him protection and will not allow Creon of Thebes to carry off him or his daughters. In reward Oedipus reveals to Theseus alone where he must die in Attica and how, when he has disappeared beneath Attic earth, his presence will be a blessing to Attica. Only Theseus sees the manner of his death, and on oath reveals it to no one except his heirs. For this service Oedipus will hold Athens unscathed from any attack that may come from the Thebans who cast him out. Sophocles also wrote a *Phaedra*, which has perished; it dealt with the adulterous passion of Phaedra, wife of Theseus, for her

stepson Hippolytus, but details are not known. It is believed that at the time of the action Theseus is supposed to be away.

In *Mad Hercules* Euripides relates how Hercules, after recovering from the fit of madness in which he killed his children, is brought to Attica from Thebes by Theseus and cleansed from the defilement of his deed. He also receives the promise of a place to dwell in recognition of his services to the Greeks, including Theseus. So too in the *Suppliants* Theseus supports the claim of Adrastus, the survivor among the chiefs who led the great Argive expedition against Thebes, to receive back the dead from the Thebans. If the Thebans will not yield, Theseus will make war on them, after putting the proposal to the Athenian people for their approval. He receives back the bodies of the Argive troops which the Athenians bury on Cythaeron, while those of the leaders are brought to Eleusis in Attica for burning before the bones and ashes are taken to Argos.

Deceived Husband

In the *Hippolytus*, Theseus has a very different part. There were two versions, of which the older, now lost, presented Phaedra in the style of Potiphar's wife, as perhaps Sophocles did, attempting to seduce Hippolytus and, when she failed, denouncing him for an attempt on her virtue. In the later one, which survives, Phaedra at first takes no action and conceals her passion until she is ill with it. Her old nurse induces her to confess it and unwisely reveals it to Hippolytus, making overtures in Phaedra's name

The bull horns one of the sacred symbols of the Minoan religion, Greece, Minoan, Late Bronze Age (1450-1400 BC). Cnossos, Crete

but without her permission. Hippolytus recoils in horror and upbraids Phaedra for advances which she did not make. Phaedra hangs herself, leaving a written message for Theseus, accusing Hippolytus of rape. On his return Theseus believes the message and curses Hippolytus, driving him into exile. As Hippolytus drives along the shore, Poseidon, carrying out Theseus's curse, sends a bull from the sea to terrify his horses. They smash his chariot and drag him until he is nearly dead. The goddess Artemis then appears to tell Theseus the truth, and he is reconciled to his dying son. Theseus appears here only as a deceived, outraged, and hasty husband and father. But in the other plays he appears as a humane ruler with a certain leaning toward democracy.

Episodes of Theseus's career are treated in Alexandrian poetry. Bion remarks that all lovers are happy, even Theseus when he went down into implacable Hades, because Pirithous was at his side. The remains of Callimachus's *Hecale* tell how the old peasant woman, Hecale, entertained Theseus on his way to capture the bull of Marathon, but was dead when he returned.

It has been argued that Theseus was originally a hero of the Ionian Greeks, who lived in the northern Peloponnese as well as in Attica and Euboea before the Dorian and West Greek invasion, so that his connection with Troezen, a Dorian city in classical times, goes back to the Mycenean period. Within Attica he seems originally to have belonged to the northeastern region about Marathon. The power of Minos over Attica could represent the power of rulers in Cnossus, who were already, in the 15th century BC, Greeks rather than Minoans, though Cnossus fell later to other Greeks from the mainland. Theseus's defeat of the robbers between Troezen and Athens

may be a fairly late development of his story, not much earlier than the 6th century BC.

Friend of Democracy

The political Theseus no doubt has ancient roots in Attic tradition. But he appears in definite form first in Thucydides, and in plays of Euripides which apply forms of thought belonging to the 5th century BC to heroic legend. According to Thucydides, Attica before Theseus's reign was divided between separate communities which had their own authorities and took little common counsel or action except in face of external peril. The shrewd and energetic Theseus abolished these local assemblies and directed their members to meet in Athens, though the rest of the local inhabitants still lived separately. By the death of Theseus, Athens had become a large and powerful state, and the Athenians date their political unity from that time. Euripides in his Suppliants even makes Theseus claim to have set the people free to exercise equal votes and to elect annual officers, an equal part of these to be chosen by the poor. Isocrates (*Panathenaicus*), Aristotle (*Politics and Constitution of Athens*), and Plutarch (*Life of Theseus*) regard Theseus's constitution as a historical creation, a mixture of various elements which was intended to be just and stable and was later gradually improved, until finally it was transformed for the worse into extreme democracy. Some oligarchs regarded Theseus's concessions to the people as the remote beginning of decay.

The truth symbolized by this treatment of Theseus, alone among epic heroes, is that Attic society, and even the Attic state, had a continuous existence since heroic or, historically, since Mycenean times. In other regions of Greece overrun by the Dorians the heroic or Mycenean society had been

swept away and no such continuity could be claimed.

E. D. PHILLIPS

Thyrsos

Ivy-twined staff tipped with a pine cone, or sometimes with a bunch of grapes and vine leaves, which was an attribute of the Greek god Dionysus and was carried by his worshippers: ivy was the plant of Dionysus and the phallic pine cone was an emblem of fertility and immortality; the grapes and vine leaves marked the god's link with wine and intoxication.

The Titans

A race of enormous, powerful gods; they roamed the earth before the Olympian gods. The Titans were the children of Ouranos (Heaven) and Gaia (Mother Earth). Ouranos and Gaia also produced the Hecatonchires (The Hundred-Handed Ones) and the Cyclopes (giant beings with a single eye). Most of the Titans are not central to Greek mythology, although they play a role in the foundational creation myths; notable Titans include Cronus, Rhea, Prometheus, and Atlas.

The Titans in Creation Myths

Ouranos, jealous of the strength and power of his offspring, casts the Cyclopes into Tartarus (the deepest region of the Underworld) so that they cannot challenge his rule. Gaia, their mother, is angered by this and encourages the Titans to rise up against Ouranos. Cronus, the youngest Titan, takes a flint sickle and castrates his father Ouranos in his sleep. Blood from this wound drops on the Earth and from it spring the Giants (another large race of immortal beings) and the Erinyes (also known as 'The Furies';

The eleventh labour of Hercules requires a transfer of Atlas' burden, but only for a short time.

ful enough, Rhea helps him mount an attack on Cronus and the Titans. Zeus slips a poison into Cronus' cup, making him vomit up the children he ate; Poseiden, Hades, Hestia, Demeter, and Hera are all released, and prepare to fight the Titans. Zeus releases the imprisoned Hecatonchires and Cyclopes from Tartarus, and this rebel army defeats the Titans who band together under the leadership of Atlas. When the war is over, the Hecatonchires are tasked with guarding the exiled Titans, and Atlas must spend his days holding up the Heavens on his shoulders. Zeus assumes leadership of the world, and the Olympian age begins. At the same time, cycles of mythical family violence are established in these early creation stories that reverberate in much of the later Hellenic material.

Prometheus: Saviour of Humanity and Trickster

Prometheus elects to fight against Cronus in the Titanomachy, and so avoids the fate of his relatives when they lose the war. He is an unusual figure in that Prometheus is not only very wise and talented, but when Zeus is inclined to be harsh with the human race, Prometheus supports and protects them. Some myths indicate that Prometheus created humans, hence his desire to help them. The first major exploit involving Prometheus and his trickster nature involves the question of what portion of a sacrificed animal is offered to the gods and what portion to humans. Prometheus disguises bones and fat to look like excellent meat, and the meat to look like bones. Zeus chooses the bones and fat for his portion, but in anger at being tricked, vows to withhold fire from humans. Prometheus steals fire from Mt. Olympus, passing it to humans so they can cook their meat and warm themselves. When Zeus discovers this further deception, he chains Prometheus to a giant boulder and has a huge eagle

hideous, winged creatures that exact revenge on filial misdeeds). From Ouranos' severed testacles, which Cronus flings into the ocean, arises Aphrodite, goddess of love. Cronus assumes power over the Earth and takes his sister Rhea as his wife. His first act as sovereign is to re-imprison the Cyclopes, and along with them the Hecatonchires.

Titanomachy, or War of the Titans

The Titanomachy was the battle waged between the younger Olympian gods, led by Zeus, Hades, and Poseidon, and the older Titan rulers, led by Atlas.

Like his father before him, Cronus is jealous and wary of those who might overthrow him. Instead of throwing his children into Tartarus as Ouranos did, Cronus devours them as soon as they are born. Rhea (like Gaia before her) is outraged by this, so she bears her youngest boy Zeus in secret, substituting a stone wrapped in swaddling clothes for Cronus to eat. When Zeus is mature and power-

(some say a vulture) eat his liver every day, and each night the liver heals, only to be eaten again the next day.

Prometheus, of all the Titans, plays a peculiar role in post-Titanomachy mythology, and so is worth some attention. His story is both a cautionary tale (be careful of the tricks you play or the dangerous things you invent) as well as an inspiration for progress (as an inventor, thinker, creator). His fire-stealing episode is echoed in other cultures whose trickster gods steal fire, and his ingenuity is similar to other characters in Greek myth, such as Sisyphus, Daedalus, and Odysseus. He is the subject of an ancient tragedy *Prometheus Bound* (controversially attributed to Aeschylus) and a lyrical drama by Percy Shelley, *Prometheus Unbound*.

FURTHER READING: Campbell, Joseph. The Hero with a Thousand Faces. *(Princeton, NJ: Princeton UP, 1968); Hyde, Lewis.* Trickster Makes This World: Mischief, Myth, and Art. *(New York: Farrar, Straus and Giroux, 1998); Aeschylus, James Scully, and C. J. Herington.* Prometheus Bound. *(New York: Oxford UP, 1975); Hesiod, and M. L. West.* Hesiod: Theogony. *(Oxford: Clarendon, 1966).*

The Story of Troy: Cassandra intercedes before Priam to obtain a Pardon for Paris; Brussels Manufactory (1515-1525)

The Trojan War

The Trojan War is a mythical battle between an alliance of Greek city states and the city of Troy. Homer describes a short segment of the decade long war in the *Iliad*, and includes further embellishments in scenes from the *Odyssey*. While the conflict has long been considered entirely mythic fantasy, in recent decades archaeological evidence strongly suggests that Troy, or Illium, was an historical city, and that it was destroyed in a large battle at about the time of the mythical conflict. The myth, however, has

inspired storytellers in poetry, theatre, film, and music for thousands of years.

Causus Belli

The cause of war, according to legend, is the abduction of Helen, the most beautiful woman in the world. Paris, prince of Troy, absconds with her, and so sets in motion the largest military expedition in Greek memory and the ultimate destruction of his home. Paris was a very attractive if fairly weak and un-warlike young man who grew up in the mountains when his mother left him to die (having been told in a dream that her son would cause the downfall of Troy). He is known to

have excellent judgment in matters of feminine beauty. So when an argument erupts between the goddesses Aphrodite, Hera, and Athena over who is the fairest, they seek out Paris to make the ruling. In what is known as 'The Judgment of Paris', the three goddesses offer the prince bribes: Athena offers him power, Hera offers him wealth, and Aphrodite offers him the most beautiful woman in the world. Paris chooses Aphrodite, who promptly leads him to Helen.

Helen had, after a hotly contested courtship, chosen Menelaus as her husband, who became King of Sparta. The other suitors, who included

Decorated pithos (large storage jar) found at Mykonos, Greece, depicting one of the earliest known renditions of the Trojan Horse

Odysseus and many other future leaders of the region, all agreed that whomever won Helen would have the protection of the rest. So when Helen ran away with Paris, the old pact still stood intact, and the Greeks amassed 1,000 ships in pursuit. Agamemnon, the most powerful of the group, takes leadership of the army, although each contingent is led by a different commander. So while Troy is a unified foe with city walls, the Greek army is a coalition whose in-fighting almost spells their defeat, as Homer relates in the *Iliad*.

The Siege of Troy

The war lasts ten years. The first nine years are glossed over, and not much is known or told other than the fact that neither side can gain any permanent advantage over the other. Homer's *Iliad* relates the events during a short period of the final year. Achilles, Greece's greatest warrior, is enraged that Agamemnon would steal his concubine after being forced to relinquish his own, the daughter of a priestess of Apollo. Because of Agamemnon's slight against Achilles, the great warrior refuses to fight and threatens

to return home. This is almost fatal to the Greek forces because Achilles single-handedly fights like an entire squadron of men, and his contingent are hardened soldiers.

In the fighting, while Achilles sulks away from the battlefield, his young companion Petroclus enters the fray wearing Achilles' armour and is killed by Hector, the prince and great champion of Troy. This brings Achilles out of his indifference and he challenges Hector to single combat. Hector knows he will be beaten, and says a tearful goodbye to his wife and son. Achilles kills him, and then in an almost obscene final gesture drags Hector's body behind his chariot, refusing to give the body to the Trojans for a proper burial. King Priam steals into the Greek encampment late at night and begs for his son's body back. In the moving scene in which Priam kneels before Achilles, the man who has killed so many of Priam's sons, Achilles' rage is lost and he understands the nature of human suffering.

The Fall of Troy

After the action of the *Iliad*, the story continues. Homer tells the story of

the Trojan Horse in Book VIII of the *Odyssey*, when a singer (not unlike Homer himself) performs for Odysseus at his request. This passage inspires Virgil's account of the fall of Troy in the *Aeneid*.

Paris, with help from Apollo, shoots an arrow that catches Achilles in his one vulnerable point: his heel. Achilles' subsequent death is marked by a funeral in which the entire Greek army and many of the gods lament his passing. Paris and Priam are killed during battle by Achilles's son Neoptolemus.

Odysseus comes up with the idea of the wooden horse: a massive horse sculpture is constructed out of sight of the city. All the remaining Greek ships pack up and sail away, as if they are retreating. The great Greek heroes hide inside the horse, which, when the Trojans find it, they think is some kind of parting gift, and so they bring it inside the city walls as a trophy. That night the heroes burst out of the horse, the Greek army returns, and they burn the city of Troy to the ground. The war is over.

Archaeological Evidence for the Trojan War

Since the nineteenth century when archaeologist Heinrich Schliemann began his quest to find the treasures of ancient Greece, the Trojan War has become more than a myth and has started to be taken seriously as a piece of history by many researchers. Parts of the story are probably mythical: Helen as the impetus for war is probably a myth, although historians have evidence for women being treated as property during the alleged time of the war, around the 12th century BC. The story of the war, however, in its larger arc as a story of conflict between the western kingdoms of Mycenea and the eastern kingdoms in ancient Turkey (probably Hittites), is historically sound. There is also evidence that the city known as Illium or Troy, on the western coast of Turkey, was destroyed at least twice, one of those times in and around the 12th century BC. New clues continue to be discovered, but more and more the evidence suggests that the Trojan War, or perhaps a series of east-west conflicts, was an historical event recorded and expanded in popular memory by lyrical storytellers like Homer.

FURTHER READING: Wood, Michael. In Search of the Trojan War. (Berkeley: University of California, 1998); Strauss, Barry S. The Trojan War: A New History. (New York: Simon & Schuster, 2007); Fields, Nic, Donato Spedaliere, and S. S. Spedaliere. Troy, C[a]. 1700–1250 BC. (Oxford: Osprey, 2004).

Troy

The principal sources of our knowledge about Troy are twofold and complementary; the Homeric epics, and archeological investigation in modern times. It is as a result of archeological investigation that there is now general acceptance of the view that there is a historical reality behind Homer; and that the tale of a ten-year siege of the city by an expedition under the command of the Achaean overlord Agamemnon from mainland Greece had a real basis. In addition, as the result of recent researches into the techniques of orally transmitted poetry, there is also wide acceptance of the theory that, no matter what the precise date may have been when the *Iliad* and the *Odyssey* were first written down in their present form, the sagas about the Trojan War and its aftermath could have been commemorated by bards soon after the actual events. These early sagas would then have formed the basis of the epic tradition, which was refined and

enlarged by succeeding generations of poets depending upon memory and improvisation. It seems likely that the Trojans and Achaeans not only had the same kind of material culture but were perhaps of similar 'Indo-European' extraction.

The name of Homer is primarily associated with the two great epic poems, the *Iliad* and the *Odyssey*. Each of them is independent but their common background is the Trojan War. The central feature of the *Iliad* is the 'Wrath of Achilles', or the quarrel between Achilles and his overlord, Agamemnon. As a result of this quarrel, Achilles refused to continue fighting and the Greeks are pressed back. Then Achilles takes up arms again and kills Hector, the Trojan prince. The *Iliad* ends with Hector's funeral.

The *Odyssey* contains much about the Trojan War too, but it starts at a point in the tenth year after the war ended. There is a council of the Olympian gods, at which it is decided that Odysseus, who has been wandering

about as a result of the anger directed against him by the sea god Poseidon, should be brought home to his kingdom of Ithaca. The nucleus is a cunning man's voyage overseas among miracles and monsters, his revenge on his enemies who took advantage of his absence, the faithful wife at home, the young son growing to maturity in the absence of his father. Though the adventures extend over ten years, all but the last are concentrated in a single section. As in the *Iliad*, a large subject is embraced in one view by focusing on a single portion.

The Towers of Ilion

Epic poetry is simply recitation; and Greek epic is written in hexameters, a single verse constantly repeated, saved from monotony by the device of a shifting caesura or 'pause' in the line. One of the features of epic diction is the use of stock phrases, many of them very old. They frequently consist of a half-verse preceding or following the caesura. The formality of these set

Woodcut from the Nuremberg Chronicle (1493)

verses, used repeatedly and without variation whenever the subject requires them, stamps them as archaic. The roots of the *Iliad* and *Odyssey* lie far back in the Mycenean Age, though the poems as a whole appear to have taken shape in Asia Minor during the tenth and ninth centuries; and they were still expanding in the seventh.

Homeric archeology is a comparative study. Its object is to interpret the poems in the light of the excavated remains, and the remains in the light of the poems. There are elements in the poems—descriptions of material objects and social usages—which have accordingly been dated to definite periods, early or late, from the fifteenth to the seventh centuries.

From a reading of Homer we gather that Troy was an extensive city, defended by mighty walls and towers and it is called either Troy (Troie) or Ilios, both conventionally described as 'well-walled', but each having more distinctive epithets. Troy is a 'broad city', 'a great city', 'the city of the Trojans', with 'deep rich soil'; it is the 'city of Priam', having 'lofty gates' and 'fine towers'; and Ilios is 'well-built', 'very windy' but 'a comfortable place to live'; it is also 'steep', 'sheer' and 'frowning', as well as 'holy' and 'sacred'; since it was the city of the Trojans ('those tamers of horses') it

not surprisingly has 'fine foals'. It has been conjectured that the city of which Homer gives us these revealing glimpses could have sheltered as many as 50,000 people. A great city indeed must have been required for the indigenous people and the many allies of the Trojans with their horses and war gear.

There was an open agora (place of assembly) in the upper part of the citadel outside the palace of King Priam. This magnificent place 'was fronted with marble colonnades, and in the main building behind there were fifty apartments of polished stone, adjoining each other, where Priam's sons slept with their wives. His daughters had separate quarters, on the other side of the courtyard, where twelve adjoining bedrooms had been built for them, of polished stone and well roofed in. Priam's sons-in-law slept with their loving wives in these.' Nearby were other palatial residences, including those of Hector and Paris, the latter built by Paris himself with the aid of the best workmen to be found in the land of Troy.

There were temples of Apollo and of Athene. The latter seems to have had a seated image of the goddess, for Hector (*Iliad*, book 6) bids his mother Hecuba to take a robe, the loveliest and biggest she can find,

the one she most prizes herself, and lay it on the knees of the goddess. She is to promise to sacrifice a dozen yearling heifers, if only Athene will take pity on the town, on the wives and children of the Trojans. Homer then describes how Hecuba went into the palace and ordered her attendant ladies to gather the old women together from all parts of the city. Then she entered her bedchamber, where she stored her embroidered robes, woven by the women of Sidon whom Paris had brought back with him on the voyage on which he had fetched Helen. One of these robes, the largest and most richly adorned, lying at the bottom of the pile like a cluster of brilliant stars, she picked out as the gift for Athene. The old women thronged after her to the shrine in the citadel, and the door was opened to them by Theano, daughter of Kisseus and wife of Antenor, whom the Trojans had chosen to be priestess. They lifted their hands to Athene, and Theano took the robe and laid it upon the lap of the goddess.

Was this magnificent city, doomed to destruction at the hands of the besieging Greek forces, conjured out of poetic imagination? Did the Trojan War really take place? The search for the site, the work of excavation, the correlation of material objects with

Laminated cuff, a so-called treasure of Priam

The site of numerous sanctuaries where many animals were sacrificed; The wells provided water to wash the altar.

Ulysses Remembers Troy

*Much have I seen and known;
cities of men*

*And manners, climates, councils,
governments,*

*Myself not least, but honour'd of
them all;*

*And drunk delight of battle with
my peers,*

*Far on the ringing plains of
windy Troy . . .*

*The lights begin to twinkle from
the rocks:*

*The long day wanes: the slow moon
climbs: the deep*

Moans round with many voices.

Come, my friends,

*'Tis not too late to seek a
newer world.*

*Push off, and sitting well in
order smite*

*The sounding furrows; for my
purpose holds*

*To sail beyond the sunset, and
the baths*

Of all the western stars, until I die.

*It may be that the gulfs will wash
us down:*

It may be we shall touch the

Happy Isles,

*And see the great Achilles, whom
we knew.*

Tho' much is taken, much abides; and tho'

*We are not now that strength
which in old days*

*Moved earth and heaven; that
which we are, we are;*

One equal temper of heroic hearts,

*Made weak by time and fate, but
strong in will*

*To strive, to seek, to find, and not
to yield.*

Tennyson, *Ulysses*

Homeric description—all this has led to impressive archeological discoveries in the past hundred years, making impossible that kind of scholarly scepticism which once dismissed the age of the Greek heroes as entirely fictitious. We have now been able to discern a basis of hard fact in many cases, though inconsistency, exaggeration, and imaginative adornment must always be taken into account as possibly operative factors.

There is general agreement that no other city in the Troad (the northwest promontory of Asia Minor) except Hissarlik has any good claim to be the site of Troy. It also seems clear that the settlement known as Troy VI was severely damaged by an earthquake at the beginning of the 13th century BC, and was succeeded by the settlement known as Troy VII(a), which had real continuity with Troy VI. Troy VII(a) was destroyed by fire about half a century later, apparently through human agency. It is therefore Troy VII(a) which has strong claims to be regarded as the Homeric Troy.

From the 4th century BC onward, Greek historians reckoned years in Olympiads, from 776 BC, though local events continued to be dated by the names of annual magistrates and calculations for earlier times were based on the traditional genealogies. It is the Parian Marble, a long inscription of the 3rd century BC, which embodies the first attempt to work out a comprehensive chronology. Some time afterward another effort was made by the Alexandrine scholar Eratosthenes, whose Chronographicae in nine books (known to us in fragments) started with the capture of Troy, dated to 1184 BC, as compared with 1209 BC. Other historians and chronographers gave different dates and their conjectures ranged over a period of two centuries. A destruction date for Homeric Troy around the middle of the 13th century BC, would roughly agree with that given by the historian Herodotus.

Golden sauceboat with two handles, discovered in the excavation of Troy.

'The archaeological Troy,' wrote Carl Blegen, 'the Troy that was built by masons, carpenters, and labourers, of rough stones or squared building blocks, and crude bricks made with straw, of wooden timbers and beams, of clay, and probably thatch for the roofing—that Troy, in its ruined state today, differs greatly, so far as its appearance is concerned, from the glamorous citadel pictured in the epic poems. But—if one is blessed with a little imagination—when one stands on the ancient hill top in the extreme northwestern corner of Asia Minor and looks out over the Trojan plain and thinks of some of the many exciting scenes it has witnessed, one cannot escape feeling that this Troy, too, has a powerful touch of enchantment.'

The ruins, called Hissarlik, he continues, occupy the western tip of a low ridge coming from the east and ending somewhat abruptly in steep slopes on the north and west and a more gradual descent toward the south. Some four miles distant to the westward, across the flat plain of the tree-bordered Scamander, and beyond a line of low hills, is the Aegean Sea. On it, to the southwest, floats the island of Tenedos—which was sacked by Achilles—and much further northward is

Imbros, where, the sorrowing Hecuba says, some of her sons who had been captured by Achilles were sold into slavery. Behind Imbros, on a clear day, one sees the twin-peaked height of Samothrace, and often when the weather is at its clearest, one can even make out the summit of Mt. Athos. Looking on all this, one remembers the old story told by Aeschylus of the fire-signals that flashed from peak to peak across the sea and land to Mycenae, announcing to Clytemnestra that Troy had been captured.

The Mound of Hissarlik

Heinrich Schliemann, a German businessman turned archeologist, started to excavate the hill of Hissarlik in 1870 and he conducted seven major campaigns before he died in 1890. His work was then continued by his architect and assistant, Wilhelm Dörpfeld, in two large-scale campaigns in 1893 and 1894. His discoveries were published in his *Troja* und *Ilion* (1902). Then, between 1932 and 1938, seven campaigns of three to four months were arranged by the University of Cincinnati, with the aim of investigating anew the stratification and other problems. The results of this work

under Carl Blegen have now been published in the series called Troy.

The evidence of inscriptions found at Hissarlik caused it to be identified more than a century and a half ago as the site of Hellenistic and Roman. However, some of those who believed in a historical reality behind the Homeric poems considered that the site could be identified in the stronghold known as Bali Dagh, above the gorge through which the Scamander flows from the hills into the lower plain. In 1822 Charles Maclaren collected, in his *Dissertation on the Topography of the Plain of Troy*, all the relevant data from the *Iliad* and compared it with the best modern maps. As a result he revived the idea, prevalent from classical to Roman times, that Hellenistic and later lay upon the same site as the Homeric Troy. Frank Calvert, some fifty years later, arrived at a similar conclusion and, in 1865, put his theory to the test of actual excavation on a small scale. This produced Roman, Hellenistic, and prehistoric pottery and other objects. When Schliemann visited the Troad in 1868, Calvert showed him the site. He agreed that Hissarlik was a more likely possibility for the site of Troy than Bali Dagh, and determined to begin his excavations there.

The Hissarlik mound had a length of about 656 feet maximum and was under 492 feet wide. It went up to about 101 feet above the level of the plain at its northern extremity. As Blegen says: 'For an administrative centre and a capital the situation was admirably suited, both for security and for economic reasons. It lay near enough to the sea to have landing places and perhaps a small port or two within easy reach, and yet far enough away to be reasonably safe from sudden hostile attacks or piratical raids. It also controlled a land route that apparently came up along the western coastal region of Asia Minor to the shortest crossing of the straits from Asia to Europe. From its vantage grounds it could no doubt likewise dominate traffic up and down the straits, and perhaps tolls of some kind were exacted from those who passed.'

Break with the Past

The archeology of Troy, then, dates back for about 5,000 years. The first five settlements belong to the Early Bronze Age and are marked by a stratified deposit of some 39 feet in thickness. From the beginning the settlement was a kind of fortified stronghold and the debris of Troy I alone

consisted of no less than ten phases of building. The fortification wall in this first phase of the occupation of the site is its most peculiarly impressive feature, some of it found standing to a height of about ten feet 5,000 years after its construction. Well-built houses were sometimes coated with plaster and there were woven mats on the floors.

Troy VI of the Middle Bronze Age shows marked and novel differences from what had gone before. Blegen is not alone in thinking that these differences indicate a clear break with the past, and the arrival and establishment of a new people endowed with a heritage of its own. This new people could well have been culturally, perhaps ethnically, closely related to the Mycenaean Greeks.

FURTHER READING: M. Forrest ed. Troy and the Early Greeks. *(Cambridge U. Press, 1973); C. W. Blegen, and others.* Troy. *(Princeton Univ. Press, 1950–58, 4 vols).*

Uranus

Uranus is the Greek name for sky or heaven, whether as a common noun or personified as a god. In the earliest Greek literature the sky is imagined as a solid roof to the world, made of bronze or iron and garlanded with stars. (For the ancients there was nothing humdrum about metal; it comes from the womb of earth, and there is an air of magic about the working of it.) Nothing is said about its shape. The sun 'goes up into' it and 'comes down from' it. It is supported by Atlas, or by pillars. It is the seat of the gods, for the peaks of Mt. Olympus, where they have their houses, reach up to it.

Considered as a god himself, Uranus is the consort of Ge, Earth. The rain that fertilizes the earth and makes things grow is sometimes (from the 5th century BC on) represented as his seed, though this may be a rationalistic interpretation of the mythical marriage rather than its basic meaning. The mythical offspring were not, for

Central part of a large floor mosaic, from a Roman villa in Italy (c. 200-250 BC); Uranus, the god of eternity, is standing inside a celestial sphere decorated with zodiac signs.

example, vegetation spirits, but Titans, Cyclopes, and ogres with 100 hands, none of whom has any place in our present world. At their birth Uranus kept them pressed down inside Earth. In her discomfort she consulted with them, and Cronus was emboldened to take an adamantine sickle and castrate his father when he came at night to resume intercourse with Ge. Various divine or semidivine beings sprang up from where the drops of blood fell on the earth. Cronus threw the severed genitals in the sea, and in the foam that formed round them Aphrodite was born. (Her name suggested 'foam'.) Cronus now became king of the gods, and Uranus played no further part in the divine history.

The episode represents a combination of two myths. One is about the separation of heaven and earth. Many peoples tell how the sky originally lay on the earth and later rose or was pushed to its present position.

Sometimes a physical link such as a tree or navel-cord has to be severed; in Polynesian myth, heaven and earth were an embracing couple, Rangi and Papa, and Rangi's arms were cut through. Secondly, we have an Asiatic myth: in the Hittite version, Heaven is king of the gods for nine years and is then castrated; gods are born from his severed members. In the Babylonian version he is less prominent. The motif of children hated by their father and confined within their mother is there, and it is a son of Heaven who overthrows the father, but the primeval parents here are Apsu and Tiamat, the subterranean waters and those of the sea.

The personified Uranus owes his existence to these oriental models. He has no other significance in myth or cult. Indian evidence proves that Zeus was the original Father Sky and consort of Mother Earth; and he remained the real Greek sky god.

This computer enhancement of a Voyager 2 image emphasizes the high-level haze in Uranus' upper atmosphere.

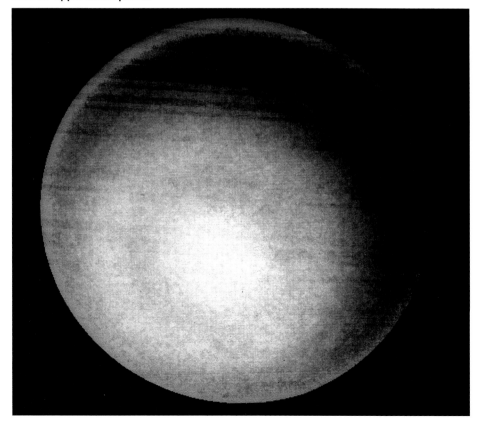

Uranus in Astrology

In 1781 Sir William Herschel identified a new planet, which was named first for King George III, then for Herschel himself and finally for the Greek sky god Uranus. The discovery of Uranus, and later of Neptune and Pluto, wrecked the traditional astrological picture of the order of the universe, in which the seven planets of antiquity corresponded to numerous other groups of seven, and round which so many religious, mystical and magical ideas had gathered. In the circumstances, it is not surprising that 'change' is the key notion which astrologers have come to associate with Uranus, especially change of a sudden, disruptive and revolutionary sort.

Astrologers say that it is only when a new planet is recognized that human beings seem to respond to its influence, even though the planet has been in existence, unrecognized, all along. They see the influence of Uranus behind all the violent and revolutionary upheavals of the modern world, from the French Revolution onward, behind the accelerated pace of change, new inventions and discoveries, and progress in science and technology, especially in the fields of electricity and magnetism. Someone strongly influenced by Uranus is likely to be highly original and inventive, free-thinking and rebellious, independent, willful, unconventional, wild and unorthodox, impatient of old systems and accepted ideas.

Some see the planet casting its shadow before it, as it were, in the American Revolution of 1776, and Uranus is believed to have played an important role in American history. It was in the ascendant sign, Gemini, when the Declaration of Independence was signed. It returned to Gemini, in an ominous conjunction with the two baleful planets Saturn and Mars, in 1860, the year before the outbreak of the Civil War. It was again in Gemini, and again in conjunction with Mars, in 1942, when the United States was again at war.

FURTHER READING: A. Crowley, Aleister Crowley's Astrology (Spearman, 1974); T. George. Uranus-Neptune-Pluto. *(Arthur Publications, 1980); J. Townley.* Uranus. *(Weiser, 1978); P. Walcot.* Hesiod and the Near East. *(Verry, Lawrence, 1966).*

Venus

The word Venus is related to English 'wish' and, more remotely, 'win'. The Latin common noun means 'charm', 'attraction', 'delight'. Its derivative verb venerari, which in antiquity also meant 'venerate', primitively signified the sacral act of alluring or enticing something from beyond mankind's power. Thus a famous literary echo of an old prayer reports the formal enticement of willingness from the god Quirinus (veneror horam Quirini). The goddess who sprang from the abstract venus forever kept the skill of wheedling.

Rome's foremost expert in religious history, Varro, was struck by the absence of Venus's name in the oldest records. Indeed Venus could not boast an old priesthood or festival or shrine at Rome. Further, Venus was unique in Italy. Etruscans spoke of Turan, 'Lady'. In the Oscan dialect the comparable goddess was Herentas, very similar in concept because the name is related to the aforementioned Latin 'willingness' and to English 'yearn'. There is reason to believe that Venus had not even been universal to the Latins of central Italy. She seems especially Roman and thus contrasts with Jupiter whom all the Indo-European speakers knew, or with Mars who, though native to Italy, was shared by all peninsular inhabitants.

Most of Venus's cult remains un-

Titian's *Venus and Adonis*, one of his *poesie*, a series of mythological paintings created in the mid 16th century.

known to us. Some Romans insisted that the month of April was named after Aphrodite, her Greek equivalent. However, this folk etymology was based on the cult of Venus on behalf of vegetable gardens. As early as the late third century her name signified the garden produce itself. The Romans consecrated gardens to Venus on 19 August, and vegetable gardeners kept the day holy.

There is no certain answer as to why Venus was related to the Vinalia, two wine ceremonies in the civil calendar on 23 April and 19 August. These festivals belonged to the sky god Jupiter. Aside from the coincidence of their worship on days of the Roman Vinalia, there is some Campanian evidence of a state cult of Venus Jovia. This worship can be construed in one of two ways. Either Venus is already identified as Aphrodite whom Zeus (Jupiter) fathered according to one Greek myth, or the goddess originated as the sky god's venus or, to use the local term, herentas. Of course,

vineyards do not greatly differ from gardens. Also, in a sense, all plants need to be coaxed or wheedled to put forth their fruits. Such coaxing may be enacted by sexual representation. Be that as it may, no clear and direct evidence of such religious practice emerges from the ancient evidence on Venus.

Produce and Prostitution

At least as early as 290 BC, Venus was somehow associated with the August Vinalia because her first temple was dedicated on that day by a patrician, Fabius, who had built it with fines exacted for ladies' debauchery. Although it stood at least 600 years, this temple's activities are rarely mentioned. Venus's epithet Obsequens, 'compliant', and the source of the building funds point to an already existing identification of the goddess with the Greek Aphrodite and the Etruscan Turan, who were definitely goddesses of female sexuality. Despite the sexual aspects of both the cult title and the ladies'

Small statue of Aphrodite bathing, known as the *Rhodes Venus*

um. Aphrodite occasionally had the epithet Aineia, which was interpreted to commemorate her maternity. The maritime route of Aeneas's legendary wanderings can be traced from one to another of Aphrodite's shrines. Some place-names of the western Italian coast preserved indications of Aphrodite in her role as protector of seafarers. Venus inherited these places as Roman rule spread.

After successive humiliations from Carthage's great general Hannibal, a direct descendant of the two Fabii observed what seems a family tradition and dedicated a temple to the true Venus Erycina in 215 BC. By this gift Fabius and the Romans placated a deity who had protected Carthage during the earlier Punic war and who was also an ancestress of the Roman people, through Aeneas who came to Latium and founded Romulus's line. Venus Obsequens had received her temple at roughly the same time as the Romans first reared a statue group of Romulus and Remus being suckled by the she-wolf. Venus Erycina had been integrated into the Roman tradition of their nonItalian ancestry. Consequently Rome's Capitoline Hill, reserved for truly Roman gods, allowed a site for Venus of Eryx.

Venus is certainly connected with the month of April by the dedication in 181 BC of a third temple on the earlier Vinalia of 23 April. This Venus, another Erycina, had been promised a temple during a war with the Ligurians of northern Italy, whom the Romans reckoned distant relatives of the Sicilians. Situated just outside the city, the new shrine reproduced the very temple on Mt. Eryx where temple prostitution still thrived. Rome's Erycine precinct attracted the city's less savoury residents. On 23 and 25 April prostitutes and the offspring of prostitution and pimping kept their holy days here. Late April and early May had become holidays given over

misbehaviour, Fabius had a personal reason for the choice of his piety. He claimed that Venus had submitted to the wishes (obsequi) of his father and himself. The two Fabii had fought together in several campaigns against the Samnites and after the last Samnite war Venus Obsequens received her temple. Unfortunately, we do not know whether the Samnite Venus was worth conciliating in war.

Venus perhaps exercised some political sway among the Latins, for there existed two large precincts a few miles southwest of Rome where Aphrodite or Frutis, sometimes called Venus, were annually worshipped by all the Latins. One or both shrines, purportedly of great age, may have actually been related in cult to the widely renowned goddess of Mt. Eryx on the western tip of Sicily. The Erycine sexual goddess was variously identified with Aphrodite and the Phoenician Ishtar. The Latin Frutis was said to have received her cult statue from Erycina.

One tradition explicitly equated Venus Erycina to the Aphrodite who bore Aeneas. Accordingly, the Trojan hero gratefully transported her cult to Cyprus, to Sicily, and to Lati-

to sexual promiscuity and stage plays. Since the third century such rites, introduced under the influence of the Greek Sibylline Books, had been consecrated to Flora, spirit of blossoming. They had their likely model in the cult of Aphrodite Antheia (Flora in Latin). For centuries the Floral Games provided notorious spectacles of sexual licence. Venus herself was not directly worshipped with Flora; nevertheless as divinity of produce and prostitution Venus belongs to the same kind of religious mentality.

The Sibylline Books reinforced the association in 114 BC, when the Romans were prompted to dedicate a temple to Venus Verticordia, 'Turner of Hearts'. Her name was intended to commemorate the acquittal of two Vestal Virgins charged with breaking their vows. Whatever the intent of the title, which is supposed to suggest the conversion from lust to chastity, Venus clearly retained her latent power of coaxing.

Political Promotion

Through Cornelius Sulla, who briefly engrossed the Republican government by his dictatorship of 82–79 BC, Venus entered the realm of personal politics. Sulla, also her devotee in other ways, adopted the style Epaphroditos, 'Aphrodite's darling', which he rendered Felix in Latin. The latter style, which he may also have applied to a Roman Venus, comprised all notions of fertility, prosperity, success, and good luck. At Pompeii a coastal colony of Sulla's veterans accorded Venus unusual prominence. The Pompeian cult perhaps combined Sulla's patroness with the town's continuing adoration of Venus Physica, Venus of Nature (physis), which preserved the Greek idea of growth.

In 55 BC Pompey the Great dedicated a temple to Venus Victrix 'the Winner', atop his theatre, which was the first permanent theatre in Rome.

Opposition to its construction was probably blunted by the consecration to Venus. At about the same time, Rome's great poet Lucretius published his philosophical poem on Nature, in which he invoked for poetic inspiration Venus, ancestress of the Aenead race, and which he dedicated to Memmius whose clan corporately worshipped Venus.

The patrician clan of Julii asserted even stronger proprietary rights of ancestral cult for Venus since they claimed direct descent from Iulus, the Trojan son of Aeneas. Julius Caesar surprised no one by emphasizing his clan's rise to power in his own person by vowing a temple to Venus Genetrix during the battle of Pharsalus, at which Pompey was defeated. Caesar raised the temple (perhaps the first built entirely of marble at Rome) in his new forum and dedicated it in 46 BC, although his adopted son Augustus completed the work. Beside the statue of his ancestress Caesar set a golden statue of Cleopatra.

In the Greek East subject provincials joined Aphrodite with deified Rome in a religious demonstration of loyalty to the Empire and to the imperial house which Caesar had generated. Ultimate expression of the Catholic loyalty of the Empire is met during the reign of Hadrian (117–128 AD). This emperor of Spanish birth devoted himself to the adornment of Rome, Italy, and the Empire, whose ideal he generously cultivated with lovely and magnificent buildings. Hadrian did much to accord the provincials a sense of merit for their role in the Empire's government. To amplify his notion of imperial unity Hadrian built Rome's largest and handsomest temple to Venus and Roma, which he situated beside the Colosseum. Adoration of Roma, a provincial concept, remained unique to this temple. Each goddess had her own precinct, placed back to back. By universal usage this double

temple was referred to as the City's Shrine. Hadrian chose to dedicate the temple on 24 April, the feast of Parilia, in order to honour Venus in her month and Roma on her birthday in the city's 888th year.

At Rome Venus was worshipped under other cult names. Most of these are easily understandable; Placida, 'pleasing'; Alma, 'nurturing'; Pudica, 'demure'. A few are most obscure, for instance Calva, 'bald'. The goddess's popularity extended throughout Italy and the Latin-speaking western Empire. She invited identification with lesser local divinities and found herself acquainted with universal notions. Thus she provides other examples of the Roman capacity to enlarge the concept and identity of their gods.

The Dead and the Sewers

Near the great cemetery on the Esquiline Hill once stood a holy grove called Libitina where corpses were prepared for burial. The profession of undertaker was also libitina. Cult for and in groves was quite common but a grove cult for the dead was extraordinary. By the Imperial age the Grove of Libitina was no more than an address, and very probably just the name of a street. From the name of the grove, or from that of its tutelary deity, the Romans thought up a goddess Libitina. At some later point they could not intellectually tolerate the plethora of insignificant divinities. Perhaps the very distaste for the subject of funerals had prepared the Romans to believe Libitina governed sexual desire (libido); thence the easy next step carried them to apply Libitina to Venus and to rear a temple to this goddess of lust. The word Libitina seems to have entered Latin from Etruscan, where it meant 'dead'. Libitina was not necessarily an Etruscan goddess, but a euphemism for death and its sequel.

Another example of a latter-day Venus can be derived from a known locality. In early times the Romans knew the Little Aventine Hill as Mt. Murcus. The valley between the Aventine and Palatine Hills was named the Murcia and was ultimately given over to the construction of the enormous Circus Maximus; this embraced a number of old religious sites, among which was an altar to Murcia. Murcia shared her name with the turning posts at that end of the racecourse. Being overwhelmed physically by the affairs and structures of the Circus and her link with the locality having been forgotten, Murcia became the subject of learned speculation. Her name was derived from the Greek myrtea, 'myrtle'. Since this shrub was sacred to Aphrodite, Murcia came to be another name for Venus. With the discovery of her new identity Murcia's cult seems to have perished.

Next and more perplexing is the case of Venus Cloacina. Cloaca is the Latin word for sewer. In uniformity with the need for a deity to oversee every place and structure, a shrine to Cloacina was put up in the Forum over the Cloaca Maxima, the town's main sewer. The Romans fancied that cloaca was derived from a verb of cleansing. Further, they supposed that the goddess of cleansing must be Venus, because the local plant used for sacral cleansing was the same as the myrtle. Finally, both Cloacina's shrine and Murcia's altar were situated over running water. This Venus was humanly represented and her statue held a flower of some kind. By involutions peculiar to the ancient mind Venus became mistress of funerals, racecourse turning posts, and sewers.

A last instance of Venus's cquisition of alien functions illustrates another Roman religious peculiarity. When the Romans entered Carthaginian Africa, they readily acknowledged the native goddess Venus Caelestis, 'heavenly'

Venus. The existence of an obscure Greek deity, Aphrodite Ourania, perhaps promoted the Romans' acceptance of Caelestis. At any rate the ground was soon prepared for the introduction of the planetary week and the convictions of astrology. In the wake of these innovations Venus lent her name to the sixth day of the new week which still keeps alive Mesopotamian astrology in Italy, France, and Spain, where Ishtar's planet is commemorated in Venus's day. Our own Friday is just a further step in the equation. 'Friday's child is loving and giving!'

The Roman Venus exhibits different modes of divinity. From first to last her state cult contributed to the

> *In astrology Venus is traditionally the ruler of love and desire, beauty, and relationships—not confined to sexual partnerships . . .*

grandeur of the Empire and the glory of certain élite clans. Venus goddess of vegetables gave way to the Venus of female sexuality, whose myth and cult are based upon Greek and oriental precedents that became peculiarly Roman only insofar as they included accounts of Aphrodite as the mother of Aeneas. Whatever else the cult of the abstract venus had once contained, the aspect of charm and allure was transferred to a female goddess of procreation.

Venus the Planet
The Babylonians connected the morning and evening star with the goddess of love, and so did the Greeks and Romans, possibly because its appearances mark the limits of night, the time of love-making. Venus is the only planet named for a female deity

and its astrological symbol is widely used outside astrology as a symbol of the female, the corresponding male symbol being that of Mars, the god who was the lover of Venus in classical mythology.

In astrology Venus is traditionally the ruler of love and desire, beauty, and relationships—not confined to sexual partnerships but extending to relationships with friends and in business. It is also considered essentially beneficent, a force making for harmony, reconciliation, peace, affection, love of beautiful things, physical attractiveness. The position of Venus in your birth chart is thought to affect all these matters, but especially your ability to enter into relationships with other people and your attitudes to beauty, the arts, and the pleasures of life. If Venus is fortunately placed, it should tend to produce a warm, gentle, sympathetic, graceful, and artistic person, contented, tactful and probably rather sentimental. The planet is particularly associated with music and is said to produce composers and musicians.

If not so fortunately placed, the influence of Venus may be less harmonious. The old belief was that Venus in conjunction with Saturn and Mercury in a horoscope threatened death by the treachery of a woman or by poison, traditionally the woman's weapon, but this has been reinterpreted by at least one modern authority to mean the threat of being dominated by a woman, or women, in life. It is often said that a man born when Venus is close to the sun in the zodiac is likely to be effeminate, his character (sun) being unduly influenced by the feminine planet. Saturn square to Venus, as in Hitler's horoscope, is supposed to indicate selfishness and egotism.

The influence of Venus on love-life varies with its placing in the zodiac.

According to Margaret Hone's *Modern Text Book of Astrology*, a person who has Venus in Taurus will be 'steadfast in love, but possessive' and 'slow to make partnership but reliable when once settled'. Venus in Gemini, however, means that 'affection is changeable and often for more than one at a time', and if Venus is in Scorpio 'love tends to be more intense, more sexual, more secretive, and passionate'. Venus in the eighth house, incidentally, is a good sign, traditionally foretelling an easy death.

In magic the force of Venus is connected primarily with love and sex, and with fertility and the teeming life of nature. Copper, as the metal of Venus, is useful in love charms, and operations of love, lust, pleasure, and friendship should be timed in the hour and day of Venus.

FURTHER READING: For the Roman goddess, see G. K. Galinsky, Aeneas, Sicily and Rome *(Princeton Univ. Press, 1969).*

Vesta

Roman goddess of the hearth, equivalent of the Greek Hestia: worshipped at home as the deity of the family hearth, her public cult was conducted in a circular shrine, the 'hearth' of the community, where a perpetual fire burned, tended by the Vestal Virgins; her favourite animal was the ass.

Vestal Virgins

Priestesses of the sacred fire of Vesta in Rome; probably the successors of the King's daughters who originally tended the fire on the royal hearth; if they let the fire go out, they were beaten; chosen as small girls, they served for thirty years, during which time they had to remain chaste.

Villa of the Mysteries

Cult centre of Dionysus at Pompeii, the town which was overwhelmed by eruptions of Vesuvius in 63 and 79 AD; murals depict the rituals of the cult.

Virgil

Publius Vergilius Maro (70–19 BC), author of the *Aeneid*, the *Eclogues* and the *Georgics*; in the Middle Ages his fourth eclogue, predicting the birth of a child who would usher in a new Golden Age, was taken to refer to Christ, and in legend he became a master magician; he guides Dante through the afterworld in the Divine Comedy.

Zeus

There is good reason to suppose that the hierarchical organization of the Olympian deities of the Homeric poems reflects the social and political conditions of the Mycenean period, when the gods and goddesses were gathered together in a single heavenly stronghold under the monarchical hegemony of Zeus. Their dwellings, built by Hephaestus, surrounded the central palace of Zeus.

The authority of the supreme male deity was now fairly stable, but it was still by no means unchallenged. The Mycenean pantheon spread its influence as the Mycenean social and economic system became dominant elsewhere. The ensuing conflict and fusion is paralleled by an increasing complexity in cult and mythology and reflected in the composition and organization of the pantheon.

In its most dramatic form this process had assumed the character of a struggle between the older conception of an Aegean goddess and a newer conception of a dominant male god, Zeus, whose name is certainly Indo-European. Crete had been the centre of Minoan civilization and had now become part of the fringe of the Mycenean. The study of the all-pervasive cult of Zeus in Greek religion helps us to understand the means whereby, and in what diverse forms, the Minoan religion, with its prime allegiance to a Great Goddess (although it was already familiar with the growing power of its own Cretan male god), became progressively reconciled with the Mycenean pantheon.

Significantly, it has been claimed that the earliest representation of Zeus occurs on the Geometric lid from a tomb at Fortetsa near Cnossus. That this representation is traditionally Cretan is indicated by the presence of birds, one of them carried on the left hand of the figure traditionally supposed to be Zeus, who strides toward a tripod. There is another bird on top of the tripod. Between the figure and the tripod is yet another larger bird with its head lifted toward the handle of the tripod.

The principal figure carries in his right hand an object which consists of three wavy verticals—the thunderbolt, or at least fire, perhaps resembling the bolts depicted on Syro-Hittite reliefs. Underneath the tripod is a human bust—perhaps the Minoan goddess herself, associated with, but not yet displaced by, Zeus. We could then have here represented a double epiphany or manifestation of Cretan Zeus and the older Cretan goddess, heralded by the birds of Minoan tradition.

The thunderbolt of Zeus was itself traditionally regarded as a means of bringing death so that immortality might be conferred. The tripod, a three-legged cauldron to be put over a fire, goes back in its origins to the 14th century BC.

The Cauldron of Rebirth

Real or simulated boiling in a cauldron is a familiar prelude to rejuvenation, immortality, and apotheosis. The infant Dionysus-Zagreus, for instance, was slain, his limbs cooked in a cauldron, and restored to life again. In the boiling cauldron mortality and old age are shed, perennial youth is gained, rebirth follows upon death, the initiate is born again. Thunderbolt and tripod can be accompaniments of initiation; and Cretan Zeus, pre-Olympian in origin, was an initiation god.

It is tempting to imagine that the mystery of Cretan Zeus himself is celebrated in this scene on the Fortetsa lid in the form of a double epiphany, reflecting the combination of the new Dorian with the traditional Cretan background, as it were newly Hellenic yet abidingly Minoan.

Background of the Gods

However that may be, other evidence illustrates the growth of the cult of Mycenean Zeus against the old Minoan background in Crete itself. Homer and Hesiod were the first to compose theogonies, to give the gods their epithets, allot them their offices and occupations, and describe their forms, in the tradition reported by Herodotus. This means that these customary Greek theogonies derived from the epic tradition, rooted in the Mycenean period.

In the Homeric Catalogue of Ships (in the *Iliad*, book 2) Crete is described as having 100 towns. Seven of these are mentioned by name, including Cnossus, Gortyna, and Phaistus, all of them from central Crete, which was apparently the chief area of Achaean occupation.

Though they are by no means principal characters in the *Iliad*, it is quite clear that the Cretan captains were of some importance, consistent with the island's contribution to the Trojan expedition, for Idomeneus and

Rembrandt painting portraying Zeus, in the form of an eagle, abducting Ganymede to serve as his cup-bearer.

Meriones had a considerable contingent of eighty ships. This number can be compared with 100 ships under the command of Agamemnon himself, ninety under Nestor, sixty under Menelaus, brother of Agamemnon, and a mere twelve under Odysseus.

Idomeneus boasts of his descent from Zeus. Like other similar leaders of the Heroic Age of Greece, he had quite a short pedigree, which goes up to a god in the third generation before the Trojan War. Aerope, his first cousin, was connected by marriage with the Atreidai, the family of his allies. She married Atreus and was herself a granddaughter of Minos. In the *Iliad*, Idomeneus kills Phaistus, son of the Maionian Boras from Tarne and the eponymous hero of this great Cretan city. There was another Phaistus in the Peloponnese, and again another in

Thessalian Achaia. The opponents of Idomeneus, Oinomaos and Alkathoos have associations with Pelops and the Peloponnese; and his father Deucalion has associations with Thessaly. The implication is that he was an intrusive northerner by extraction, a bringer of strife to Crete before he went to Troy.

Europa and the Bull

Zeus, the god ancestor of Idomeneus, the one member of the Olympian pantheon with an Indo-European name, rose to his eminence with the growing power of the Achaeans. The result was that, in Crete, the name of their sky god was attached to a Minoan deity, whose original ritual and character can be discerned from the evidence of later times. It was not until after the Minoan period that this originally secondary deity, this youthful god, pushed his way to the forefront in a variety of forms and under a variety of names.

The myth of the Minotaur implies that he was identified at Cnossus with the bull; and the story of the love of Queen Pasiphae for the Minotaur may derive from a form of the sacred marriage, the male partner in the ritual being played by the king masked in the head of a bull. The sacred marriage was closely involved with the fertility of the crops. This association is clearly to be observed—as is also the association with central Crete—in the famous legend of Zeus and Europa.

An archaic kind of Europa, riding on a bull, features in the earliest (5th century BC) coins of the city of Gortyna and also of Phaistus. The type persists on the coins of Gortyna throughout the fifth century. Their pictorial character has plausibly suggested a derivation from local frescoes. This relation is even more conspicuous in the fourth-century coins both of Gortyna and of Phaistus. On one type of coin from Phaistus Europa is sitting on a rock and is welcoming with her raised hand the bull who is approaching her. A coin series from contemporary Gortyna tells vividly the story of the marriage of Zeus and Europa, with Zeus changing from a bull into an eagle. Coins of Cnossus, probably struck in 220 BC, when that city was closely allied with Gortyna, are similar to the Gortynian type which features Europa; and Europa on the bull remained as one of the chief coin types of the Roman province of Crete —probably struck at Gortyna between 66 and 31 BC.

It appears to be likely that the final evolution of the male deity from a bull into an anthropomorphic Zeus, the Zeus who later became involved with Europa, must have occurred in the Mycenean period. Zeus is featured as the partner of Europa not only in Hesiod, but already in the *Iliad*. Animal

sacrifices continued to be conspicuous in the rituals of Zeus, the victims normally being either rams or, more frequently, oxen. Both of these animals are associated with sky gods in general and with Zeus in particular. They were the most precious victims that pastoral peoples could offer, considered to be most possessed of fertilizing power and most essential to their economic survival. Various traditions combine to associate mainland settlers at Gortyna, or its neighbourhood, with the Arcadian area where the Achaean dialect survived. It is therefore perhaps significant that Gortynian Zeus shared the title of Hekatombaios ('to whom hecatombs are offered') with the Arcadian Zeus.

A celestial Zeus of Gortyna called Zeus Asterios ('Starry Zeus') was known to Byzantine writers and he was associated with Europa by earlier writers including Hesiod and Bacchylides. After his affair with Europa, Zeus reputedly gave her in marriage to the Cretan king Asterion (or Asterios, or Asteros) who, childless himself, reared the children of Zeus and Europa; and, according to the Byzantine writer Tzetzes, Sarpedon, Minos, and Rhadamanthys were sons of Zeus Asterios. The Minotaur was also called Asterios or Asterion. There were sacred herds of cattle at Gortyna, a cult of a solar deity called Atymnos, brother of Europa, whose early death was mourned; and an inscription of the 5th century BC confirms the worship of the sun.

The art and the literary and numismatic evidence of historical times all indicate how the sacred marriage of Zeus and Europa combined Mycenean with Minoan—and even more primitive— traditions of cult. Europa often features in art on the bull, holding in one hand his fertilizing horn and in the other hand a flower, symbol of her fertility and also of earlier magical associations before the bull had been deified.

The marriage of Zeus and Europa traditionally occurred in or under a plane tree near a stream at Gortyna. Coins of Gortyna of the 5th century BC show a goddess in a tree, generally considered to be Europa possessed by Zeus in the form of an eagle and thus identified with Hera. A bull's head, however, is apparently often fixed to the trunk of the tree. The tree on the coins seems to be a pollard willow and not a plane tree. Yet we need not go so far as to accept the suggestion that Europa was actually a willow goddess and that Zeus, as a nursling of the willow, might naturally be mated with a willow bride. Magical plant and tree associations of this kind must have existed long before either Zeus or Europa. Such earlier connections were indicated in the mention of the tree where the sacred marriage took place and the stream nearby, where the goddess bathed.

Putting Away Childish Things

The cult of the goddess Leto at Phaistus, not far away from Gortyna in southern Crete, is of particular interest. We have evidence to prove that Cretan youths, when they reached the last stage of initiation into manhood and citizenship, cast aside their boys' garments before assuming their warriors' costumes. The formality of this particular ritual was embedded in the festival which was known at Phaistus as the Ekdysia ('casting off'), during which the youth cast off his boys' clothes. This festival was associated with the local cult of Leto and was connected with the myth of Leucippus, who was changed from a girl into a boy. According to the myth, Galatea, daughter of Eurytus and wife of Lamprus, bore a daughter; and she persuaded Leto to let the girl change sex when she grew up.

The change was commemorated in the Phaistian festival of the Ekdysia.

When the Phaistians married they lay down beside the statue of Leucippus, which was presumably in the sanctuary of Leto. The festival and the mythology suggest a combination of fertility, initiation and marriage ritual. The youths of Phaistus were apparently initiated into manhood, citizenship and marriage at the same period of life. The local Leto, as her epithet Phytia ('causing growth') indicates, promoted growth and fertility in the young. When growth had been promoted, the boy died and was reborn as a man, casting away his boy's clothes and dressing like a man.

Leto Phytia and her Phaistian festival were rooted in the earliest stratum of Cretan religion. It has been suggested that, because the cock was dear to Leto (as to all women in childbirth), since he stood by to lighten her labour, Leto Phytia was somehow related to Zeus Welkhanos of Phaistus, whose sacred bird was the cock. Coins of Phaistus in the period from about 430 to 300 BC show Welkhanos as a youthful, beardless god, his right hand caressing a cock; on the reverse side there is a bull. The Cretan identification of Zeus with Welkhanos is also confirmed by lexicography.

The discovery of numerous tiles with the name of the god Weukhqnos (Welkhanos) was made years ago at neighbouring Hagia Triada. Significantly, the temple of Zeus Welkhanos was here built upon the ruins of the old palace of Hagia Triada. An associated month name and spring festival is attested in three other towns of Crete.

A. B. Cook (author of *Zeus*) thought the meaning of Welkhanos could have been 'god of the willow-tree', confirming his idea that Zeus at Phaistus, as at Gortyna, was consort of a willow goddess. For he had a cock (instead of his usual eagle), since the

cock, as the crest of the Phaistianl-domeneus, had a long-standing mythical association with the town. There was also a tradition that Idomeneus was descended from the sun, sire of Pasiphae, and that the cock was sacred to the sun. Though these associations may be true, there is no reason but to suppose that Cook's identification strained the evidence.

It is nevertheless possible to conclude, from the nature and provenance of the cult, that Zeus Welkhanos was a product of the Minoan god of fertility. There is clear similarity between the coins of Phaistus showing Welkhanos with a cock in the branches of a tree and the coins of Gortyna showing Zeus, Europa, and the eagle. The cock, like the eagle, seems to signify a bird epiphany. Welkhanos must surely have

> *The weather god, lord of storms, rain, lightning, and thunder, who acquired supremacy in his mountain stronghold . . .*

been yet another male partner in a sacred marriage with the old Minoan mother goddess.

Thunderbolt and Aegis
The evidence about Zeus Welkhanos and the representation (if it be of Zeus) on the lid from Fortetsa serve alike to emphasize the difficulty of clearly distinguishing Olympian Zeus from the specifically Cretan Zeus. The weather god, lord of storms, rain, lightning, and thunder, who acquired supremacy in his mountain stronghold, had an earthly prototype in the Mycenean Great King. Nevertheless, the Cretan Zeus who survived with such dominant traits of his original nature long after the Olympian pantheon became supreme in offi-

cially sponsored religion, is but one symbol—though one of outstanding importance—through which old prehistoric cult exercised its influence. The later Zeus, Olympian though he might be, exhibited himself in many forms, as is evident in those various distinguishing epithets attached to his name, which not only reveal his many-sided nature but often a pre-Olympian basis.

In eastern Crete, 'the Cretan-born Zeus' was specifically associated with Dicte by the epithet Diktaios (Dictean). The geographer Strabo expressly connected the temple of Dictean Zeus with the old Bronze Age population of the area. Although the Hellenic temple which stood on the site of the Minoan town of Palaicastro had been destroyed, sufficient numbers of votive offerings were found there in the course of archeological investigation to define its position; and the site of the alter was fixed by a bed of ashes. It was the discovery of the inscription of the famous 'Hymn of the Curetes', addressed to Zeus of Dicte, which confirmed with certainty that the temple was that of Dictean Zeus. Or again, there is Zeus Idaios ('of Ida'), similar to Dictean Zeus, mentioned in a much-discussed fragment of *The Cretans of Euripides*, delivered by a chorus of inspired devotees of Zeus.

The ancient Greeks themselves believed that the Pelasgians were the aboriginal inhabitants of Greece and they tended also to associate Pelasgians with Carians (people from southwest Asia Minor) and the Leleges of the Greek islands. The name survived in the ancient shrine of Zeus Pelasgios at Dodona in Epirus, in northwest Greece. Here was the most ancient oracle in Greece, the divine responses obtained from the rustling of sacred trees and from brazen vessels suspended from them. The cult of Zeus Karios ('Carian Zeus'), centred at Mylasa, the Carian capital, was also found in Boeotia and Attica, in mainland Greece.

'The portion of Zeus is the broad heaven among the clouds in the upper air,' says Homer in the *Iliad*. Hence a repeatedly recurrent Homeric epithet of Zeus is the Cloud-gatherer, sending rain, lightning, thunder. Small wonder that altars have been found in Greek houses dedicated to Zeus Kataibates—Zeus who descends (in thunder and lightning)—and sacrifices were made on these altars to appease him and ward off destruction from the house.

Beside the thunderbolt, the aegis (skin shield) is a peculiar attribute of Zeus. In keeping with his rise to eminence in the Heroic Age of Mycenean Greece, Zeus, as god of manly strength and prowess, was especially honoured at two of the four great athletic festivals of Greece, the Olympian and the Nemean, besides many others. From the 4th century BC onward, Greek historians reckoned time in Olympiads, the periods corresponding to the Olympic Games, which were quadrennial and claimed uninterrupted celebration from 776 BC.

The sacred precinct of Zeus at Olympia, the Altis, was surrounded by a wall with several entrances. In the southern part stood the great temple of Zeus, with the famous gold and ivory statue of Zeus by Pheidias, which was classed as one of the seven wonders of the world until it perished in 462 AD, and which was more praised in antiquity than any other work of art.

Lord of the City State

Zeus was of supreme importance in the daily life of the Greek city state. As Nilsson explained, in *A History of Greek Religion*: 'Just as the father of the household is Zeus's priest, so Zeus himself in the patriarchal monarchy of earlier times is the special protector of the king and hence the supreme custodian of the social order. Thus in Homer Agamemnon is under the special protection of Zeus. The god was not dethroned with the fall of the monarchy. As Zeus Polieus he is the divine overlord of the city state.'

As protector and guardian of the house he was Zeus Herkeios ('Of the front court'). As Zeus Ktesios ('the Acquirer') he was similarly protector of house and property. Hence Nilsson's conclusion that where Zeus appears in the shape of a snake under such names as Ktesios, Meilikhios ('the Kindly One') and Philios ('the Friendly One'), the name of Zeus had been added to the house deity which appeared as a snake, because Zeus was also protector and guardian of the house. A deity, male in later Greece, female in the Minoan Age, developed out of a domestic snake cult.

Zeus was also protector of the fugitive suppliant, as Zeus Hikesios. He had a part to play in the sanctity attaching to the duties of friendly hospitality (Ksenios). From the beginning of the 5th century BC, there grew up, in the city of Athens and its neighbourhood, a special class of resident aliens called metoikoi. They were attracted by the opportunities of trade in a flourishing commercial centre, and the government encouraged them, despite the fact that, as foreigners, they were really excluded from civic rights and from public ceremonies associated with the official religion of the state. Nevertheless, once a year, at the national festival of the Panathenaea, these resident aliens were not merely permitted to take part but were allowed special marks of honour. They also had a separate Zeus Metoikios as their special patron.

As the governments of the city states, like that of Athens, tended to become more democratic in form, they still continued to have allegiance in council and assembly to Zeus as, for example, to Zeus Agoraios ('Of the market place'). That epithet was not peculiar to Zeus, but no doubt derived from the location in the market place of a shrine or altar of the deity to whom it applied. Functional shades of meaning must have been derived from the various functions of the agora, the market place, chiefly as a place of assembly and also as a market place in the strict sense. Zeus Agoraios would therefore have been a special patron of those mustered in assembly at the agora. From this special association with the assembly of citizens, Zeus Agoraios could be described in literature as patron of eloquence or of public supplication.

In later antiquity, among the more sophisticated, as religious belief tended to become more monotheistic, there was a tendency for Zeus to become conceptualized as the one, single god, the beginning and the end of all things.

R. F. WILLETTS

FURTHER READING: A. B. Cook, Zeus (Biblo & Tannen reprint, 3 vols); M. P. Nilsson. Minoan-Mycenaean Religion. *(Lund, Sweden, 1950); M. P. Nilsson.* A History of Greek Religion. *(Greenwood, 1980); W. K. C. Guthrie,* The Greeks and their Gods. *(Beacon Press, 1968); R. F. Willetts.* Cretan Cults and Festivals. *(Greenwood, 1980).ed from them. The cult of Zeus Karios ('Carian Zeus'), centred at Mylasa, the Carian capital, was also found in Boeotia and Attica, in mainland Greece.*

Glossary

Allegorical — A story or poem with details that have a hidden, parallel meaning, used as commentary on social or political issues.

Allurements — Charms, either material or emotional, to attract someone.

Amplitude — Greatness in size and effect, full, and abundant.

Anemone — Brightly coloured varieties of flowers in the buttercup family.

Antiquarianism — Interest in and dealing with things and ideas from long ago.

Archaic — Old-fashioned and outdated.

Bereavement — The process of mourning, expressing grief for the death of a loved one.

Citadel — A fortress that protects a city and its people in case of attack.

Connivance — Consent, encouragement, and participating in doing something bad or illegal.

Consecration — The formal act of making something holy.

Dais — A raised platform where speakers, honoured guests, or notable figures are placed before an audience.

Deification — Being made into, or treated like, a god.

Disdain — To regard something as being beneath one's consideration.

Disillusion — Disappointment when you realize something isn't as good as you thought it was or would be.

Edict — An order or command issued by someone in power.

Egalitarian — Believing that all people are equal and should be treated the same way in all respects.

Enigmatic — Difficult to understand, puzzling.

Epithets — Apt descriptions that describe different. characteristics of a person, particularly used by Homer.

Gadfly — A flying insect that infests and lives off cattle and deer by biting them; the word is also used to describe a person who is annoying on purpose in social settings.

Inferred — Meaning taken from something not explicitly stated.

Initiatory — Introductory, doing what is required to begin something new.

Lamenting — Expressing great sorrow, mourning, or grief.

Libations — Ceremonious drinks, taken by participants and often used as an offering to deities.

Manifestations — A perceptible showing that embodies a defined set of criteria.

Metamorphosis — Transformation from one form or being into another.

Nomadic — Not remaining in one place for long, usually used to describe the habits of a person or people.

Pantheon — All of the gods and goddesses of a religion taken as whole; also, an ancient domed temple in Rome built in honour of all the deities.

Paramour — A lover, especially one met in secret.

Posterity — Known to all future generations; history-making.

Primordial — Existing at or from the beginning of time, being the first in origin.

Progeny — The offspring or children of a person, animal, or plant.

Purification — Cleaning and removing any pollution or unwanted element.

Ramifications — The resulting consequences of an action, often having an unexpected or complicating effect.

Scurrilous — Saying or suggesting awful, untrue things about someone; slanderous.

Tenacious — Persistently clinging to an idea, person, or an opinion.

Theogony — The genealogy of gods; a family tree of deities.

Tractable — Easy to lead and work with.

Votaries — Those who have made vows to do religious service, such as a monk or nun.

Index